RUSSIA IN THE 21st CENTURY

This book demonstrates that Russia intends to reemerge as a full-fledged superpower before 2010, challenging America and China and potentially threatening a new arms race. Contrary to conventional wisdom, this goal is easily within the Kremlin's grasp, but the cost to the Russian people and global security would be immense. A sophisticated strategy is proposed to dissuade President Vladimir Putin from pursuing this destabilizing course. The book also explains why the Soviet Union imploded, why Western experts missed the signs of the collapse, and how Russia has metamorphosed into an authoritarian regime instead of pursuing a transition to fully democratic free enterprise. It demonstrates that the Soviet Union was "structurally militarized" and that Russia's military-industrial complex is intact. The Cold War image of the Soviet Union as a westernizing, mass consumption society committed to "peaceful coexistence" is exposed as a statistical illusion. A critique of American foreign policy making is also provided that emphasizes the confusion caused by tampering with evidence to conform with public expectations and the damage to the national interest caused by attempting to satisfy a consensus of particular special interests.

Steven Rosefielde is Professor of Economics at the University of North Carolina, Chapel Hill, and Adjunct Professor of Defense and Strategic Studies, Center for Defense and Strategic Studies, Southwest Missouri State University, Springfield. The author or editor of eleven books on Russia and the Soviet Union, he has also published more than a hundred articles in journals such as the *American Economic Review, European Economic Review, Economica, Soviet Studies*, and *Europe-Asia Studies*. Professor Rosefielde is a member of the Russian Academy of Natural Science and was a Fellow of the Carnegie Corporation of New York from 2000 to 2003. He has served as a consultant to the Office of the Secretary of Defense as well as advised several directors of the U.S. Central Intelligence Agency and the U.S. National Intelligence Council. Professor Rosefielde has also worked continuously with the Swedish Defense Agency and the Central Economics and Mathematics Institute (Moscow) for more than a quarter century and with the Center for Defense and Foreign Policy (Moscow) for more than a decade.

Praise for *Russia in the 21st Century*

"In this timely and important work, Steven Rosefielde, a foremost expert on Russia, underlines the extent to which Russia's past is part of the present, and sets its conditions on the future. The result is a disturbing picture, conveying neither the end of history nor Russia as a normal state."

– Pekka Sutela, *Bank of Finland and the Helsinki School of Economics*

"This is an important book that effectively challenges much of the conventional thinking about Russia and the path it will take. Professor Rosefielde has been ahead of Western intelligence communities on the USSR and now Russia for many years, and I believe he continues to be ahead with this book. Many of its conclusions are chilling. The author argues persuasively that Russia will be less inclined to follow the liberal and globalist ideas of the West and far more challenging to the West than commonly expected. Moreover, Russia's military industrial complex is dormant but not gone and Russia has the resources – and plan – to resurrect itself as a great military power. Such conclusions are based upon extensive original research in Russian as well as English sources, keen analysis, and nearly unassailable logic."

– William Van Cleave, *Southwest Missouri State University*

RUSSIA IN THE 21st CENTURY

The Prodigal Superpower

STEVEN ROSEFIELDE
University of North Carolina, Chapel Hill

CAMBRIDGE
UNIVERSITY PRESS

CAMBRIDGE
UNIVERSITY PRESS

University Printing House, Cambridge CB2 8BS, United Kingdom

One Liberty Plaza, 20th Floor, New York, NY 10006, USA

477 Williamstown Road, Port Melbourne, VIC 3207, Australia

314-321, 3rd Floor, Plot 3, Splendor Forum, Jasola District Centre, New Delhi-110025, India

79 Anson Road, #06-04/06, Singapore 079906

Cambridge University Press is part of the University of Cambridge.

It furthers the University's mission by disseminating knowledge in the pursuit of
education, learning and research at the highest international levels of excellence.

www.cambridge.org
Information on this title: www.cambridge.org/9780521545297

First published 2004

A catalogue record for this publication is available from the British Library

Library of Congress Cataloging in Publication data
Rosefielde, Steven.
Russia in the 21st century : the prodigal superpower / Steven Rosefielde.
p.   cm.
Includes bibliographical references and index.
ISBN 0-521-83678-6 – ISBN 0-521-54529-3 (pbk.)
1. National security – Economic aspects – Russia (Federation)
2. Military-industrial complex – Russia (Federation)
3. Russia (Federation) – Military policy.
4. Security, International.   I. Title: Russia in the
twenty-first century.   II. Title.
HC340.12.Z9D4453   2004
338.4´7355´00947 – dc22   2004045110

ISBN 978-0-521-54529-7 Paperback

In memory of
David Rosefielde, Bill Lee, and Robert Levy

CONTENTS

FIGURES AND TABLES

ACRONYMS

ACW advanced conventional weapon

ALCM air-launched cruise missile

CER cost-estimating relationship

CBW chemical-biological warfare

CFE Conventional Forces in Europe treaty

CIA Central Intelligence Agency

DIA Defense Intelligence Agency

DOD Department of Defense

GDP gross domestic product

Genshtab general staff

GNP gross national product

Goskomstat Soviet state statistical agency

Gosplan Soviet state central planning agency

Gossnabsbyt' Soviet state wholesale allocation system

GRU Main intelligence administration of the Russian general staff (Glavnoe Razvedovatel'noe Upravlenie)

Khozraschyot economic cost accounting

IW information warfare

KGB Komitet Gosudarstvennoi Bezopasnosti (Soviet Committee on State Security)

MBMW machine building and metalworking

MEAC Military-Economic Analysis Center (CIA)

MEAP Military-Economic Analysis Panel (CIA)

Minatom Ministry of Atomic Energy

MIRV multiple independently targetable reentry vehicle

MOD Russian Ministry of Defense

MVD Ministerstvo vnutrennikh del (Ministry of Internal Affairs)

NATO North Atlantic Treaty Organization

NMD national missile defense

OPK oboronnyi-promyshennyi kompleks (defense-industrial complex)

OSD Office of the Secretary of Defense

PGM precision guided munitions

RDT&E research, development, testing, and evaluation

RMA revolution in military affairs

Roskomstat Russian statistical agency

Rosvooruzhenie Russian arms export agency

SORT Strategic Offensive Arms Reduction Treaty

START Strategic Arms Reduction Talks

SNA System of National Accounts

TNC tactical nuclear weapon for conventional war fighting

TNW tactical nuclear weapon

TVD teatry voennykh destvii (theaters of military operations)

UAV unmanned aerial vehicle

VPK voennyi promyshlennyi kompleks (military-industrial complex)

PREFACE

Specialists and amateurs alike frequently hold strong views about Soviet and Russian military-economic potential, but their attitudes are seldom consistent. During the Cold War, it was fashionable to speculate that the East and West were converging, that systems were becoming mixed, that both sides shared a common interest in peace and would gradually reduce their military forces. Accordingly, analysts like Franklyn Holzman argued that the Soviets spent less on defense than America and inter alia that the healthy economic growth indicated by Goskomstat and CIA statistics was primarily attributable to the workability of the "reformed" command system. But in the aftermath of the Soviet collapse, it has become just as fashionable to blame the USSR's demise on its excessive defense burden and the deficiencies of central planning. And, of course, transitologists and now the European Union have officially proclaimed Russia a "market economy,"[1] suggesting "blue skies" ahead, without a military cloud in the sky, since the contemporary defense burden is said to be half and the absolute dollar value less then a tenth the American level. Western economic and security advice to the Kremlin follows this script, stressing further liberalization without the slightest recognition that Russia's defense-industrial complex is just as large as ever and that Russia's economic and security drift is against the "globalist" tide. It is easy to understand the diverse partisan interests shaping these "approved" contradictions and even to sympathize in some regards with the disingenuousness, but insofar as policymakers believe what they say, their happy talk obstructs the resolution of serious problems vital to both Russia and the West. It is in our mutual interest to see Russia scrap "structural militarization" in favor of an "optimal" security strategy and to substitute "economic liberty" for the system of authoritarian economic sovereignty and privilege seeking installed by Boris Yeltsin and rationalized by Vladimir Putin. This book constructs an analytic foundation for such an initiative by explaining why Russia will ensnare itself in a Soviet-style quagmire unless it structurally demilitarizes and westernizes its political economy. It isn't enough to offer the counsel of perfection and for Putin to say amen. The bear has to be genetically recoded.

METHODOLOGY

This book employs "standard" western economic theory and quantitative methods to analyze Soviet and Russian civilian and military-industrial potential and performance. It relies on the microeconomic utility-optimizing principles of Adam Smith and his modern mathematical successors, especially Vilfredo Pareto, to establish a benchmark for evaluating Soviet and Russian possibilities. Following Abram Bergson's precepts on welfare economics, this book employs the familiar Pareto standard as a handy and widely understood referent, not as a uniquely valid ideal.

Best Sovietological practices, including adjusted factor costing where applicable, are applied throughout to handle the special problems posed by Soviet institutions, Soviet accounting, and Marxist price fixing. My approach differs from Bergson's and the CIA's here in only one regard. Like Bergson, for the years after 1963 I reject the claim that ruble values measure consumers' or planners' utilities (marginal rates of product substitution), but I go further, denying that they reflect "production potential," that is, marginal rates of enterprise product transformation "on average." This means that, whereas most Sovietologists seem to believe that Soviet ruble factor cost or adjusted ruble factor cost tells us something important about Soviet neoclassical supply-side possibilities, I insist that such statistics are opaque indicators of both demand and supply. The nuance matters because if Bergson is right, western and Soviet growth statistics can be validly compared as oranges and oranges on the supply side. If he is wrong, comparisons of these statistics are inherently ambiguous, providing only an illusion of comparability.[2]

My standard of verification also departs significantly from Bergson's. Dating as early as 1953, he argued that Soviet data were "reliable and usable," including subaggregates, except in infrequent cases where there was strong evidence of doctoring. This attitude, adopted before he recomputed his famous GNP growth series to assess Soviet data reliability, might be likened to a qualified auditor's report that acknowledges improprieties but judges the overall result satisfactory. As guides to Soviet performance, properly computed output and combined factor productivity growth series were considered ipso facto reliable in precisely the same degree as the underlying data. This turned out to mean in practice that Bergson's perception of Soviet performance was exactly what he computed. Although he considered other viewpoints, he never gave any ground regarding the possibility that his capital series were overstated by hidden inflation or that his dollar estimates of comparative Soviet size were too high. Nor did the Soviet collapse give him pause. He acted as if his axioms were sufficient to gauge the truth and were unfalsifiable, unlike Enron's auditors in similar circumstances, who amended their appraisals. Bergson's method consequently was conviction driven and therefore unscientific judged from the strict requirements of the hard sciences. The CIA acted differently. It possessed a lax attitude toward what constituted compelling evidence of falsification, and it freely adjusted official data to suit its presumptions. This elastic interpretation of Soviet data "reliability" enabled it to craft reality to its liking while claiming that it was rigorously adhering to Bergson's strictures. This book, by contrast, takes the position that blind faith in the "usability" of Soviet subaggregates and undisciplined data manipulation are both unwarranted in the wake of the Soviet disunion. Bergson and the CIA should have amended their analyses after the events of 1991 but didn't. This book doesn't repeat their mistakes.

Relatedly, it was also discovered that the convictions shaping Sovietological attitudes and the CIA's manipulation of Soviet data were governed by "public culture" – socially approved ideas about what the world ought to be. These "idols," as Francis Bacon observed centuries ago, turn science into sophistry and garble public discourse. Therefore, pains have been taken to explain not only how flaws in Bergson's and the CIA's axiologies caused them to get the Soviet Union and Russia wrong but why these errors occurred. My method in its entirety thus begins with scientifically tested, improved axiologies of markets and plans and then moves ahead to an examination of the principles, values, and convictions determining initial axiomatic choice and policy perceptions to prevent preconceptions from biasing results and conclusions.

ACKNOWLEDGMENTS

Work on this text began in 1987 after completion of the second edition of *False Science: Underestimating the Soviet Arms Buildup.* The Earhardt Foundation provided initial funding, but the collapse of the Soviet Union raised too many uncertainties to permit finishing the project. Research continued sporadically thereafter. For a time it seemed as if Russia might dismantle its military-industrial complex and structurally demilitarize, but by 2000 the momentum shifted, and I once again began a comprehensive assessment of the possibility that Russia was heading back to the future.

Financial and moral support for the undertaking was generously provided by the Carnegie Foundation of New York, under the Carnegie Scholars Program (Carnegie Scholar 2000), International Peace and Security division, established by President Vartan Gregorian in 1999. I am indebted to it and the Earhardt Foundation for their kind assistance. Some of my ideas were also developed under a grant from the University of North Carolina Institute for the Arts and the Humanities. Special thanks goes to Patricia Rosenfield, chair, Carnegie Scholars Program, and special advisor to the vice president and director for strategic planning and program coordination, for her constant encouragement and for organizing two Carnegie Scholars Program colloquia. The Bank of Finland Institute for Economics in Transition provided me with valuable research support during the spring of 2004.

My intellectual debt is equally immense. I relied heavily on William Lee's deep knowledge of Soviet and Russian weapons systems and the inside machinations at the Central Intelligence Agency and the Defense Intelligence Agency. He knew the evasions and half-truths and guided me through the minefields. Vitaly Shlykov, former deputy chairman of the Russian Defense Council under President Boris Yeltsin and consummate

VPK and GRU insider, performed a role similar to that of Virgil, acting as guide to the Soviet/Russian perspective for more than a decade. We were introduced by Joseph Churba, president of the International Security Council, and have worked continuously with each other ever since, with the kind assistance of Jan Rylander, director of the Swedish Defense Agency (and chairman of WEAG Panel II, a nineteen-nation R&D cooperative organization). Lieutenant General Viktor Samoilov, former director of Rosvooruzhenie (Russian state arms sales agency, 1994), and Col. General Valery Mironov, Soviet commander in chief of the Northwestern TVD (1991) and former defense minister of Russia, also helped me with specifics.

William van Cleave, professor and department head, Defense and Strategic Studies Department, Southwest Missouri State University, and J. D. Crouch, associate professor, Defense and Strategic Studies Department, Southwest Missouri State University (and former assistant secretary of defense for International Security Policy), occasionally coached me on military developments, as did Stephen Blank, professor of national security studies, Strategic Studies Institute, U.S. Army War College, and Alexander Belkin, Center for Foreign and Defense Policy (Moscow).

Thanks too is due the Central Intelligence Agency for the fine quality of its documents, for its excellent conferences, and for debating with me over the years. James Noren's and Noel Firth's comments on my analysis were especially helpful, as were Abe Becker's critiques and contacts with CIA directors Stansfield Turner, Bill Casey, Robert Gates, Robert Inman, and James Schlesinger (also secretary of defense). Prior assistance by OSD Director of Net Assessment Andrew Marshall, Deputy Assistant Secretary for Intelligence Patrick Parker, Derk Swaine, and David Epstein provided an invaluable background. The Defense Intelligence Agency and the National Intelligence Council also helped in various ways.

My grasp of Russian economic realities leaned heavily on the contributions of others. Professors Abram Bergson, Alexander Gerschenkron, Anne Carter, and Wassily Leontief provided the basic training. Academician Yuri Yaremenko, director of the Institute for National Economic Forecasting; Academician Valery Makarov, director of the Central Economics and Mathematics Institute; Georgii Kleiner, deputy director of TsEMI; Emil Ershov, professor at the Higher School of Economics, Moscow, and former deputy director of the Institute for National Economic Forecasting and Goskomstat SSSR; Alexander Bulatov, professor at Moscow State University for International Relations; Aleksei Ponomarenko, professor at the Higher School of Economics, Moscow, and former deputy director of Goskomstat (RF); Kirill Bagrinovsky, professor at TsEMI and Moscow State University; Slava Danilin, head of laboratory, TsEMI; Maya Shukhgalter; and Evgeny Gavrilenkov, former director of the Higher School of Economics and now chief economist at Troika Dialog were but a few of the Russian colleagues who continuously informed and challenged my understanding of Russia's unfolding reality.

Stefan Hedlund generously shared his works in progress and scrutinized my analysis. Those providing comments and criticisms included Jan Rylander; Jan Leijonhielm, Department Head, Swedish Defense Research Agency; Wilhelm Unge, senior researcher, Swedish Defense Research Agency; Professor Lennart Samuelson; Eugene Kogan, guest researcher, Stiftung Wissenschaft und Politik; Colonel Ret. Heikki Hult, Finnish National Defense College; Pekka Sutela, head, Bank of Finland Institute for Economies in Transition; Professor Julian Cooper, Centre for Russian and East European Studies, University of Birmingham; Professor Gertrude Schroeder, University of Virginia; Professor Franklin Holzman, Tufts University; Professor Peter Wiles, London University; Professor Mario Nuti, Comparative Economic Systems, University of Rome; Professor Sabrina Ramet, Trondheim University; Peter Havlik, deputy director, Wiener Institut fur Internationale Wirtschaftsvergleiche; Leon Podkaminer, staff economist, Weiner Institut fur Internationale Wirtschaftsvergleiche; Professor Jacques Sapir, Etudes en Sociales Responsible Russie ex-URSS, IRSES-MSH, Paris; Eric Brunat, deputy resident representative, United Nations Development Programme, Russian Federation, former executive director of the Russian European Center for Economic Policy in Russia and vice-president of the University of Savoie; Ivan Samson, professor of economics, PEPSE(lab) Espace Europe, UPMF, University of Grenoble; Professor Xavier Richet, University Sorbonne Nouvelle, Paris; Jean Francois Huchet, associate professor of economics, University of Rennes; Bruno Dallago, professor of economics, University of Trento; Professor Philippe Debroux, Soka University, Hachioji; Charles Wolf, Jr., senior economic advisor and corporate fellow, RAND; Igor Birman; Professor Murray Feshbach, George Washington University; Stuart Goldman, specialist in Russian and Eurasian Affairs, Congressional Research Service; John Hardt, senior specialist in post Soviet economics, Congressional Research Service,

Library of Congress, and adjunct professor in economics, George Washington University; James Millar, professor of economics and international affairs, George Washington University; Anders Aslund, director, Russian and Eurasian Program, Carnegie Endowment for International Peace; Peter Reddaway, professor of political science, George Washington University; Nicholas Eberstadt, Henry Wendt Chair in Political Economy, American Enterprise Institute; Ted Karasik, RAND; Dan Goldberg, Department of Defense; Judith Shelton, adjunct professor; Ronald Childress, professor of law, University of South Carolina; Keith Bush, Director of Research at the U.S.–Russia Business Council; Professor Odelia Funke, University of Maryland; and John Wilhelm.

Japanese colleagues who offered comments and criticisms included Tad Sano, vice minister for international affaires, Ministry of Economy, Trade and Industry, Japan; Professor Masaaki Kuboniwa, Hitotsubashi University, Kunitachi; Professor Shinichiro Tabata, Hokkaido University; Masumi Hakogi, emeritus professor of Tohoku University (Graduate School of Cultural Studies) and professor of international economics, Hiroshima University of Economics; Professor Yoji Koyama, Niigata University; Professor Satoshi Mizobata, Kyoto University; Professor Ken Morita, Hiroshima University; Professor Kumiko Haba, Hosei University, Tokyo; and Aiko Tomiyama, lecturer, Niigata University; Kaoru Nakata, State Department, Tokyo.

Special thanks go to Professor Quinn Mills, Harvard University, and Professor Ralph William Pfouts, University of North Carolina, Chapel Hill, who regularly discussed most of the themes addressed in this volume with me over the years. Professor Robert Levy, University of California, San Diego, patiently schooled me in the psychological and anthropological aspects of public culture, power networking, and noneconomic behavior as these issues bore on Russia and western national security policy making. Professor Francis Fukuyama, School of International Political Economy, Johns Hopkins University, was kind enough to explain many subtle aspects of his "end of history" theory to me in Nanjing. Howard Stein, visiting professor of African and African American Studies, University of Michigan, Ann Arbor, improved my understanding of the Washington consensus and problematic aspects of G-7 misassistance to Russia. Associate Professor Janine Wedel, School of Public Policy, George Mason University, and Joseph Stiglitz shed further light on the problem.

Natalia Vennikova coauthored some of the underlying essays supporting this text and untiringly assisted me with Russian source materials. My graduate research assistants Yabin Sun and Xilong Chen, along with many undergraduate volunteers, including Lauren Ghiloni, did yeomen service, as did Nancy Kocher, who smiling endured typing seemingly endless textual revisions. My wife Susan and daughter Justine provided continuous encouragement, and my son David was a never-ending source of insight and inspiration. My gratitude to everyone is immense. I of course am solely responsible for the book's content.

RUSSIA IN THE 21st CENTURY

INTRODUCTION

The corpse of the Soviet Union was still warm when Francis Fukuyama heralded the "end of history" in 1992, using a phrase reminiscent of Karl Marx's utopian prediction that history would stop once the world had become fully communist.[1] For a decade, it seemed that the "idea of the West"[2] – liberal, democratic, humanitarian free enterprise – had vanquished its "Muscovite" authoritarian rival[3] and would reign supreme. As in Marx's adolescent idyll,[4] peace, harmony, prosperity, and happiness would flourish forever under a new world order once the post-Soviet transition was complete. Whatever the Soviet economic and military realities may have been, they couldn't deflect Russia from its progressive course or form the basis for transmuted conflict.

Of course, few expected smooth sailing and no one expected perfection. The "end of history" was only a metaphor conjuring a glimpse of the paradise that might be attained if the West had the pluck and wit to press forward. Western leaders did not flinch. They embarked on ambitious programs of liberalization, democratization, market building, globalization, and arms reduction, but with mixed results. The transformational depression in the former Soviet Union (far deeper than the drop in consumption during World War II), the financial crises of 1998, flagging growth, widening global economic inequality, nuclear proliferation, the Balkan wars, the Arab–Israeli crisis, Indian–Pakistani brinkmanship, 9/11, and the Iraq war in 2003 have all been discouraging, but it can still be argued that, though history continues to unfold, liberal democratic free enterprise has taken root throughout Eurasia and a revival of superpower rivalry is unthinkable.

Russia is more open than at any time since the Bolshevik revolution. Economic liberty, including the right to own productive assets and engage

1

in private business, has been greatly expanded. People are making headway transforming paper civil rights into realities, and democratic institutions are being built despite the persistence of political authoritarianism.[5] But the dead hand of the past hasn't completely withered. Russia has "modernized" itself by adopting most of the trappings of the West, but it has not become westernized. Its consumers still aren't economically sovereign, its government isn't democratically responsive to the electorate, and Russian society is blatantly unjust.

Kremlin leaders have been chastened by the dissolution of the Soviet Union and the hyperdepression that ensued, but old reflexes remain, together with the paradoxes. Russia's economy is depressed, but the leadership expects to recover lost ground. The country has no capacity to compete in the global consumer goods market, but it is a leading arms exporter. Its military-industrial complex and armed forces are in disarray, but it plans to repair the problem by 2010. And while Russia's geopolitical reach is narrowly circumscribed, the Putin administration confidently anticipates reclaiming the federation's status as a great power. The word "superpower" is still taboo,[6] but if greatness is attained, dormant capabilities will be rediscovered.[7]

The unthinkable is thinkable, and given Russia's vast mineral and intellectual wealth, it is doable as well. The main obstacles, as during the Communist era, are the corruptness, inefficiency, and inequity of its system. Should the leadership try to reconstitute its full military capacities using the economic mechanism it has today, Russia will become a colossus with feet of clay.[8] It will have enormous military power and considerable global influence, but the level of consumption for everyone except a small coterie will remain Spartan. Having rid itself of the "no-frills" system it possessed during the Communist era, it will end up as a structurally militarized managed market successor to the Soviet Union.

Sacrificing consumer welfare and social justice for heightened power and privilege seems prodigal, even to postmodern skeptics.[9] The priorities appear antiquated, yet its systems, along with the psychology and culture of the Russian people, are pressing Russia in this direction. "Rational expectationalists" aren't fazed. They recognize that many other countries reject the West but are confident that constructive dialogue and engagement can bring them around.[10] They may be right. Perhaps tirelessly repeating the mantra of liberal, democratic, humanitarian free enterprise will suffice to make the Kremlin a reliable ally and partner in peace.[11]

This book, however, explains why it is more likely that Russia will reemerge as a "prodigal superpower" with a colossal military burden, docile oligarchs, and no-frills living standards for a subservient majority – a superpower frustrated by deterrence, economic backwardness, and popular discontent because it cannot say one thing yet do another and prosper.[12] The gap between the western ideals Vladimir Putin espouses and the actions of Russia's oligarchs, bureaucracy, security services, military-industrial complex, and mafia, not to mention the behavior of the new Russians, seems too great to prevent the nation from sliding back to the future.

Russia's fate depends largely on the insightfulness and resolve of its head of state. Putin or his successors will have to go beyond declarations of idealist intent and the kind of paper reforms that primarily advance oligarchic consolidation by repressing the forces of authoritarianism and privilege sufficiently to make "westernization" work. The leadership could have an epiphany. It could realize that feigning democracy and free enterprise while entrenching hierarchy and power is not only unjust but counterproductive. Or that incorporation into the European Union and globalization could save the day. More likely, the leadership will need better outside coaching before it is able to pursue the policies that are best for Russia. Further, it will need not only to have explained what must be done and why[13] but also to be confronted with the potential consequences of denial. Russians know or can easily learn what to do (*chto delat'?*), but for cultural and selfish reasons they seldom act in accordance with the national interest.[14] They recognize this flaw and are scathingly self-critical, but they have nonetheless become adept at using humor, rationalization, and self-deception to avoid modifying their behavior. Giving correct counsel is therefore futile unless the prescriptions are complemented by the reality principle. Whenever Russia's leaders say one thing but do the reverse, to their own and the West's detriment, they must be reprimanded.[15]

This policy approach will be rejected by those who deny Russia's habituation to authority and privilege or interpret it as an "infantile disorder" best treated with forbearance. These analysts must be required to defend their position by presenting evidence substantiating that Russia is on the path toward westernization, not just modernization, as occured in the Soviet Union during the twentieth century. The counterthesis – that Russia is trapped in a Muscovite authoritarian mold that gravely impairs the competitiveness of its civilian economy and that prods its leadership toward reconstituting its dormant military power – also calls for proof. Supporters of this postition need to establish that past efforts at western-ization failed; that the success of Putin's economic, political, and military reforms remains doubtful; that a military-industrial revival is technically feasible; and that the "end of history" isn't at hand.[16]

Three of these tasks are simple conceptual and statistical exercises. It is now widely conceded that the liberal reforms following Stalin's death didn't westernize the USSR, that Russia's contemporary economic sit-uation is precarious,[17] and that history will continue to unfold in unex-pected ways. But the prospects for military-industrial rejuvenation are more controversial. Those who believe that the West is best assume that other economies cannot generate enough wealth and know-how to be militarily competitive and tend to downplay conflicting evidence. On the other hand, those who recognize that nondemocratic societies can suc-cessfully modernize argue that modernization can only be accomplished by subordinating military to civilian interests.

Both attitudes are understandable but misguided. Inferior systems can compensate for low productivity by concentrating resources and talent in the military-industrial complex, trading reduced living standards for power. Similarly, post-Soviet authoritarian societies can modernize by borrowing technology without paring their defense. This book shows that the Soviet Union succeeded in both these regards and explains why Russia can do better.

Vladimir Putin is barred from rebuilding a superior war machine nei-ther by economic necessity nor by democratic rationality. Will he tread this path? Social science cannot provide a definitive answer, but various forces are jointly prodding the Kremlin back toward full rearmament.

Should Putin embrace the pursuit of heightened military power, west-ern solicitude won't stay his hand. He will have to be persuaded that the short-run security and economic gains to be derived from fifth-generation military reindustrialization will not offset the long-term harm to Russia's ruling elites – that in the final analysis Muscovite market authoritarian-ism will subject Kremlin leaders to the same frustrations that destroyed Soviet power. This book tries to make the case that current trends to-ward authoritarianism and greater military power will both lead to a dead end and should be rejected now lest they soon become irreversible.

Table I.1. *Soviet defense burden 1928–90: Defense spending as a percentage of GNP*

	Bergson	CIA
1928	1.0	
1937	6.2	
1940	13.8	
1944	38.8	
1950	10.3	
1951		24.2
1955	10.2	19.5
1960		14.5
1965		16.0
1970		15.4
1975		15.5
1980		15.3
1985		14.9
1990		13.8
2000		13.2

Note: Bergson's estimates are derived from the official Soviet defense budget and are valued in established 1937 ruble prices. The CIA's numbers are valued in established 1982 ruble prices. The estimate for 2000 was computed by Rosefielde in 2000 dollars using CIA methods.

Source: Abram Bergson, *The Real National Income of the Soviet Union since 1928*, Harvard University Press, Cambridge, MA, 1961, p. 46, table 3, p. 48, table 4, pp. 61, 364. Noel Firth and James Noren, *Soviet Defense Spending: A History of CIA Estimates, 1950–1990*, Texas A&M University, College Station, 1998, pp. 129–30, table 5.10 (table 6.4, this volume).

The main points to grasp are these:

1. The Soviet Union was, and Russia remains, structurally militarized. The Soviet economy was, and the Russian economy has the dormant potential to be, dominated by (a) the security concerns of the leadership, the genshtab (general staff), and the VPK (military-industrial complex) on the demand side, supported by an immense military-industrial asset base with superior embodied technology constantly improved by large RDT&E outlays, and (b) a priority factor allocation support system on the supply side. This assertion is substantiated by the defense burden statistics in Table I.1, which show that the military's share of GNP has been continuously in the double digits since the late 1930s.

2. The CIA's published estimates understate the defense burden because its weapons cost–estimating procedures took inadequate account of improving Soviet military technology and purported "constant" weapons prices were improperly lowered yearly as "productivity" gains reduced real input costs. A MIG25 produced in 1990 under this "input cost" convention was counted in the agency's real weapons growth series as being worth only 90 percent of the same fighter built in 1989, even though the ruble price was stated to be the same. The resulting downward bias is obvious. No country computes statistics this way for comparison with other nations' real defense output, and the method was never publically vetted. The agency covered up the downward bias by falsely claiming Soviet weapons weren't being rapidly technically improved and attributing the discrepancy between its misconstructed prices and those directly collected in the Soviet Union to "hidden inflation." Donald Burton (CIA), however, completed a study in the early 1990s demonstrating that Soviet weapons indeed were being continuously improved, which, together with unclassified DIA weapons production data, clearly shows, that the Soviet defense burden was not only higher than the agency reported but was rising rapidly (chap. 3). The agency was alerted to the problem of rising real weapons growth by the information obtained directly from the books of the Soviet Ministry of Defense, which revealed that the agency's weapons estimate was only a quarter of the 1970 but it chose to ignore the threat because it alleged that the Soviet military machine-building series was distorted by "hidden inflation." The agency's mishandling of this matter was governed by its conviction, partly based on public cultural values, that the Soviet Union was gradually demilitarizing and by its unwillingness to consider the alternative.

3. In the late 1980s, the Soviet defense burden (using the DOD's broad definition) was in the vicinity of 30 percent of GNP, according to Vitaly Shlykov and Academician Yuri Yaremenko, who independently audited the numbers for the Central Committee of the Communist Party.

4. Soviet weapons procurement grew rapidly, for the most part at double-digit rates, throughout the post-Stalin era, including the waning years of the Gorbachev administration.

5. The Soviet economy didn't collapse because it couldn't adjust to reductions in weapons production, as the CIA (Noren and Kurtzweg) hypothesized (reductions that never occurred, according to Shlykov and William Lee). It was undone by a wave of insider plunder precipitated by the green light Gorbachev gave to "spontaneous privatization," managerial misappropriation, asset stripping, and entrepreneurial fraud, all under the guise of "liberalization."

6. The West failed to grasp the reality of Soviet structural militarization because the CIA misleadingly argued that post-Stalin weapons growth was close to zero and that while the defense burden was immense it was steadily declining, indicating the mounting importance of civilian concerns. The agency also confusingly and contradictorily claimed that the main cause of the burden being so high was weapons price inflation, encouraging some scholars like Franklyn Holzman to assert that the Soviet defense burden wasn't much larger than officially claimed and was smaller than America's. This conviction was so firmly embedded that Holzman failed to recant even after Gorbachev revealed that Soviet defense spending in 1989 was twice his estimate. Other Sovietologists reinforced these mischaracterizations by sweeping the issue of structural militarization under the rug, focusing their attention on civilian topics, implying by omission that the defense sector was peripheral.

7. The gray eminence shaping western views of Soviet economic performance and potential was Abram Bergson. During the early years of the Cold War, when people entertained the possibility that socialism might displace capitalism and intellectual attention was concentrated on the great Soviet challenge, Bergson took the position, based on his analysis of Oscar Lange's economic theory of socialism, that Soviet economic planning was viable and that the USSR could conceivably best the West. And he argued with conviction in 1953 that Soviet data were "reliable" and "usable" enough to sustain these judgments before undertaking the requisite calculations to prove them. But a decade later, he had a change of heart, concluding on the basis of a series of Rand studies and his own textbook that "efficiency," "productivity," and "productivity growth" were central planning's Achilles' heel. Thereafter, the majority of his work and that of the CIA was dedicated to corroborating this prophesy. Both were able to show that Soviet economic growth was decelerating and that factor productivity was falling because technological progress wasn't fast enough to offset the rate of increase of new capital formation. But this implied neither declining living standards nor economic collapse. Most Sovietologists, following Bergson's lead, argued that while the rate of per capita consumption growth would surely fall below the "golden age" rate in the West, it would converge to an asymptote high enough above zero to keep the system viable. Socialism wouldn't bury capitalism, but neither would it fade quietly into the night.

8. These attitudes dovetailed with the nostrums of public culture. Soviet communism, viewed from the perspective of consensus cultural values like tolerance, diversity, and conflict avoidance, was seen as a legitimate social experiment that hadn't turned out as well as its architects had hoped but that nonetheless offered the prospect of learning and constructive reform. During the early years, it had sometimes misbehaved and threatened its neighbors, but it was liberalizing and putting militarism behind it. This left Soviet leaders with two choices. They could coexist harmoniously with the West, accepting the material shortcomings of their system, or they could transition to democratic free enterprise. Either way, there would be a happy ending, without armed conflict or internal collapse.

9. These cultural verities, together with Bergson's conception of Soviet economic potential and his assumption that western recomputations of Kremlin statistics from subaggregates were reliable and usable, explain why the West was blindsided by the Soviet Union's dissolution. Everyone should have known better. How could a country that criminalized business, entrepreneurship, and private property; fixed prices; and shouldered a double-digit defense burden have increased per capita consumption more rapidly than the United States and Europe for most of the postwar period, as the CIA's series indicated? The answer obviously was that the data were corrupt. Gorbachev proved it when he acknowledged in 1989 that the official Soviet defense budgetary statistic excluded weapons, and Bergson's own Rand study of USSR growth during 1928–37 similarly revealed that Stalin's aggregate growth claims couldn't be reconciled with any weighting of the subaggregate data. Sovietologists and the CIA, for diverse reasons, wanted to believe that the numbers were good enough and fell victim to their wishful thinking.

10. The Soviet collapse testifies amply to the fact that living standards were more nearly stagnant, as Gorbachev complained, than steadily improving, as Bergson's conception of planning required. Charles Wolf, Jr., and Henry Rowen's Team B portrayal of the Soviet Union as an "impoverished superpower" came closer to the mark, but in the final analysis Shlykov's characterization is best. The communist version of Muscovy was a "pushek i masla" regime, imposing Spartan living standards on its subjects in order to maximize military preparedness.

11. The postcommunist epoch has been a tale of two paradigms: "globalism" and "cultural determinism." The first envisions the former Soviet Union embracing peaceful, democratic free enterprise as a rational, universal ideal. Gorbachev's, Yeltsin's, and Putin's reforms are presumed to be virtuously motivated, and the glitches that have arisen, like Russia's fifteen-year hyperdepression, are ascribed to policy errors. Institutional obstacles are acknowledged but deemed inconsequential. This globalist preconception isn't new. It is a variant of the Cold War faith that rational Soviet leaders would eventually liberalize. The counterhypothesis is that Russia is unique, not universal – that the emerging postcommunist system is more strongly influenced by its Muscovite heritage than the logic of westernization. The government is liberally autocratic and has a democratic veneer, just as under Czar Nicholas II. The "commanding heights" of the economy, as the Bolsheviks used to say, are managed and controlled by insiders, oligarchs, and rent seekers beholden to the president, who at his discretion as a rent grantor can confiscate the assets they "administer" or can otherwise revise their user privileges. Authoritarian politics are in command, not markets, and the state apparatus strongly reflects the aspirations of the security services, the genshtab, and the VPK. The closed and opaque character of the system fosters moral hazard and stultifying corruption.

12. The evolution of the Russian economic mechanism, the state bureaucracy, and presidential power and the federation's military modernization plan all point to the Kremlin returning back to the future.

13. Russia has an intact military-industrial complex, a genshtab, an approved military modernization blueprint, and the mineral wealth to reactivate its dormant structurally militarized potential. Supply-side constraints don't preclude a return to prodigal superpowerdom.

14. Russia's future is culturally "path dependent" but not inevitable. Westernization is demonstrably better than Muscovite prodigal superpowerdom, and Putin is clever enough to evaluate the alternatives dispassionately, if he can be coaxed past his wall of denial.

15. Muscovite culture has conditioned him and most other Kremlin leaders to suspend their disbelief, assuming that they can reconcile opposites. Gorbachev thought that he could enrich his inner circle through "spontaneous privatization," improve productivity, democratize, expand weapons production while "disarming," and advance the people's welfare all within the parameters of party autocracy. Putin appears to similarly believe that markets without the rule of law and democracy will provide his administration with the best of both worlds, free enterprise–driven prosperity and vast military and political power.

16. Persuading Putin that Russia is on the wrong path will require more than cogent logic. The West must modify its public culture–approved strategy of compliments and bribes – cheerleading insincere liberalization and providing lavish assistance – by confronting the Kremlin with reality and insisting that it forswear prodigal superpowerdom and medieval Muscovy.

17. The West is disinclined to tackle the problem head on. It prefers to chant the mantra of the Washington consensus and employ influence payments. It too is befuddled by globalist rhetoric. In this regard, Putin is no more to blame than the West.

18. Nonetheless, it is important to try and break with the tried and disproven eclectic engagement methods of the past because the reemergence of Russia as a Muscovite prodigal superpower threatens to destabilize world security and is certain to blight the lives of most Russians.

1

AFTER "THE END OF HISTORY"

FROM COEXISTENCE TO THE END OF HISTORY

The prevailing perception of Soviet economic and military potential and hence post-Soviet possibilities was forged during the late 1950s and early 1960s by scholars connected with Harvard and MIT such as Abram Bergson, Alexander Gerschenkron, Simon Kuznets, Evsei Domar, Joseph Berliner, Franklyn Holzman, and Marshall Goldman.[1] In an intellectually polarized era during which the Soviet Union was heralded as a socialist savior and damned by John Maynard Keynes as a "slave state," these scholars appropriated the middle ground by offering sophisticated "theory-normed" positivist theories and impressive scholarship.[2] Socialists were mollified by calculations showing extraordinary feats of growth during the 1930s using one convention, while Stalin's detractors were placated by humdrum results arrived at using another. The fears of those impressed by the Soviet Union's economic and military challenge during the 1950s were validated, but comfort was offered by predictions of the waning of the communist economic and military miracles and by proclamations of the superiority of markets over central planning in the long term. Although this supposed superiority was unwelcome news for socialists, they could find solace in the Soviet Union's purported egalitarian virtues; its rejection of militarism; its steadily improving living standard; and the possibility of democratic, market socialist reform, peaceful coexistence, and global systemic convergence. Patience was the watchword. If you didn't like what you saw today, tune back tomorrow for a brighter day, whatever that might be.

The confection was irresistible. Not only did it offer something for everyone, but it appeared to uphold the "idea of the West": enlightenment "public cultural values" motivating individual and societal action. It confirmed America's faith in the superiority of democracy, markets, social justice, tolerance, diversity, and conflict avoidance while affirming the power of reason as an engine of peaceful coexistence and constructive reform.

But it was based on mistaken assumptions. With the benefit of hindsight, we can see that the Soviet Union hadn't assimilated the idea of the West, nor found a way to successfully navigate to it. Although internal performance measures like GDP growth suggested that central planning was a viable and even competitive economic system, they were belied by direct perceptions of a widening gap between western and Soviet per capita consumption.[3] Moreover, the economy was far more militarized than was conceded, and the quality of life was a pale shadow of what socialists thought it to be. The Bolsheviks had stumbled upon a formula for barracks socialism, a strategy that Vitaly Shlykov (former deputy chairman of the Russian Defense Council) dubbed "pushek i masla" (guns and margarine),[4] which offered vast military power, Spartan consumption, and social regimentation tolerable in an epoch of revolutionary ascetism but insufferable as leaders and the populace began to suspect that the grayness of existence would never end. The Cambridge School wasn't oblivious to the monotony, futility, and bleakness of Soviet life but refused to believe that it was regime threatening. It thought that Gorbachev's vision of market communism offered sufficient hope for a better future – that the system would evolve and endure.

What went awry? The Cambridge School concedes nothing.[5] Together with the Central Intelligence Agency,[6] it denies that any of its concepts or calculations were flawed. Nor does it admit to having misappraised the complex possibilities of communist modernization and reform. The transition process merely heightened the Soviet leaders' appreciation of the long-term deficiencies of administrative command planning more than anticipated and fortified their resolve to bear short-term adjustment costs. Once Gorbachev, Yeltsin, and Soviet liberals came to grips with the possibilities of improving economic efficacy, they rejected half measures, moving vigorously toward constructing their brand of western social democracy. Some members of the Cambridge School may have been converted to the "Washington consensus" along the way, disavowing the durability of pluralist coexistence,[7] but they didn't admit to being otherwise mistaken.

Their position is misleading. It mischaracterizes what the Soviet Union was and what it is becoming. It is based on a myth of Soviet and post-Soviet westernization that obscures contemporary economic potential. The USSR from the outset was an authoritarian, military mobilization regime with a proletarian revolutionary ideology; it has since metamorphosed into a mixed system that is composed of demobilized, physically managed subnetworks and inefficient markets and that allows a privileged coterie to live prodigally off the resources that once sustained the USSR's military-industrial complex (VPK). Russia's future, which may see a reversion to a military mobilization regime, remains shackled to this Muscovite authoritarian identity.[8]

THE IDEA OF THE WEST

The countervision of Russia as a modernizing state heading toward its European home is best conceptualized in terms of the economic and political aspects of what Samuel Huntington calls the "idea of the West."[9] For a nation to be classified as western, its people must be rational, individualist utility seekers who possess or embrace consumer sovereign markets, democratic governance, social justice, and pluralism responsive to the people's will – in other words, something approximating either the American free enterprise or the European Union social democratic ideal.

Westerners find these principles founded on humanism, enlightenment rationality, a Lockean social contract, and the "rule of law" appealing because they reconcile deeply felt cultural values like individualism, self-reliance, self-actualization, and equal opportunity with social harmony. Economic liberty makes it possible for everyone to receive precisely what he or she earns, while the social contract, the Golden Rule, the rule of law, and rationality foster fairness by eradicating market power, privilege, and discrimination.[10]

Democracy complements Pareto (competitive) efficiency by pairing consumer sovereignty with popular governance.[11] Just as economic liberty under the rule of law ensures that demand is responsive to product supply, so too does democracy obligate political representatives to act in accordance with their constituents' desires.

For strict libertarians, this means that the state's role is restricted to promulgating and enforcing laws that empower free enterprise, preserving the sanctity of commercial contracts, and providing for the national defense. But the idea of the West is also compatible with social democracy, which in the interests of social justice expands these duties to encompass economic regulation and transfer of wealth as long as these don't unduly degrade economic liberty and consumer sovereignty. Social democracy, the European Union's idea of the West, is from this perspective merely free enterprise in which a revised Lockean social contract tempers competition with a heavy dose of communitarian compassion originating in the sensibilities of the electorate. As in libertarianism, sovereignty is held to come from below. It is never imposed by self-anointed rulers.[12]

Sophisticated advocates of democratic free enterprise and social democracy recognize that markets and electoral democracies don't always operate as they should. Markets can be rigged and governments may disregard opinion polls.[13] Indeed, despite authoritative claims to the contrary, it isn't clear that people and government regulators carry their utility searches far enough to really matter. Individuals cannot rationally process more than a few complex consumption and business choices at any given point in time,[14] and often Paretian optionality cannot be achieved because decisions are distorted by impaired judgment and psychopathology. Likewise, Arrow's paradox proves that a government cannot act in accordance with its constituents' micropreferences, as required by the notion of political consumer sovereignty.[15]

These complications and others can be addressed by invoking concepts like "bounded rationality," which in effect acknowledge that neither the free enterprise nor the social democratic version of the idea of the West can generate outcomes closer to perfection than our limited human intellectual capacities allow. This stricture applies to the narrow conception of utility maximization based on the prevailing state of knowledge and to expanded models that encompass learning. Although the idea of the West is frequently depicted in majestic terms as a self-regulating political-economic system composed of renaissance men and women fully actualizing their material and human potential, reality is less Olympian. Bounded rationality, impaired judgment, psychopathology, and habits that influence "rational expectations," together with power seeking, cause western economies to significantly underachieve their ideals. For this reason the "idea of the West" throughout this volume refers to an aspirational ideal, not to real western practice.

It should also be recognized that "public cultural" values like the idea of the West are seldom complete blueprints for action and are therefore less coherent than many suppose. Rules are needed to deal with special situations. Should cigarette companies have the right to advertise? Should cell phones be permitted in concert halls? Under what conditions is affirmative action justified? And what sanctions are appropriate to deter violations of the Golden Rule? Opinions vary about permissibility and consequently about the real meaning of the idea of the West.

The efficacy of western public culture moreover is limited in another significant way. People may be hypocritical. They may fail to practice what they preach, their actions belying the idea of the West because they adhere to subcultural, shadow cultural, or countercultural values. While they pay lip service to the Golden Rule, they may feel that all is fair in love and war and deliberately seek to succeed at other people's expense. Or they may publically counsel patience on the premise that reason will prevail but act to preempt on the counterassumption that opponents are unreasonable.

All these qualifications clearly are important to appraising the merit of the idea of the West, but they aren't fatal. Advocates remain convinced that free enterprise and Paretian social democracy are far better than their competitors. They generate higher living standards, faster growth, and a superior quality of life.[16]

UNIVERSALISM

Most westerners steeped in their own cultural milieu find it difficult to believe that anyone could reject free enterprise, democracy, social justice, tolerance, diversity, and conflict avoidance because they consider authoritarianism and economic illiberality reprehensible (except when it is claimed that they are progressive) even though they know that the privileged resist the sharing of wealth and power. Consumer sovereignty, in their view, promotes prosperity more effectively, is fairer, and fosters social tranquility better than the alternatives. It is also inclusive. Any nation can westernize regardless of geography, race, ethnicity, and religion by founding its system on the principles of economic and political liberty – on the sovereignty of individuals, in other words, not the tyranny of the powerful. Further, because it is tolerant of diversity, the idea of the West is universal in the broadest sense. Westernization is not only ubiquitously suitable, it is best for every member of society as he or she perceives well-being in a competitive world under the rule of law. Unlike the particularistic regimes of the rest, the west is inherently global. It doesn't require states or religious fundamentalism, only the adherence of individuals everywhere to a Lockean social contract and the principles of mutual respect and fairness.

The validity of this lofty set of enlightenment claims has been deconstructed and challenged for centuries. The ensuing dialogue has clarified assumptions and possibilities. It has not been proven, and cannot be, that the West must always be best, but the idea of the West seems most promising.

CONVERGENCE

The idea of the West has sufficed since the eighteenth century to sustain the conviction that progress will lead to the globalization of democracy, economic liberty, prosperity, and universal peace. Through a process of emulation and prosleytization, inferior civilizations, it is argued, will adopt the idea of the West. They will be encouraged in their resolve by the possibilities of "catch-up." Neoclassical economic theory, especially the Stolper-Samuelson price equalization hypothesis, explains how all "western" nations should achieve the same high frontier living standard, even if there are barriers to international labor migration.[17] Universal attainment of this standard will come about through the transfer of capital and technology. Since, by assumption, newly westernizing states will be competitive free enterprise systems operating under the rule of law, rich countries will be drawn by low wages and other factor costs to invest in poor countries until profit rates and factor incomes globally equalize. As capital and technology flow toward the less developed westernizing nations, their growth will exceed the long-term "Golden Age" rate of the advanced countries, allowing the poor not only to prosper but to ultimately reach the global best standard. The same reasoning applies in the political sphere. Westernizing states with primitive democracies that favor privilege will import the best electoral practices of the advanced nations until, after a protracted period of reform, their politicians and administrators will be transformed into agents of the people's will. Consumer and popular sovereignty, along with common living standards, will reign everywhere, accompanied no doubt by world government and international harmony.[18] The idea of the West in this way has an influence that goes far beyond the contestable proposition that the West is best. With only modest embellishment, it becomes a visionary blueprint for transition, a benchmark for international relations, and a prophesy that brooks no skepticism.

KRUGMAN'S DICTUM

But suppose that some backward nations remain obstinately benighted? Paul Krugman deduces that they will remain backward on the grounds that, by rejecting the idea of the West, they will ensure their own inefficiency.[19] Their living standards will be substandard because they will necessarily misallocate factors and combine them with inferior technologies. And their growth will be retarded by insufficient foreign investment and inefficient technological transfer. Their domestic research and development will be similarly impaired, and they will misselect new technologies. Not only will deviant societies remain absolutely poor, but the gap between rich and poor will continuously widen. Democracy outside the West will flounder, there will be no world government, and international relations will deteriorate.

Few scholars have been this forthcoming. While it is commonplace to assert the West's superiority, to espouse the converse is considered narrow-minded. Multicultural defenders of rival civilizations take umbrage at the suggestion that nonwestern economies must underperform, just as socialists refused to acknowledge the superiority of markets during the Cold War, pressuring adherents of democratic free enterprise to be circumspect. While western officials, especially those associated with institutions like the International Monetary Fund, tirelessly preach the blessings of westernization, they often contradict themselves by predicting the convergence of all modernizing societies regardless of their political, economic, and cultural orientations. By conflating modernization with westernization, they extol the gospel without provoking the ire of nonbelievers.

Perhaps looking the other way is wise, especially for theorists who harbor doubts about whether the practice of democratic free enterprise closely approximates the ideal. But Krugman's dictum serves as a useful reminder that Russia's future may depend more on embracing the idea of the West than optimists concede. For backward nations like Russia, donning the cloak of democracy and economic liberty, borrowing technology, and modernizing won't in and of themselves bring about convergence, unless they also westernize.

EXCEPTIONALISM

Evidence substantiating Krugman's dictum abounds. The gap between rich and poor nations has been steadily increasing, despite the modernization of the majority of less developed states. Only eight nations – Japan, Taiwan, Hong Kong, Singapore, Malayasia, South Korea, Thailand, and China – have managed a sustained catch-up during the past four decades, and only the first four achieved living standards comparable with those of America and the advanced states of western Europe.[20] These successes, rare as they have been, demonstrate that some nonwestern societies may be exceptions to Krugman's dictum, even though Japan's waning fortunes augur otherwise. The performance of the rest also might not differ as much as expected from the West because America and the EU fail to adhere sufficiently to their own principles, special circumstances may apply, and nonwestern systems may exhibit compensating virtues or adopt asymmetric strategies that enable them to offset failures in some areas with successes in others.

The Soviet Union and now Russia have been frequently perceived in these terms. From the early days of Nikolai Bukharin and Evgeny Preobrazhensky's *ABCs of Communism* through the Stalin years, many were convinced that the Kremlin had discovered a superior socialist alternative to democratic free enterprise,[21] while others were impressed more narrowly by its resource mobilization model. Today, many in leadership roles continue to expect a miracle,[22] even though they cannot articulate its principles. We will later consider the possibility of a miracle in detail, but it is useful to observe from the outset that, despite the formidable evidence substantiating that the West really is best, there are nagging doubts that often prod scholars to contend that nonwestern systems are as valid as their western cousins. A good example of the analytic consequences of this thinking is provided by the "Cambridge paradox." Although most

Sovietologists in the Harvard circle and the CIA never seriously doubted that democracy and economic liberty were better than "socialist" central planning after the midsixties, they nonetheless subscribed to the view that Soviet postwar GDP and per capita consumption growth had kept pace with those of western countries until communism self-destructed in 1991,[23] without any explanation of why this seemed reasonable. Transitologists like Anders Aslund who foresee smooth sailing for Putin display a similar logical inconsistency.[24] They believe in the superiority of the idea of the West but also in the likelihood that societies that flout it will miraculously excel or swiftly transition to democratic free enterprise. The possibilities of exceptionalism and maturation make such outcomes thinkable[25] but hardly provide solid ground for a dispassionate consensus. While Putin may validate the dreams of Russia's Slavophiles, any sober assessment of the Kremlin's prospects must assume he won't, absent a rigorous demonstration of how such a Muscovite utopia can be realized.

SUMMARY

- American and European perceptions of and prescriptions for international security are blinkered by their "public culture," which Samuel Huntington aptly describes as the idea of the West.
- The idea of the West includes individualism, rationality (enlightenment reason), economic liberty, democracy, social justice, tolerance, diversity, conflict avoidance, and a proclivity to temporize on the assumption that rational self-interest will eventually impel rivals to amicably resolve their conflicts.
- Tolerance, pluralism, and conflict avoidance encourage analysts and policymakers to downplay the deficiencies of rivals even though their economic and political systems violate all the axioms of western public culture.
- This "approved contradiction" prevented analysts and policymakers from correctly assessing the Soviet Union's performance and potential.
- This assessment failure was predictable because inefficient economic systems and antidemocratic regimes matter. It should have been obvious that, despite the Soviet Union's public mantras of perfect planning and wise communist state governance, the shadow reality was severely inefficient and dysfunctional.

- Most Sovietologists are in denial. They reject Krugman's dictum, continuing to assert they were right, and in line with the "Washington consensus" they apply the same failed principles (e.g., of "convergence and rational self-restraint") in diagnosing Russia's economic and security prospects.
- What they call "transition theory" is merely the threadbare public cultural claim that all is well because it will end well.
- But all wasn't well and isn't well, nor will it be well unless Russia is understood as it is, not as we desire it to be.

2

PRODIGAL SUPERPOWER

BLINDSIDED

Almost no one saw it coming until moments before the crash. Why were Sovietologists blindsided? Didn't they know that the USSR's criminalization of business, entrepreneurship, and private ownership was sure to impair its global competitiveness? Were they dozing on the job? The answer isn't hard to find. Sovietologists weren't asleep at the watch. They were beguiled by their numbers and axioms and the theories that supported them, and they failed to pay adequate attention to other early warning signs. For those too young to remember, the consensus in the West – a consensus that reflected a protracted theoretical debate on the feasibility of Soviet socialism[1] – was that the economic performance of the USSR was mediocre given its economic backwardness but good enough to allow it to survive permanently in a state of peaceful coexistence. Official statistics published by Goskomstat (the State Statistical Committee), adjusted to reflect the western concept of gross domestic product (GDP), showed the USSR's national income and per capita consumption growth outpacing America's during the period 1955–89, with defense spending as a share of GDP persistently falling after 1969.[2] The USSR's margins of superiority weren't great, and the growth rate noticeably decelerated after 1968, as it had in Europe and Japan , but if no one in 1991 expected the West to implode, why fret about the USSR?

One possible reason for worry was that Soviet economic statistics were unreliable. However, western calculations broadly confirmed Goskomstat's findings. CIA estimates of the USSR's GNP during the years 1951–87, computed using 1982 ruble factor cost weights, are shown

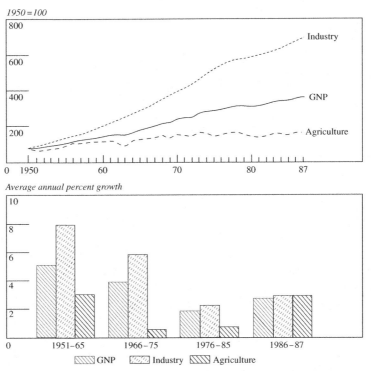

Figure 2.1. USSR: Trends in GNP and Industrial and Agricultural Output, 1950–87.
Source: Central Intelligence Agency, *Measures of Soviet Gross National Product in 1982 Prices*, Joint Economic Committee of Congress, Washington, DC, November 1990, p. 5.

in Figure 2.1. According to these estimates, the USSR's GNP grew at a rate of 3.9 percent per annum, well above the American rate for the same period. Table 2.1, taken from a study of the period 1951–80 and containing statistics calculated using 1970 ruble factor cost weights, corroborates this picture, although three European countries, Germany, Spain, and Italy, equal or excel the Soviet standard. Per capita consumption estimates reported in the same study and presented here in Table 2.2 give a favorable but less rosy impression. While living standard growth in the USSR outpaces the rate for America, the UK, Sweden, and Norway, the performance of the French, Germans, and Spaniards is notably superior. In any case, not bad for a country that criminalized business, entrepreneurship, and private property.

Table 2.1. *Average annual rate of growth of national product for selected OECD countries (GDP) and for the USSR (GNP), 1951–79*

Country	Growth rate
USSR	4.8
America	3.4
Finland	4.2
France	4.6
Germany	5.1
Italy	4.8
Netherlands	4.4
Norway	4.1
Spain	5.3
Sweden	3.4
UK	2.7

Source: USSR: Measures of Economic Growth and Development, 1950–80, Joint Economic Committee of Congress, December 8, 1982, p. 20, table 1.

Professional opinion broadly supported the CIA's figures (as do post-Soviet recompilations),[3] even though many thought the estimates too conservative. The only really controversial issue was the defense burden, which the agency estimated at 15 percent (military expenditures as a

Table 2.2. *Average annual rate of growth of per capita consumption in selected OECD countries and the USSR, 1951–79*

Country	Growth rate
USSR	3.0
America	2.2
Finland	3.4
France	3.9
Germany	4.6
Italy	4.0
Norway	2.5
Spain	4.1
Sweden	2.2
UK	2.2

Source: USSR: Measures of Economic Growth and Development, 1950–80, Joint Economic Committee of Congress, December 8, 1982, p. 22, table 3.

percentage of GNP). Some analysts, like Franklyn Holzman, placed the figure below that for America,[4] whereas others, like William Lee, put it above 20 percent.[5] But beyond the size issue, most agreed with the CIA that the burden hadn't grown after 1970 and that the weapons component was declining.[6] A net assessment therefore didn't support a case for collapse, although by 1989 the agency did begin to portray some developments since 1980, like flagging per capita consumption growth, as menacing.[7]

FALSE SCIENCE

What is wrong with this picture? Western analysts, who knew that statistics for Lenin were instruments of the class struggle and that machine building was the system's strong suit and consumption its Achilles' heel, persuaded themselves that Goskomstat's machine-building numbers were particularly unreliable, and they compounded this misjudgment by contending that Soviet fiat prices could measure neoclassical production potential with correct "factor cost" accounting. The details of this story have been recounted elsewhere, but the essentials deserve attention here.[8]

Back in the bad old days of Stalin, Soviet economic performance claims were seemingly preposterous. The growth rate for aggregate net material product (NMP; i.e., GDP minus nonproductive services) in the years 1928–37 was purported to be 16.7 percent per annum.[9] As with similar claims made later by Chairman Mao, few economists took them seriously. Western specialists, most notably Abram Bergson, therefore set out to evaluate their internal consistency with an eye toward producing a reliable alternative.[10] He proceeded by recalculating NMP from published subseries data, adjusting the results to reflect the western concept of GNP, and finally converting them to what he considered "production potential" measures computed using adjusted ruble factor costs. The first step proved to be the most critical. No matter how he weighted component subseries, he couldn't generate NMP or GNP growth rates greater than 11.9 percent.[11] The precise discrepancy wasn't important. What counted was that official aggregate growth rates were 40 percent higher than the figures recomputed from the Soviet's own subseries, proving that Moscow's aggregates were "freely invented," index manipulated, or the result of serious inadvertent error.

Table 2.3. *Soviet economic growth by sector of origin (CIA estimates: ruble price weights)*

	Compound annual rates					
	1950–55	1955–60	1960–65	1965–70	1970–75	1975–80
Ruble factor cost	6.4	6.4	5.0	5.4	4.0	2.8
Adjusted factor cost	5.4	5.9	5.0	5.3	3.7	2.7

Method: The adjusted factor cost GDP growth rates are taken directly from table A5. The ruble factor cost GDP growth rates are computed by aggregating the GNP components in table 5 with the CIA's established price value added shares for 1970 reported in table 11.

Sources: CIA, *USSR: Measures of Economic Growth and Development, 1950–80,* Joint Economic Committee of Congress, Washington, DC, December 8, 1982, p. 41, table 11, pp. 63–4, table A5.

A judgment, however, still had to be rendered as to whether the subaggregates themselves were reliable and also whether they could be given a plausible economic interpretation, since the underlying prices were determined administratively by the State Price Committee, not competitively by the market. A lively debate preceded Bergson's recomputations of Soviet GNP growth on both issues and was broadly resolved by the early 1950s.[12] The consensus was that the subaggregates should be assumed innocent until proven guilty (i.e., could provisionally be taken as roughly reliable)[13] and that, while adjusted ruble factor costing couldn't reflect the "consumer utility standard"(consumers' preferences), on average it could be interpreted as approximating the neoclassical supply-side "production potential" criterion given planners' preferences.[14] Henceforth, it became heretical to allege without sufficient cause that subaggregates significantly exaggerated achievements or to reject them as meaningless, for growth estimates at established prices tracked adjusted ruble factor cost series closely (Table 2.3) and supplementary index number theoretic tests confirmed that both series were well behaved.[15]

This sealed Sovietology's fate. The gap between the official Soviet growth rates (adjusted to reflect the concept of GDP)[16] and the western recalculations from subaggregates dwindled from more than 4.8 percent for the period 1928–37 to .5 percent for the period 1961–90.[17] Sovietologists – including those in the CIA, who selectively "low-balled" growth by substituting physical for official value subaggregates (Table 2.4), liberally interpreting Bergson's notion of "reasonable doubt"[18] – had willy-nilly become certified external auditors confirming the basic accuracy

Table 2.4. *USSR: Comparison of CIA estimates of industrial*
growth with official Soviet statistics, 1961–80 (percent)

	Industry		Machinery	
	CIA	Soviet	CIA	Soviet
1961–70	6.3	8.6	6.6	12.1
1971–80	4.0	5.9	5.1	9.9
1981–87	2.2	3.9	2.4	6.3

Source: CIA, *Measures of Soviet Gross National Product in 1982 Prices,* Joint
Economic Committee of Congress, Washington, DC, November 1990, p. 23.

of Goskomstat's post-Stalin figures. They could pride themselves on
exposing the overstatement between official aggregate growth rates and
their recalculations from subaggregates, but they couldn't sufficiently
challenge the reliability of the per capita consumption growth statistics
when perceptions or theory conflicted with numbers crunched in accordance with approved procedures. The best they could do was substitute
physical series for value sector of origin series whenever evidence of hidden inflation seemed compelling or convictions drove them to it, hoping
Goskomstat hadn't made undisclosed adjustments for the "quality" of the
physical mix. Consequently, while they may have lamented the shoddy
quality of Soviet consumer goods, they couldn't take Gorbachev's warning cries of "zastoi" (stagnation) appropriately to heart, because their
own numbers showed Soviet per capita consumption still growing.

Ironically, though the majority of Sovietologists missed Gorbachev's
alert,[19] certain that adjusted Goskomstat consumption statistics were
sufficiently "reliable," they ignored the other great early warning sign,
the Soviet arms buildup, because, as will be explained in chapter 3, they
mistakenly supposed military machine-building data were extraordinarily upward biased. The Soviet world of their untestable and elastic numerical conjuring consequently seemed to be stably decelerating and
benign.

But the illusion couldn't stand up to Soviet reality. Gorbachev and the
Communist Young Turks who advised him knew better. Frustrated with
the Soviet Union's material squalor, its structural militarization, and their
own limited prospects, they launched, with mixed motives, a series of ill-
conceived reforms that eventually tore the Soviet Union asunder, leaving
the CIA and Sovietologists scratching their heads.[20]

POSTWAR PERFORMANCE

We will never know precisely how badly the Soviet economy performed because, as widely suspected, the problem came not only from above but from below. Sovietologists did a laudable job of uncovering the free invention and indexing antics of TsSU (the Central Statistical Agency) – or, as Harrison would have it, its inadvertent errors[21] – by recalculating aggregate Stalin era national income from official subaggregates. But they could not accurately gauge the overreporting of physical output and the falsification of value data. The first type of distortion is easily understood. Producers simply overstated their output and explained away delivery deficits as spoilage. Or they added mud to grain and measured the "improvement" in tons.[22]

The second type, however, is more interesting. The problem is rooted in the deficiencies of Soviet administrative price formation. Like many of his contemporaries, Karl Marx believed that value was intrinsic and inhered in the quantity of labor. The prices of goods and services accordingly could be computed by aggregating direct and indirect (capital services) labor time, allowing for skill differentials if desired. Philosophical qualms about labor input being the ultimate arbiter of value aside, labor value theory made no allowance for some types of product and service improvements. If better designs enhanced quality (utility) without altering labor input, original and improved product prices must be the same, even though superior items were clearly preferable. This confronted Soviet systems directors with a dilemma. They could adhere strictly to Marxist labor value theory and accept the consequences, or they could bend Marxist principle to recognize the value of qualitative improvements, including those embodied in new goods. Without admitting heresy, price setters adopted rules raising unit prices "appropriately" above *sebestoimost* (prime cost), throwing the door open to abuse for anyone who benefited from falsely claiming that product characteristics had been improved.

The phenomenon was insidious because the Soviet state had an interest in promoting qualitative improvements and new goods but lacked effective methods for measuring competitive hedonic benefit. Likewise, while auditors in principle could verify whether enterprise managers adhered to the cost and "value" pricing rules for new and improved goods, in practice "red directors" (enterprise managers) had considerable leeway that they and their supervisors were tempted to exploit because overpricing

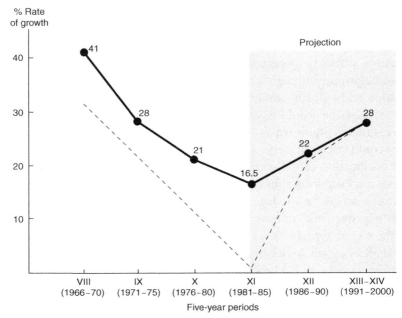

Figure 2.2. Growth rates of national income in the USSR over five-year periods, 1966–2000.

Source: Abel Aganbegyan, *The Economic Challenge of Perestroika*, Indiana University Press, Bloomington, 1988. (Used by permission of Indiana University Press and The Random House Group Limited.)

helped give the leadership the erroneous impression that some plans had been fulfilled. Spurious innovation (false claims to have created new products) from their perspective was a victimless and riskless crime. Although extraordinary profit and productivity growth provided telltale traces of hidden inflation, the problem was mitigated by periodic price reductions or could be concealed with deceptive cost accounting. Moreover, if what Vladimir Kontorovich has recently asserted is correct, there wasn't any need to fret about concealment because pressure to engage in overpricing often came from above.[23]

Hidden inflation in these and other ways became the great corrupter of Soviet statistics.[24] "What is the difference between three- and four-star Soviet cognac?" goes one joke. The punchline – "The number of stars on the label" – effectively conveys the point. Figure 2.2, prepared by Abel Aganbegyan, chief economic advisor to Gorbachev, illustrates his perception of the phenomenon as exemplified in postwar Soviet economic performance (represented by the dashed line). No wonder Gorbachev had no qualms condemning "zastoi" when the Goskomstat's statistics showed per capita consumption catching up with America's. Although the invisible character of the fraud (the mislabeling of inflation as "value added") shields the illusion of growth from precise quantification, it is reasonable to infer, given the USSR's unceremonious collapse, that much of its consumer prosperity was a mirage.

The same presumption holds for the rest of the economy, though it is least applicable to military machine building, because World War II, if nothing else, proved the Soviets could mass-produce competitive combat weapons; the Defense Intelligence Agency's satellite reconnaissance photos documented the post-Stalin arms buildup; William Lee's estimates indicated that 80 percent of Soviet RDT&E (research, development, testing, and evaluation) was devoted to defense, including weapons-building technology; and there were no anonymous consumers. Weapons were designed by the military-industrial complex (VPK) for the Ministry of Defense and the general staff (genshtab), who knew their goods and were ill-disposed toward flimflam that eroded the purchasing power of their budgetary allocations. On balance, and in light of the USSR's collapse, it seems safe to conclude that Soviet economic growth during 1955–89 was slower than America's, Europe's, and Japan's, as competitive market theory suggests and Bergson expected after 1963,[25] with the brunt of the adjustment being borne outside the defense sector.

INTEPRETATION

Consideration also needs to be given to the possibility that the dissonance between the statistical record and Soviet disunion has a complementary explanation. Perhaps adjusted factor cost estimates of Soviet growth didn't meaningfully measure technical efficiency and production potential. This appears to be an important aspect of the riddle of postwar Soviet economic growth. Steven Rosefielde and R. W. Pfouts have shown mathematically that adjusted factor costing doesn't measure marginal rates of product transformation given linear homogeneous production functions, as claimed.[26] Soviet managers were prevented by numerous quantitative constraints from basing their production decisions on relative prices, and even if the constraints were nonbinding, they had no knowledge of western adjusted factor cost prices and therefore could not have been governed by them. Insofar as red directors took prices into account, they relied on official wholesale ruble factor cost prices, and consequently, as originally surmised by Lord Lionel Robbins, Ludwig von Mises, and Frederich von Hayek, neither adjusted factor cost nor Soviet fiat prices measure neoclassical production potential or consumer utility. Soviet managers and planners doubtlessly strove to economize, given false prices, but they were unable to optimize planners' or consumers' utilities.[27]

BEHIND THE "HUMAN FACE"

The USSR revealed by scrubbing away the Sovietological assumptions of subaggregate reliability, spurious weapons innovation, and neoclassical meaningfulness isn't pretty. Instead of a planned socialist system rapidly improving consumption standards for the broad masses against the odds[28] while holding the line on defense, we are confronted with a "prodigal superpower." Beneath the gilding, the Soviet Union turns out to be a structurally militarized economy that consumed an inordinate share of GDP from the mid-1930s onward and an expanding share after 1955 (see chap. 3), exhibited subpar aggregate growth, and provided a nearly stagnant mangy dog living standard, just as Gorbachev perceived it.[29] Its virtue from the leadership's perspective is obvious. The command economy was the wellspring of the leadership's privileges and the Soviet Union's vast military power. This had been enough for Stalin's successors, until Gorbachev crystallized the desire of the Communist Party's Young Turks for more. The Sovietologists had been right in one sense: The system could have continued chugging along if its leaders had been content. The physical management system that girded it was much more complex than central planning[30] and very robust. But by sweeping its warts under a rug of treacherous assumptions, the Sovietologists failed to appreciate how easily things could become unglued by simmering discontents intrinsic to the Muscovite system.[31] They missed the signs then, and they aren't doing a conspicuously better job now discerning the emergence of Russia as a prodigal superpower.

SUMMARY

- Sovietologists, even free enterprise libertarians like Warren Nutter, overestimated Soviet economic performance because they directly or indirectly allowed the principles of tolerance, diversity, and conflict avoidance characteristic of western public culture to dull their judgment.

- Sovietologists shielded themselves from criticism by allowing the "facts" to speak for themselves, though these "facts" were misleading and in addition were misconstrued; by pretending that adjusted factor costing made prices approximately proportional (on average) to marginal rates of enterprise transformation; and by occasionally tampering with the evidence, substituting physical for real value production series on pretexts Bergson would not have approved.

- Output statistics were said to reliably measure "production potential," that is, "technically efficient" supply, and sometimes "systems directors' preferences" as well.

- CIA estimates of Soviet GNP growth were declared reliable in the same sense, even though the USSR's economic performance was inexplicably better than market theory implied was possible.

- The CIA did take some account of "spurious innovation" and "hidden inflation," especially in the military machine-building sector, but the adjustments were misguided and, with regard to weapons, mismotivated as well. The agency falsely erased Soviet weapons growth but confirmed official consumption growth statistics. The average postwar GNP adjustment for the period 1951–90 was approximately 1 percentage point.

- These finding were strong but wrong.

- The Soviet economy wasn't technically efficient; neither aggregate production nor per capita consumption grew faster than in the West; weapons growth wasn't negligible; planning didn't provide a competitive living standard; and the compensatory benefits of "communism," whatever these might have been, weren't enough to keep the population from rejecting the USSR's inferior economic system.

- The verdict of history must be that the Cambridge School, the CIA, and western socialists were misled, the Cambridge School and the CIA by their cultures, premises, convictions, and methods, the socialists by the chimera of scientific planning.

- All three remain in varying degrees of denial. They neither repudiate their estimates nor are willing to explain the incompatibility of these estimates with Paretian theory and the fall of Soviet communism.
- Their refusal to contemplate their errors and/or learn the pertinent lessons distorts their perceptions of Russia's contemporary economic potential.

3

STRUCTURAL MILITARIZATION

The most important aspect of the CIA's mismeasurements was the false readings they gave of Soviet economic potential. The numbers made it seem that the USSR could gradually normalize to a mass consumption society or do so more swiftly by curtailing military outlays. Gorbachev's revelation that living standards were stagnant implied a very different problematic. The USSR was losing in the great living standards race with the West because administrative command planning wasn't up to the task. And what Gertrude Schroeder has called the post-Stalin treadmill of economic reform did little to improve the USSR's economic capability.[1]

The system, however, was good for something.[2] As World War II and subsequent Defense Intelligence Agency (DIA) studies clearly demonstrated, the Soviet economic mechanism was capable of mass-producing competitive combat weapons. Central planning allowed the leadership to concentrate its best research and development, material, and human resources on the task without worrying that market forces would bid them away, a prioritization that paid conspicuous dividends in terms of military and international political power. This ability to focus resources on the development and production of weapons, together with the importance placed on military power by Stalin and his successors, led to the Soviet Union's "structural militarization." In other words, supply-side comparative advantage priority access to resources and the demands of the Soviet general staff (genshtab), the military-industrial complex (*voennyi promyshlennyi kompleks* [VPK]), and the Kremlin coalesced to drive the Soviet economy. Instead of pitching resources down a black consumption hole, Moscow learned to live with and love structural militarization, a phenomenon the CIA's costing methodology prevented it from grasping.

WESTERN DEFENSE ESTIMATES

Cold War era appraisals of Soviet defense activities were developed based on the same premises as were used for the analysis of national income. It was assumed that most Soviet statistical subseries, after being factor cost adjusted, were "usable" (unless there was compelling evidence to the contrary) and that they provided meaningful measures of production potential. Adjusted factor costing was permissible because it conformed to SNA procedures, even if the results didn't measure "production potential." The same principle applied to transforming data from Marxist to western accounting standards. But tampering with the evidence was strictly prohibited unless adjustments were carried out for the purpose of sensitivity testing and the results were treated accordingly. More specifically, the CIA couldn't substitute physical for value subseries and claim that it was legitimately operating within the parameters of Bergson's method and SNA procedures or that its results were "unbiased."

Most analysts also believed that official subseries were complete,[3] that the components reported accurately reflected official NMP and GNP statistics, and that the official aggregate defense budgetary expenditure statistics were correct, given Soviet definitions.[4] They therefore believed that total Soviet defense spending and components could be reliably compared with American defense expenditures by adjusting Goskomstat's numbers to fit U.S. defense-accounting conventions. Although there was some appreciation of the fact that Soviet pricing and profit policies could have been devised to understate defense costs,[5] most analysts thought that Soviet and western defense activities could be satisfactorily compared by ascertaining the definitional boundaries of the Kremlin's aggregate and subseries expenditure and production statistics.

Sovietologists approached this accounting classification game with relish, applying the same principles of sufficient "usability" that served them so badly in assessing aggregate Soviet economic performance. The guiding rule was the false premise that Goskomstat statistics were only fudged at the margins.[6] The analysts reasoned that the aggregate defense budgetary statistic included all core defense activities – uniformed military manpower (soldiers), operations and maintenance, procurement (of weapons and other durable military equipment), military construction (of barracks, fortifications, airfields, etc.), and RDT&E (research, development, testing, and evaluation) – although some defense expenditures were hidden

Table 3.1. *CIA and Goskomstat estimates of total Soviet defense spending 1960–75 (billions of rubles)*

		CIA	
	Goskomstat	Prerevision	Postrevision
1960	9.3	14.3	28.5
1961	11.6	14.9	29.7
1962	12.6	15.5	30.9
1963	13.9	16.1	32.1
1964	13.3	16.7	33.3
1965	12.8	17.4	34.7
1966	13.4	18.1	36.1
1967	14.5	18.8	37.5
1968	16.7	19.8	39.5
1969	17.7	20.8	41.5
1970	17.9	21.0	42.0
1971	17.9	21.8	43.5
1972	17.9	22.5	43.0
1973	17.9	23.8	47.5
1974	17.7	24.8	49.5
1975	17.4	(25.8)	51.5

Source: Steven Rosefielde, *False Science: Underestimating the Soviet Arms Buildup*, Transaction Publishers, New Brunswick, NJ, 1987, pp. 186–7, table 13.11, p. 253, table 19.2.

in other budgetary categories. Paramilitary forces, like troops of the Ministry of Internal Affairs (MVD) and the State Security Committee (KGB), and perhaps dual-purpose items, like the long-range Backfire bombers assigned to them, were considered subsidiary or were assumed to be covered elsewhere.[7] The analysts supposed further that Goskomstat's definitions of military manpower, operations and maintenance, procurement, military construction, and RDT&E broadly corresponded with America's, reducing the problem of concealment to the simple tasks of adjusting the official defense budgetary figures in light of estimates of military-related activities concealed in other categories and checking the plausibility of the aggregate using the CIA's costing methods.[8] Before 1975, the agency's "building block" and adjusted budgetary estimates exceeded Goskomstat's aggregate defense expenditure entry by approximately 50 percent since 1960 (Table 3.1).[9] Most of this disparity stemmed from the CIA's nonprocurement defense estimates, which were easily reconciled with its Soviet GNP accounts (see Table 3.2).[10] And procurement

Table 3.2. *CIA prerevision estimates of the*
structure of Soviet defense activities 1970
(billions of rubles)

MBMW	5.5
Construction	0.6
RDT&E	8.0
Outlays, necessary	5.6
Military personnel	5.3
Total	23.0

Note: The total in the original table is 25 billion rubles, which reflects the range technique used by the CIA. There is no discrepancy.

Source: Steven Rosefielde, *False Science: Underestimating the Soviet Arms Buildup*, Transaction Publishers, New Brunswick, NJ, 1987, p. 294, table A11.

was so small, 5.5 billion rubles, that it fit well with the "other machine-building" subsector of the reconstructed Soviet input-output table, allowing for minor concealment in other categories. The burden of defense (the military share of GNP) in 1970, according to the agency's reckoning, was approximately 6 percent, although higher figures could have been generated with the broader definitions of defense activities sometimes applied later.[11]

New information obtained directly from the books of the Soviet Ministry of Defense in 1975 revealed that procurement expenditures alone for 1970 may have been greater than Goskomstat's aggregate defense budgetary entry and thus shattered the Sovietologists' illusion that official statistics were "reliable." Bergson himself swore Goskomstat's defense budget figures were accurate for the period 1928–58, yet suddenly there was incontrovertible evidence this wasn't so, at least for the years 1969 and 1970. The CIA grudgingly conceded its misassumption, but only on this particular, and then set about salvaging whatever else it could with an eye, first, to justifying its prior judgment that Soviet defense spending was nonthreatening and, second, to restoring the prestige of its methodology. It accomplished these goals by attributing its 200-percent weapons underestimate to a single glitch: outdated ruble weapons prices that understated procurement costs. There had been no weapons miscount, nor qualitative misappraisal. Soviet weapons were merely more expensive.[12] In a twinkling of an eye, the estimate of 1970 Soviet defense spending went from 6 to 13.6 percent of GNP (Table 3.3), but the underlying trend

Table 3.3. *Soviet defense expenditures as a share of GNP (ruble estimates: percentage)*

	Goskomstat	CIA Prerevision	CIA Postrevision
1960	5.5	10	18
1965	5.4	8.3	15.7
1970	5.3	6.0	13.6
1975	3.9	5.7	12.8

Source: Steven Rosefielde, *False Science: Underestimating the Soviet Arms Buildup,* Transactions, New Brunswick, NJ, 1987, p. 201, table 14.2.

was unaffected because the agency claimed there had been no change in its perceptions of Soviet weapons programs.

The CIA's prerevision weapons series had reported "zero" growth for 1960–74, and its postrevision rate for 1976–84 (Table 3.4) was the same, causing both the defense (Table 3.5) and procurement burdens to fall as GNP expanded. These statistics seemed incompatible with the DIA's physical production and deployment statistics,[13] but were upheld nonetheless because the CIA claimed that its new ruble weapons price data were accurate and trumped the physical evidence. The CIA couldn't be swayed, even though it new weapons ruble price collection was slender, was indirect, and wasn't fine enough to evaluate whether weapon components had been qualitatively improved. Nor was the CIA chastened by a negative "peace dividend." As the computed defense burden diminished, Soviet growth decelerated, contrary to the CIA's prediction.[14]

These "blemishes" aside, the CIA weathered the storm well from its perspective. It had been compelled to raise the USSR's defense burden above America's, but it left the downward trend generated by the direct costing methodology intact. And although it had to abandon the "usability" of the defense budgetary statistic, all wasn't lost, because Peter Wiles conjectured that the Soviets treated weapons for accounting purposes as "capital" covered by the Fund for the National Economy rather than as defense.[15] Hence, it could be claimed that the defense budgetary statistic really was usable if properly decoded.

Of course, it was nonsense to suggest that an official aggregate defense budgetary statistic that excluded weapons wasn't deceptive just because arms were concealed as capital, especially when the Soviets challenged

Table 3.4. *Soviet military procurement 1976–84 (billions of 1970 rubles)*

	CIA	Rosefielde
1976	23.4	38.3
1977	23.4	41.7
1978	23.4	45.5
1979	23.4	49.6
1980	23.4	54.1
1981	23.4	57.9
1982	(23.4)	61.9
1983	(23.4)	66.3
1984	(23.4)	70.9
1976–84 compound annual rate of growth (percent)	0	8
1989	(23.4)	90.5

Method: The CIA's 1983 series is calculated by accepting the agency's 1982 series figure for 1976 and setting all subsequent figures at the same value in accordance with the deputy director for intelligence's testimony provided in *Allocation of Resources in the Soviet Union and China – 1983*, Joint Economic Committee of Congress, September 1983, p. 306. The Rosefielde series is computed by applying the growth rate displayed by the CIA's noncivilian machine-building series for 1976–80 (9 percent per annum) to the 1976 base year figure reported in table 13.1, column 6, p. 158 (*False Science*). Estimates for 1981–4 are calculated with the DIA's estimate of military machine-building growth in 1981–3 (7 percent per annum). See DIA, *USSR: Military Economic Trends and Resource Allocation – 1983*, August 1983. These conventions are utilized in lieu of the extrapolated ex-post weapons growth rate for 1960–70 (12.9 percent per annum) because no new independent observations have been acquired from the books of the Soviet Ministry of Defense and because the machine-building statistics suggest that the pace of the Soviet arms buildup has decelerated. The subperiod 1984–9 is extrapolated assuming a continued decline to 5 percent. A more precise estimate couldn't be calculated because the DIA ceased publishing its military machine-building series. Lee estimates weapons growth during 1984–8 at 7 percent per annum. See William Lee, *Trends in Soviet Military Outlays and Economic Priorities 1970–1988*, United States Committee on Foreign Relations, Republican Staff Memorandum, Washington, DC, July 30, 1990, p. 8, table A-7.

Source: Steven Rosefielde, *False Science: Underestimating the Soviet Arms Buildup*, Transaction Publishers, New Brunswick, NJ, 1987, p. xix, table R2.

America to reduce its defense spending to an equivalent share of GNP – a proposal championed by Becker.[16] But Wiles's conjecture served the CIA well when Mikhail Gorbachev finally admitted in 1989, fifteen years after the "bombshell," that the official aggregate defense budgetary statistic was only a third of the "true" figure, largely because it excluded

Table 3.5. *Soviet defense activities 1976–84, including military pensions and RDT&E (valued in billions of 1970 rubles)*

	CIA	Rosefielde
1976	53.3	69.2
1977	54.4	73.7
1978	55.5	78.6
1979	56.6	83.8
1980	57.5	89.4
1981	58.8	94.3
1982	60.0	99.5
1983	(61.2)	105.1
1984	(62.4)	110.9
1976–84 compound annual rate of growth (percent)	2	6.1

Source: Steven Rosefielde, *False Science: Understanding the Soviet Arms Buildup*, Transaction Publishers, New Brunswick, NJ, 1987, p. xxiv, table R5.

procurement.[17] Although the disclosure made a mockery of the CIA's premises during the early years of the Cold War through the mid-1970s and suggests that Soviet counterintelligence may have deliberately tried to deceive America into reducing its defense burden to the Soviet level,[18] the revelation was shrugged off and spun as confirmation that the CIA's direct costing methodology was reliable after outdated ruble weapons prices were replaced with new data. The agency, after all, had always said that Goskomstat's defense budgetary entry was understated (but not by 200 percent), and Gorbachev had provided partial confirmation.

THE WHOLE TRUTH

Neither Gorbachev's glasnost numbers nor the CIA's higher estimates constituted the whole truth.[19] Both were severely downward biased. The main problem in the CIA's case stemmed from its mishandling of Goskomstat's military and civilian machine-building statistics rather than those for manpower,[20] military construction, and operations. The data in Table 2.4 comparing the CIA's estimates of Soviet industrial sectoral growth for 1961–87 with Goskomstat's corresponding figures for Russia reveal that the CIA's machine-building growth estimates were

approximately half Goskomstat's. Despite its insistence that Soviet subseries data were "reliable," the CIA had chosen to violate its own rule
against data tampering by marking down the growth displayed by the
official Soviet machine-building statistics. It had been compelled to do
so by a profound dilemma. Thanks to its tenacious claim that the 200-
percent error in its weapons estimate for 1970 was attributable to "cost"
and not real value added, its direct costing growth estimates of Soviet
procurement were much lower than those indicated by the reconstructed
Goskomstat military machine-building subseries.[21] Soviet statistics were
screaming that the CIA was misinterpreting its ruble weapons prices, but
the agency was out to lunch.

Had it chosen to adhere to Bergson's admonitions against tampering with official subseries, the CIA would have been forced to reject
"outdated" ruble weapons prices as the source of its infamous defense-
spending underestimate, shifting attention to other methodological flaws,
especially its faulty use of "learning curves," and acknowledging that it
was wrong both about magnitudes and trends. But since it had dug in
its heels, one of the pillars of its methodology had to go. The decision
went against "usability" and for protecting improper "learning curve"
procedures because hidden inflation provided a convenient rationale for
maintaining its conviction that the Soviet Union was gradually demilitarizing. Although VPK price gouging made absolutely no sense in the
Soviet institutional context, the agency wouldn't reconsider its position
and instead set about purging the "unreliable" Soviet military machine-
building subseries, along with the civilian machine-building series, by replacing them with a subseries called SPIOER (Soviet Physical Indexes
Office of Economic Research), which contained its zero-growth weapons
figures and a "physical" civilian subseries, even though it acknowledged
that the technique inherently biased machine-building growth downward
by assuming weapons and other machinery were unimproved throughout
the Cold War.[22]

Had the agency stuck to its and Bergson's "usability" premise, or split
the difference, its estimate of the Soviet procurement burden in 1984
would have been nearly triple and its estimate of the total defense burden
nearly double its published figures (Tables 3.4 and 3.5), both valued in
constant 1970 ruble prices. The disparity in current prices, however, was
negligible because, while the agency denied that higher prices reflected
value added, it illogically treated "hidden inflation" as a "real" cost.[23]

The CIA's estimates of the defense share of GNP were also too low due to the exclusion of some paramilitary forces.[24] The activities of these forces, often indistinguishable from full-fledged military undertakings in the Soviet case[25] and under the direct control of the general staff (genshtab), were extensive and had no significant American counterparts. U.S. Department of Defense (DOD) calculations for the "cost of Soviet Empire" derived from CIA data added roughly 10 percentage points to the Soviet defense burden, increasing it from the familiar 15-percent figure to a mean of 25 percent.[26] This number, ten times larger than Goskomstat's defense budgetary statistic, would later turn out to be consistent with Politburo data and informed GRU (military intelligence) opinion[27] and help clarify the squabble over whether the Soviet Union was structurally militarized. If Goskomstat's revised defense budgetary statistic is accepted, a case can be made that the USSR's and America's military spending were not dissimilar, but if the CIA's "building block" method is used and the USSR's military expenditures are augmented by paramilitary outlays, the exorbitance of the USSR's defense effort is unmistakable, despite the downward bias caused by the CIA's mishandling of the Soviet military machine-building subseries and its misattribution of improved weapons technologies, and hence value added, to "hidden inflation."

DOLLAR COST ESTIMATING

During the Cold War, pride of place was usually accorded to the ruble estimates, especially those computed at adjusted factor cost, for they purportedly measured "production potential" and "opportunity costs" and hence illuminated the terms according to which guns were traded for butter at the margin. As explained in chapter 2, the Cambridge School's characterization of these matters is mathematically and operationally incorrect because managers were constrained from competitive profit maximizing, the product and factor prices of Goskomtsen (the state price committee) only reflected fiat *sebestoimost'*, and managers had no knowledge of Bergson's adjusted factor cost prices. Procurement and defense burden statistics consequently didn't measure scarcity values at the margin or on average and therefore were more opaque than previously conceded. We don't have a clear perception of the economic value of defense activities in the numerator or of GNP in the denominator, and therefore we must

Table 3.6. *Soviet and American defense activities*
1976–84, excluding military pensions and RDT&E
(valued in billions of 1978 dollars)

	USSR		U.S.
	CIA	Rosefielde	DOD
1976	120.8	141.0	84.0
1977	123.2	147.0	85.9
1978	125.7	155.0	86.9
1979	128.2	162.6	91.4
1980	130.8	170.7	93.8
1981	133.3	177.8	99.6
1982	136.0	185.4	108.4
1983	(138.8)	193.3	116.1
1984	(141.5)	201.5	126.7

Method: The CIA's postrevision figure reported in table 13.10
(*False Science*), column 1, is extrapolated to 1984 at 2 percent
per annum in accordance with the testimony of Robert Gates,
Deputy Director for Intelligence, CIA, to the Joint Economic
Committee of Congress: "Our latest dollar estimates show the
same trend since they are based on the same estimates of quantities of Soviet weapons. The estimated dollar cost of Soviet
defense activities grew at slightly less than 2 percent over the
1976–81 period, a percentage point below the long term average. Procurement costs in dollar terms did not grow during the
1976–81 period" (*Allocation of Resources in the Soviet Union
and China – 1983*, p. 307). The Rosefielde series is computed by
subtracting the CIA's weapons procurement estimates in table
13.2, column 2 (*False Science*), from its estimates of total Soviet
defense outlays, table R4, column 1, and then adding back the
author's Soviet weapons estimates reported in table R1, column
4. The DOD series measures total American defense expenditures less military pensions and RDT&E in accordance with the
CIA's definition of total Soviet dollar defense outlays. The estimates are taken form Department of Defense (Outlays), com-
puter printout, FY85, tables 6–11, and have been converted to
a calendar year basis expressed in 1978 calendar year prices.

Source: Steven Rosefielde, *False Science: Underestimating the
Soviet Arms Buildup*, Transaction Publishers, New Brunswick,
NJ, 1987, p. xxii, table R4.

treat burden statistics as a fuzzy indicator of nominal resource allocation.
However, some of the fog can be dispelled by considering the CIA dollar
estimates of Soviet defense activities.

Value measures computed in dollars ideally reflect the domestic
American opportunity costs of producing guns and butter according to
Soviet specifications. They illuminate neither domestic Soviet opportu-
nity costs nor global values because Moscow couldn't market its industrial

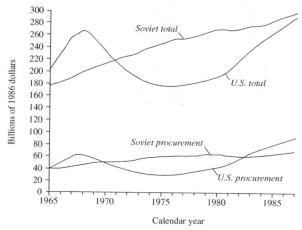

Figure 3.1. Cost of U.S. and Soviet defense activities, 1965–87.
Source: United States Central Intelligence Agency.

products in the West. Dollar estimates inform us what it would have cost to produce goods with characteristics the DOD, its civilian overseers, and consumers dispreferred. Such values only can be instructive to the extent individual analysts believe that Soviet and American defense activities were close substitutes.[28] With this caveat, it is still easily demonstrated why the USSR was considered a military-industrial superpower. The data presented in Table 3.6 indicate that the dollar cost of defense activities with Soviet characteristics surpassed American defense spending during 1976–84 by 20 percent on average. Figure 3.1 illustrates the CIA's perception of the expenditures of the two countries for the period 1965–87.[29] While it goes without saying that the market value of Soviet defense activities would have been less than their dollar replication costs, it is equally obvious that the scale of these activities was impressive and consistent with the official judgment that the Soviet and American defense efforts were roughly on a par. Soviet defense activities weren't an illusion, even though nearly invisible in Goskomstat's statistics, and they must have constituted an enormous share of the unknowable market value of the USSR's aggregate product because its weapons were more exportable than its industrial consumer goods.

This impression is underscored when a fundamental methodological error marring the CIA's dollar cost estimates is remedied. Goods and services of nonmarket economies must be directly costed for comparative purposes because their foreign exchange rates aren't determined by the forces of supply and demand. The CIA accordingly computed the dollar cost of weapons with Soviet characteristics from American engineering data and derivative parametric cost-estimating relationships (CERs).[30] These procedures were sound in principle, as was the use of learning curves to adjust the unit costs as serial production expanded. The unit cost of the first MIG25 hypothetically manufactured in the United States would greatly exceed the cost of the hundredth unit due to increasing marginal productivity. The same adjustment could also be rationalized by assuming that the reduced cost of the hundreth MIG25 unit was the consequence of accumulated learning – "mastering new technology" – rather than increasing returns in what is called Stage II.[31] On either interpretation, the dollar factor cost of any specified unit could validly serve as a constant price for computing real growth.

However, once these constant prices were set, proper indexing required they remain invariant. Unfortunately, the CIA's Military Economic Analysis Center (MEAC), failing to grasp this point, reduced its "constant" prices as serial production expanded in subsequent years in the Soviet Union. MIG25s produced in 1990 were valued, for the sake of example, at 90 percent of the same fighter in 1989, even though the unit prices were said by the agency to be "constant." This irregular convention, which violated the SNA standard, resulted in an artificial, systematically downward biased real output series that could not be challenged by outsiders, who neither knew anything about the convention nor had independent dollar cost data at their disposal to measure the distortion. Moreover, the problem was compounded by MEAC's application of old CERs for one system to new weapons without adequate adjustments for qualitative microcharacteristic improvements. If a MIG25 and MIG17 had the same weight, and other macroparameters were equal, then they were assigned the same dollar cost, even though comparison with analogous American weapons would have quickly revealed that the procedure disregarded high-cost improvements in avionics.[32]

This downward bias only came to light derivatively. The CIA's direct cost ruble procurement estimates weren't typically calculated from engineering and CER ruble weapons data. They were merely transformed from the dollar series using a handful of ruble-dollar conversion coefficients, and the results generated, as subsequent weapons price collection disclosed, were roughly half the actual values (see Table 3.4). Real Soviet procurement activities and correspondingly the defense share of the USSR's GNP consequently were far higher than the CIA's published statistics indicated. The magnitude of the disparity, narrowly defined to exclude paramilitary activities in accordance with DOD conventions, can be gleaned by comparing the author's dollar cost estimate of Soviet defense spending adjusted for the CIA's "learning curve" bias with counterpart DOD data for the United States. The Soviet advantage is approximately 63 percent for the years 1976–84 (Table 3.6), which, discounted as before for the lesser desirability of the USSR's defense characteristics, still conveys the strong impression that the dollar value of Moscow's military activities were far greater than the dollar value of Washington's during the Cold War.

Proof of this contention has recently been provided by Noel Firth and James Noren, who acknowledge that prices in real output "growth" indexes should not be downward adjusted sequentially year by year for "learning." No country in the world computes real growth indexes in this way, and the CIA didn't adjust U.S. data similarly in order to avoid mixing "apples with oranges" in its defense comparisons.

But Firth and Noren sophistically counterclaim that it is valid to annually downward adjust real "input cost" growth series, as if this is common practice or Bergson used the procedure when he was the director of the Russian Economic Subdivision of the OSS.[33] This is a distinction without a difference. There are no other examples of "input cost" growth series handled in this manner because the word "real" always means constant prices, not input and output prices adjusted for annual productivity changes. The "concept" was never vetted in the literature, and no user of CIA statistics could have imagined that the "real" estimates of SOVA (the CIA's Office of Soviet Analysis) had been calculated in this way.

Firth and Noren also try to save the day by presenting a figure (reprinted here as Figure 3.2) purportedly demonstrating that the magnitude of "learning curve" adjustments were trivial by comparing "real" Soviet procurement growth defined alternatively as "resource price" (input cost) and "output price." But their own table reveals the truth. It reports that Soviet procurement in 1970, computed in 1982 prices, was 32.1 billion rubles, whereas the CIA's graph puts the figure for the same year at approximately 40 billion rubles. The difference is the "learning curve" adjustment.[34]

The essence of our detective story is distilled in Figure 3.3, which compares the CIA's military procurement series in 1970 and 1982 learning

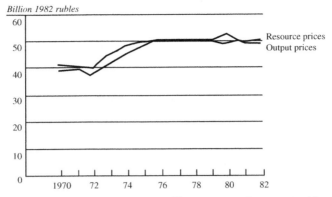

Figure 3.2. Soviet procurement as measured in two types of constant rubles. Two different measures of the annual value of Soviet procurement are shown. Both represent the levels of state set prices in the base year 1982, and both eliminate the vagaries of the Soviet price-setting system within a product group. The constant resource price line reflects cost reductions over time from learning. The constant output price line is based on the constant resource prices for the second year of production normalized to the constant resource price total in 1982. The constant resource price series is a better measure of the quantity of resources used in production, and the constant output price series is a better measure of the volume of output.

Source: United States Central Intelligence Agency.

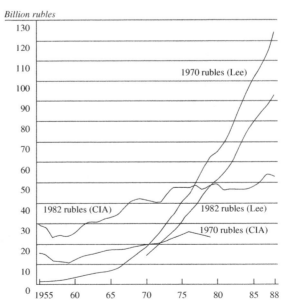

Figure 3.3. Estimates of Soviet military procurement by CIA and Lee. CIA estimates in 1982 rubles were compiled in 1985 and differ somewhat from more recent estimates. (Used by permission from Texas A & M University Press.)

Table 3.7. *Soviet military procurement 1960–75 (billions of 1970 rubles)*

		CIA		
	Rosefielde	Prerevision	Postrevision 1	Postrevision 2
1960	5.5	5.5	12.5	12.5
1961	6.1	5.6	13.0	13.0
1962	7.0	5.6	13.5	13.5
1963	7.9	5.7	14.1	14.1
1964	8.9	5.8	14.6	14.6
1965	10.1	5.8	15.2	15.2
1966	11.4	5.8	15.8	15.8
1967	12.9	5.7	16.4	16.4
1968	14.5	5.6	17.1	17.1
1969	16.4	5.6	17.8	17.8
1970	18.5	5.5	18.5	18.5
1971	20.9	5.6	19.2	(18.5)
1972	23.6	5.6	20.0	(18.5)
1973	26.6	5.7	20.8	(18.5)
1974	30.1	(5.7)	21.6	(18.5)
1975	33.9	(5.7)	22.5	(18.5)
Compound annual rate of growth (percent)	12.9	0.2	4.0	2.6

Method: Rosefielde: The best adjusted procurement growth rate, discussed in chapter 12 of *False Science*, is used to extrapolate Soviet arms growth for 1960–79. The base year estimate for 1960, 5.5 billion rubles, is the agency's and has been confirmed with the residual method. *Prerevision CIA:* The CIA prerevision 1955/60 ruble series was computed using the direct cost method. According to Donald Swain, Deputy Chief, Military-Economic Analysis Center, OSD, CIA letter dated August 9, 1977, the prerevision series grew on an intraperiod basis at the long-term rate for 1960–75. This has been taken into account by assuming that Soviet procurement grew 1.2 percent per annum during 1960–5 and fell at the same rate thereafter (1960–70). *Postrevision 1 CIA:* The CIA's "best" residual method estimate for 1970. *Postrevision 2 CIA:* The same as postrevision 1, except that the figures for 1970–5 have been reestimated in accordance the agency's 1983 series. See table 3.5.
Source: Steven Rosefielde, *Underestimating the Soviet Arms Buildup*, Transaction Publishers, New Brunswick, NJ, 1987, pp. 158–9, table 13.1.

curve–adjusted rubles with William Lee's estimates. The series in 1970 prices best illustrates the cumulative magnitude of the CIA's underestimate and its misreading of weapons growth during the Gorbachev years, disparities confirmed by Rosefielde's independent calculations (Tables 3.4 and 3.7).[35]

NUMBERS, PRIORS, AND POLICY MANAGEMENT

The CIA continues to deny that it underestimated Soviet weapons and defense expenditures, citing internal audits and friendly outside reviews.[36]

Table 3.8. *CIA estimates of Soviet weapons procurements 1980–9 (1982 ruble prices: billions)*

1980	50
1981	48
1982	50
1983	49
1984	50
1985	51
1986	52
1987	55
1988	54
1989	50

Source: Central Intelligence Agency and Defense Intelligence Agency, "The Soviet Economy Stumbles Badly in 1989," presented to the Technology and National Security Subcommittee of the Joint Economic Committee, Congress of the United States, April 20, 1990, published in *Allocation of Resources in the Soviet Union and China*, Joint Economic Committee, April 20, 1990, p. 40, fig. 4.

Noel Firth and James Noren have written an informative and wily history of the record, claiming among other things that the CIA didn't adjust its ruble dollar ratios to rationalize the forced quadrupling of its Soviet procurement estimates in 1975 but merely found better prices (which raised the ruble–dollar ratio!).[37] They also selectively report series to cover tracks. Their procurement numbers frequently do not match those disseminated to the national security community in the 1970s and 1980s at various levels of classifications (see sources for Tables 3.1 and 3.4). Their data imply a compound annual growth rate for 1960–80 of 3.3 percent, compared with a rate of 1.4 percent reported by CIA analyst Derk Swain (see Figure 3.1). The rate (with intraperiod oscillations) actually claimed from 1970 to 1989 in unclassified sources was zero. CIA and DIA testimony in the Joint Economic Committee of Congress publication *Allocation of Resources in the Soviet Union and China* (April 20, 1990) confirms the trend for 1980–89 (see Table 3.8).

The doggedness of Firth and Noren's narrative has many explanations, most of which need not detain us. However, a few aspects of the narrative are illuminating. The agency's outlook throughout was colored by the Sovietologists' premise that Goskomstat's data, even the defense budget

Table 3.9. *Soviet munitions spending*

Year	1928 rubles	1937 rubles	1928 index	1937 index	1928 burden	1937 burden
1928	0.2	0.4	100	100	0.6	0.2
1929	0.3	0.5	150	125		
1930	0.4	0.7	200	175		
1931	0.4	0.8	200	200		
1932	0.4	0.8	200	200		
1933	0.5	0.9	250	225		
1934	1.7	2.9	850	725		
1935	2.8	4.8	1400	1200		
1936	4.8	8.2	2400	2050		
1937	5.7	9.5	2800	2375	6.7	3.4
1938	7.4	12.3	3700	3075		
1939	11.9	19.9	5950	4975		
1940	16.1	26.8	8050	6700	17.0	6.5
1944	38.4	64.1				
1945	34.6	57.6				
1950	15.2	25.3				6.2
1953	21.7	36.1				
1955	23.6	39.4				6.5
1958	21.7	26.8				
Growth (percent)						
1928–37	39.5	37.3				
1937–40	42.2	41.3				

Note: Powell's munition data were provided by Bergson, who in turn derived the figures in current rubles as a residual from the official defense budget by subtracting soldiers' wages and subsistence. The ruble figures are factor cost in 1928 and 1937 prices. The burden is computed as the munitions share of Bergson's estimates, in corresponding prices.

Source: Raymond Powell, "Industrial Production," in Abram Bergson and Simon Kuznets, *Economic Trends in the Soviet Union*, Harvard University Press, Cambridge, MA, 1963, p. 178, table IV.9. Abram Bergson, "National Income," in Bergson and Kuznets, *Economic Trends in the Soviet Union*, table 1.1. Abram Bergson, *The Real National Income of the Soviet Union since 1928*, Harvard University Press, Cambridge, MA, 1961, p. 46, table 3, p. 88. table 17.

statistics, were reliable, "subject to modest adjustment." These numbers, like Bergson's postwar estimates (Tables 3.9 and 3.10), painted a picture of a civilian-oriented developing nation that was spending heavily on investment and moderately on defense (official budget) and seeking to gradually diminish its defense burden by keeping military outlays below the rate of aggregate growth. Its devious practice of downward adjusting "constant" prices for "learning"[38] enabled the CIA to square this picture with the otherwise contradictory figures generated by

Table 3.10. *Soviet defense spending*

Year	Current rubles (billions)	1937 rubles (billions)	Current burden (%)	1937 burden (%)	Military manpower (thousands)
1928	0.8	1.9	2.4	1.0	562
1937	17.4	17.4	6.2	6.2	1750
1940	56.5	45.8	13.0	13.8	3500
1944	135.7	118.0	30.2	38.8	12000
1950	80.8	42.4	8.9	10.3	4000
1955	105.4	62.0	8.9	10.2	5500

Source: Abram Bergson, *The Real National Income of the Soviet Union since 1928*, Harvard University Press, Cambridge, MA, 1961, p. 46, table 3, p. 48, table 4, pp. 61, 364.

the direct cost "building block" method both before and after the 1975 bombshell.

Since the problem was called to the agency's attention at the highest levels as early as 1981, those responsible for the numbers must have strongly believed that the spending "trend" displayed by the official defense budgetary statistics for 1969–88 and for 1989–91 (after Gorbachev admitted that the pre-1989 figures excluded weapons) was more reliable than its core preadjusted dollar series or alternative estimates by Lee, Rosefielde, and others. This predilection is clearly revealed in Firth and Noren's text by their claim that Gorbachev's "half-true" post-1988 defense budgetary statistics, combined with direct costing evidence, confirm that the economic burden of defense caused the Soviet Union to significantly curtail military programs, despite the fact that the evidence for the trend and the causality was equivocal.[39]

The same predisposition was evident in the CIA's interpretation of the pre-1975 numbers, when the burden was supposed to be a manageable 6 percent, and thereafter, when it was compelled to raise the baseline to 15 percent. Thus, while its persistent denial of fundamental error was variously motivated, overconfidence in the "reliability" of selected Soviet statistics and the conviction that the USSR's "high" defense burden discouraged any further arms buildup seem to have been primary. The agency always thought that the defense burden would compel Soviet leaders to embrace the idea of the West, whether the real number was 6 or 15 percent, a conviction supported by a strong public cultural preference for "rationality"-assured conflict avoidance, and it steadfastly refused to recognize the possibility of structural militarization.

STRUCTURAL MILITARIZATION

The scale of Soviet weapons production and defense spending is remarkable, especially in light of the postcommunist downward revision in Russian (Soviet) purchasing power parity (dollar–ruble ratios) as computed by Aleksei Ponomarenko, then deputy director of Goskomstat (see Appendix 3.1), which indicates that America's GNP was treble the USSR's in 1989.[40] Despite all the ambiguities of Soviet defense and national income statistics, current dollar estimates confirm that the Kremlin devoted a disproportionate share of the nation's resources to military activities, a finding in line with the ruble defense burden data and corroborated by defense manpower data. The best estimates indicate that the Soviet military-industrial complex employed 16 million people as well as supporting 6 million soldiers (including paramilitary troops) and up to 20 million reservists.[41]

Was this behavior a rational response to an exogenous threat or an endogenous characteristic of the Soviet productive system, with implications for contemporary Russia? The evidence points toward the latter. Soviet weapons procurement grew rapidly (see Tables 3.4 and 3.7) regardless of the global military balance or the waxing and waning of the Cold War, and its eventual slowing was due to the effects of aggregate growth retardation. The only plausible explanation for the post-Stalinist regime's unrelenting arms buildup, assuming that the leadership didn't intend to "liberate" Western Europe, is systemic. Bureaucratic inertia has sometimes been suggested, but Vitaly Shlykov, deputy chairman of the Russian Defense Council during the Yeltsin administration, attributes the behavior to structural militarization, a more sinister concept.

The bias toward excessive defense spending was the joint consequence of the attitude of the Kremlin toward mass mobilization preparedness and the activism of the Soviet military-industrial complex (VPK), reflected in Bergson's defense activities estimates for 1928–55 (Table 3.10). Stalin and his successors, influenced by the USSR's victory over Nazi Germany, believed that the USSR's national security depended on massive conscript armies, numerical superiority, robust hardware, advanced technologies, and extensive military-industrial capacities and reserves – factors that would allow it to fight and win prolonged wars against other mass armies and defend against blitzkrieg assaults.[42] This predisposed them toward outspending their postwar adversaries (who were more impressed with the German strategy Donald Rumsfeld recently described as the first "revolution in military affairs")[43] and made Kremlin leaders receptive to the blandishments of the VPK, which found it convenient to advance institutional interests while serving the country. The general staff (genshtab), the Ministry of Defense, and the VPK never tired of discovering new vulnerabilities or devising programs to redress them, and they usually succeeded in an economy where consumers and rivals could not compete for resources in the marketplace.[44] Nor was the leadership swayed toward moderation by "guns and butter" arguments because experience had taught them that planning was ill suited for creating an affluent society. "Militarization" in this way was woven into the economic fabric on both the demand and the supply sides of the equation.[45] There was no automatic civilian circular flow from worker income to consumer goods production and back to income. The dominant circuit began with the workers but was immediately diverted to the politburo and genshtab. Purchasing power was appropriated by the leadership and provided to the VPK, generating incomes siphoned off again by the state. Authoritarian Kremlin leaders were content to substitute power for prosperity, and their preferences couldn't be overturned by the ballot or the ruble.

Shlykov underscores this reality with two insights. First, he points out that the Kremlin wasn't entirely oblivious of consumer needs. Structural militarization was pursued through a policy of "guns and margarine" (*pushek i masla*), which provided the population with a "no-frills" living standard while freeing all other resources for defense. Second, this militarization continued unabated as technological progress increased GDP because military doctrine required the MOD and VPK to plan not just for the "worst" case but for the unimaginable as well. There could never be too much defense. Where the revolution in military affairs called for "optimization" under constraint, the *pushek i masla* approach mustered resources for unbounded needs.[46]

In a direct response to the proceedings of the conference entitled the CIA's Analysis of the Soviet Union 1947–1991, held at Princeton University on March 9 and 10, 2001, Shlykov, a consummate military intelligence and military-industrial complex insider, declared that the entire American intelligence community, including Team B, miscounted weapons, underestimated programs, underappraised costs, and misgauged the sustained mobilization capacity of the Soviet system.

Data on Soviet weapons production remain secret, scattered, but declassified published statistics show that the United States more often underestimated, rather than overestimated the size of the Soviet Union's military arsenal. For example, the Americans believed that the Soviet Union deployed 30,000 nuclear weapons and 500–600 tons of enriched uranium. But in reality, the figure was 45,000 weapons and 1,200 tons, according to Viktor Mikhailov, former Russian Minister of Atomic Energy. The Americans were also mistaken about Soviet tank inventories. They thought that the USSR had a little more than 50,000 tanks, at a time when it had 64,000 or even 68,000 according to another source.[47]

This myopia, understated by Shlykov because of Russian security laws, was attributed to an enormous *mertvaia zona* (dead zone), a blind spot regarding the "Soviet Union's unique war mobilization regime."[48] He asserts that the VPK system, over which he presided in various capacities, was designed to fight and win a prolonged war against all adversaries. Contrary to CIA and even Team B estimates, which were based on the assumption that the Soviet leadership was operating under an American-style rational expectations model, the Kremlin was going for broke.

This mentality is difficult for outsiders to appreciate because it is the antithesis of the idea of the West and could require unpleasant countermeasures. But it isn't illogical for a risk-averse government that likes to keep its options open, and it is consistent with the facts. Although most Sovietologists and the CIA were loath to believe that the Kremlin could be so "unreasonable" and misadjusted their data accordingly, the Soviets never abandoned structural militarization.

SWORDS INTO PLOUGHSHARES

It might seem to follow directly that the Kremlin's exorbitant allocation of resources to defense was a principal cause of Soviet postwar growth retardation and the system's ultimate collapse. This surmise cannot be disproven, for economic growth might have been invigorated by transferring resources from defense to RDT&E, by foreign technology transfer, and by investment, but the obvious benefits of a one-time transfer of resources to civilian activities aside, little could be expected from the Communist planning system. While the leadership proved that it could administrate a hundred-odd weapon systems, there were too many civilian options for microplanners to cope with. There is no reason to suppose that technological progress in the civilian sector could have been raised to the standard in military machine building or that consumer product characteristics could have been made responsive to demand in the Soviet supply-side system.[49] Although structural militarization wasn't an inextricable aspect of the Soviet productive control system, it played to the system's strength and in this sense may have been the course of least resistance. Swords simply could not have been converted into ploughshares in a way that would have saved the system from itself, and Moscow's failure to structurally demilitarize therefore should not be considered the root cause of Soviet disunion.

SUMMARY

- The Cambridge School and the CIA persistently understated the share of Soviet resources allocated to defense and the size of its military programs.
- The bias toward understatement became embedded in the CIA's direct weapons-costing methodology. Outdated cost-estimating relationships (CERs) failed to capture improvements in Soviet weapons technologies, and supposedly "constant" ruble and dollar prices in its real weapons series were lowered many percentage points every year, purportedly to capture the gains from "learning" as unit production expanded. Not only was this procedure statistically illegitimate, but the very existence of the technique was concealed so that congressional and executive users couldn't judge for themselves whether the procedure was misleading.
- Whenever SOVA's misestimates were exposed by new intelligence and official Soviet military machine-building subseries, the discrepancy was attributed to "hidden inflation," forcing the CIA into the position of claiming that its lightly adjusted civilian GDP series were "usable" and that official Soviet military machine-building statistics were "unusable" as a result of being heavily distorted by "spurious innovation."
- These contortions enabled the agency to maintain its public culturally approved conviction that the USSR was gradually demilitarizing but caused it to miss the big picture.

- The most important attribute of the Soviet production system was its structural militarization. The institutionally embedded demand for weapons was unbounded, and supply capacities were continuously expanded. As a consequence, the defense share of GDP rose to 25–30 percent during the postwar period, with the civilian share diminishing reciprocally. Contrary to the CIA's series, which showed the USSR's real per capita consumption growing more rapidly than America's, the only economic success the Kremlin ever achieved was mass weapons production.
- Structural militarization was a burden because it inhibited systemic change, but the USSR's massive defense spending wasn't primarily responsible for its low living standard, as resources couldn't have been effectively reallocated to high value added consumption under the Kremlin's central planning regime.
- These characteristics, which were missed entirely by the Cambridge School and the CIA, permanently consigned the USSR to the status of a prodigal superpower.
- The office of the secretary of defense grasped the problematic better than most but never fully appreciated the staying power of structural militarization. Also, its vision of Soviet reality was frequently dismissed as parochial.
- Few in West today appreciate that Russia remains structurally militarized, that its economic potential isn't significantly better than under communism, and therefore that it is at risk of drifting back to becoming a prodigal superpower.

APPENDIX 3.1

COMPARATIVE SIZE

Doubts about the value of Soviet goods and the quality of growth always abounded, and these seemed to be confirmed by Moscow's inability to export significant quantities of industrial manufactures to the developed West. But this and other tests didn't settle matters because it could be counterargued that East-West trade was impeded by Cold War restrictions or that socialist and capitalist tastes were incompatible.

Many claimed that Soviet goods weren't so much inferior as they were different,[50] a distinction that inclined purchasing power parity statisticians to value the USSR's GDP in dollars by matching similar items without further concern for the characteristics that made Soviet wares undesirable. This cost-side approach accorded well with Abram Bergson's concept of production potential,[51] as it emphasized technical productivity rather than demand-responsive characteristic choice. It allowed analysts to infer that dollar estimates served both as useful measures of the American opportunity costs of producing goods with Soviet characteristics and as a rough reflection of the value the global market placed on Russian products.[52] Lost in the shuffle was the possibility that Soviet goods were dispreferred in both the East and the West and that purchasing power parities had to be adjusted to account for this fact.

Using hindsight, the impact of these valuation conventions can be seen in the CIA's and Goskomstat's comparative Soviet–American dollar size estimates. Both show that Soviet GDP was two-thirds of America's.[53] Both portray the USSR as the world's second largest economy, with a first-tier per capita income just shy of the Western European mean, making Russia a military and consumer great power.

The debacle that followed the disintegration of the Soviet Union has brought about a radical reassessment of the Soviet Union's and Russia's economic standing. Specialists often continue to insist that their Soviet era calculations were right, but few outside the community believe them, particularly with regard to foreign trade, where it was often alleged that weak Soviet industrial exports to the West reflected COCOM barriers, not the inferior quality of the products.[54] When the Cold War was finally over and trade restrictions were repealed, the Russians still couldn't export their industrial products to the West.[55] The appropriate prices for these unsaleable exportables therefore should have been based on similarly worthless American goods, if indeed there were any, not valuable analogues. In case anyone missed the point, Russia's GDP could be computed through its managed exchange rate, which delivered a comparative size estimate only a small fraction of the old purchasing power parity estimates (for Russia).

Faced with this new reality, and assisted by the purchasing power parity pricing conventions adopted globally in the 1993 Standard National Accounts (SNA) methodology, which discounted some inferior characteristics, especially in services, analysts marked purchasing power parities down to roughly half the old CIA and Goskomstat levels. Following the near halving of physical production during the Yeltsin mistransition, Ponomarenko estimated Russian per capita GDP in 1995 at $3,750,[56] displacing Russia from the first tier to the lower part of the third tier, outside the ranks of the developed West. This figure has been revised upward in SNA 96 and SNA 99, which dropped adjustments for inferior services, but the precise figure is neither here nor there. What matters is the confirmation by OECD, World Bank, Goskomstat, and UN statisticians that proper characteristic matching associates the Soviet Union's collapse with poor quality growth.[57]

4

WHAT COULD HAVE BEEN DONE?

POWER AND PROSPERITY

The great irony of Soviet communism was that administrative command planning proved more suitable for weapons production than communalist abundance. Judging by the continuous rise in weapons production during 1985–8 documented by Lee (Fig. 3.3), Gorbachev, like his predecessors, appreciated military power but wanted more options as well, for a variety of contradictory reasons. We know with hindsight (see chaps. 5 and 6) that insofar as he sought to extricate the USSR from structural militarization and westernize it, he failed – that the USSR metamorphosed from a prodigal superpower founded on physical systems management (nonmarket) principles into a structurally militarized mixed economy with perverse Muscovite characteristics. Could this unfortunate outcome have been averted if structural demilitarization and democratic free enterprise had been Gorbachev's highest priorities and he had received better advice? The question is important because it sheds light on the gap between Russian public rhetoric and objective possibilities critical for assessing past actions and future prospects. The answer, which requires a detailed understanding of Soviet institutional realities, is sketched below. It will also serve here as a platform for analyzing what actually transpired later.

The USSR's productive strengths and weaknesses can be traced to its authoritarianism. The Bolsheviks constructed a productive mechanism based primarily on physical systems management principles rather than the "value" principles of markets. This mechanism allowed the state to organize and control factors, output, and distribution without external interference. The criminialization of private ownership, business, entrepreneurship, negotiated prices (including wages), and hence markets is a direct consequence of this authoritarianism, even though such prohibitions were rationalized as defensive measures forestalling capitalist revanche. Each prohibition curtailed a specific dimension of economic liberty. Outlawing business prevented people from bettering themselves by freely supplying customers with desirable goods and services. They were proscribed from producing, assisting, or engaging in profit-seeking commerce. Banning entrepreneurship denied innovators the opportunity to create new enterprises or to improve old ones, including state facilities. Nationalizing the means of production kept would-be investors from influencing state managers, and price fixing shielded managers from fluctuations in consumer demand. If the state chose to disregard transactors' preferences by undercompensating workers and overcharging buyers, it could do so with impunity because businessmen had been "liquidated" as a class and "red directors" (state enterprise managers), workers, and peasants had little room for maneuver. "Antiparasite" laws and material necessity forced employees to build Soviet "pyramids," but the Bolsheviks still had to deal with the problem of efficiency.

Mechanisms were needed to mobilize and efficiently utilize resources from the systems directors' perspective. Soviet leaders, with the assistance of the State Planning Agency and the State Statistical Agency, could determine the broad contours of aggregate and sectoral demand, but the details inevitably were left to government ministerial, administrative, and managerial functionaries and enterprise employees. Despite the suggestive imagery of "command economy," Gregory Grossman's felicitous term, the system wasn't optimally controlled.[1] Leaders, planners, ministers, and heads of main departments (*glavki*) could issue all the macrocommands they wished, but meso- and micro-decision-making regarding the 27 million goods in the official nomenclature were beyond their capacity.[2] By default, designers had enormous latitude in determining the characteristics of investments, weapons, and consumer goods. Workers had limited control over the intensity and quality of their labor. Red directors were empowered to classify employees (and hence effective wage rates), select input and output mixes, informally acquire scarce intermediate inputs (*tolkachi*), and organize production. Ministries had discretion over micro-input and production assignments, and the wholesale network exercised judgment in distributing retail goods. The State Price Committee and the incentive committees enjoyed some independence, and the State Bank had the power to advance credit.

Contrary to much conjecture, the Bolsheviks, like the Nazis after them, discovered that mobilizing resources wasn't difficult. Stalin found that he could achieve high levels of aggregate effective demand by ordering red directors to fulfill ambitious production plans and construction agencies to build new plants, employing otherwise redundant labor. The Paretian task of manufacturing goods consumers wanted was replaced with the simpler task of producing what was assigned (liberally construed), backed by the state's willingness to purchase as much output as enterprises could muster. Compliance with plan directives was encouraged by the threat of severe sanctions, including terror, and by the offer of material incentives. Red directors received handsome bonuses for overfulfilling physical output targets before the war and, to an increasing extent, for profit maximizing (subject to state-set wages and output prices) during the post-Stalin era. The leadership hoped that profit seeking would not only stimulate red directors to work harder but guide them toward better product mixes at minimum ruble cost.[3] To accomplish these objectives, workers were told that only those who worked would eat, while red directors, operating under the principle of "one-man rule," both coerced workers with punitive sanctions and used piecework bonuses to spur them toward greater exertion and productivity,[4] within the limits imposed by Soviet "job rights constraints."[5] As a consequence, functionaries, workers, and peasants alike generally were overfully employed and were induced or compelled to work hard, despite jokes to the effect that they "pretended to work and the state pretended to pay them." Indeed, most strata were underpaid, not only because the military absorbed such an enormous share of resources but because the state found it expedient to underpay them.

Physical systems management wasn't confined to manufacturing and agricultural enterprises. Productivity and growth required supporting services, including education, science, RDT&E, design, engineering, infrastructure, interindustrial allocation, retail distribution, foreign trade mechanisms, and technology transfer and diffusion. Each of these was handled in the same way. Institutions were tasked to physically maximize unconstrained by market demand and value. They were permitted to behave like Paretian rational actors, optimizing where they could, including through informal barter operations, as long as they remained insulated from consumer sovereignty and concealed their self-seeking from public scrutiny.

Forced, incentivized mass production in all its aspects, however, wasn't the panacea the Kremlin hoped it would be. No matter how ardently the systems directors tried, they could not construct a set of carrots and sticks that guided individual utility seekers to do for the leadership what it couldn't do for itself – identify the outputs that would maximize the people's welfare, allocate resources efficiently, and distribute final goods and services optimally. Authoritarian physical systems management could not evolve beyond its prehistoric roots. It was a dinosaur with a massive body and a pea brain, perfectly suited to superpower squalor but not the *dolce vita* many in Gorbachev's generation craved. They wanted guns and roses, like America had, and were determined to get them, even if it meant the command economy had to go. But how should this be done? The Bolsheviks had already failed the first time round to construct a well-functioning economy, and breaking with the established order was fraught with peril. How should they structurally demilitarize and deconstruct physical systems management this time to avoid transitioning to market authoritarianism and economic catastrophe (*katastroika*)[6] while assuring a Paretian outcome. Should they construct democratic free enterprise gradually or adopt authoritarian shock tactics, as they did in 1917 and 1929? The reformers opted for tradition on the pretext that a radical break with communism was the only viable path to the future and based on the claim that it wouldn't cause anything worse than a brief dip in living standards.[7] This zeal for the radical option reflected both the realization that physical systems management was a material dead end and Gorbachev's and Yeltsin's baser desire to enrich themselves and create an affluent circle of loyal supporters. These two leaders may also have believed they were helping the people, but they did nothing to protect their assets or assure their welfare. Given the low priority placed on the people's well-being, methodically dismantling the Soviet physical management system seemed pointless. Gorbachev and Yeltsin thought they had to scuttled it and replace it with a supply mechanism responsive to the inner circle's consumer demand. And this is precisely what they did, Gorbachev by allowing red directors, entrepreneurs, and "spontaneous" privatizers to disorganize the physical management control mechanism, which created havoc in interindustrial supply, and Yeltsin by voiding most state procurement contracts and rescinding guaranteed state production purchases (shock therapy). Some analysts have suggested that they had no choice, that there was no surgical way to break with the past.[8]

They are mistaken. Gorbachev and Yeltsin could easily have have chosen a democratic, free enterprise path if they had gone about it correctly.

The main priorities should have been to (1) prevent resource control from falling into the wrong hands, (2) redirect physical systems management toward civilian needs, (3) transform physical into market value–based systems management, (4) adopt market-facilitating cultural reforms, (5) establish the rule of contract law, (6) build market institutions, (7) implement self-purchase privatization, (8) provide lump-sum compensatory dividends for those unable to participate in self-purchase privatization, and (9) create competitive asset markets. This agenda is consonant with the approach advocated by the Washington consensus, but its focus and sequencing are drastically different. While private business, entrepreneurship, and ownership needed to be resuscitated, they could have been phased in gradually after the resource base was protected from pillage, structural demilitarization was well underway, worker welfare was protected, and dysfunctional aspects of Russia's predatory culture were quarantined. Likewise, equity wouldn't have been disregarded in the vainglorious pursuit of efficiency on the pretext that "omelettes cannot be made without breaking some eggs."

Implementation of this program would have been straightforward. The organizations responsible for physical systems management, including Gosplan (State Planning Agency), Gossnabsbyt' (State Wholesale Network), Gosbank (State Bank), and the supervisory ministries, would have been preserved initially and then phased out by gradually circumscribing their authority as market institutions developed apace. The leadership should have commenced structural demilitarization by reducing weapons, military construction, and defense RDT&E procurement orders while agreeing to purchase consumer goods produced by the VPK without limit, in accordance with prevailing practice. Had this been done, the VPK would have immediately pursued its interest by expanding civilian production without serious complication because 40 percent of VPK production under Communism consisted of consumer goods. To further facilitate the process, the leadership should have granted VPK managers wider discretion in running their firms, giving them a semblance of the rights of western firms, as Deng Xiaoping subsequently did, without granting them formal ownership.[9] It could then have allowed ownership rights to be earned by setting "strike prices" at which manager-worker groups could buy assets that had been devoted to civilian market operations. Firms should have been privatized in this way only when they demonstrated that their initiatives passed the competitive test.[10]

These liberalizing and internal privatization programs could have been concurrently introduced outside the VPK and supplemented with cultural reform, the establishment of the rule of law, and market institution building. As liberalization gained momentum, competition would have slowly determined how control over resources should have been reallocated between the VPK and civilian consumer goods producers, with the pool of transferable resources expanding due to reduced state defense procurement. The rational allocation of ownership could have advanced by gradually enlarging firms' right to buy and sell assets and carry out mergers and acquisitions. Throughout the process, the state would have had to remain vigilant against embezzlement and misappropriation of government assets. If these efforts succeeded to the degree they have in China, the Kremlin would have received ample funds from asset sales to compensate those who received a less than average amount of assets or were left out of the process entirely. Structural demilitarization pursued in these ways would have avoided all the traumas created by Yeltsin's shock therapy, and Ronald McKinnon's "Order of Economic Liberalization," preoccupied as it was with financial stabilization, would have been superfluous.[11] There would have been no oligarchs, mafia plague, or culture of corruption, and vested authoritarian interests opposed to popular sovereignty would have been diminished. Ironically, after the horses have left the corral, Vladimir Putin is now contemplating adopting aspects of this script.[12]

Neither structural demilitarization nor a democratic free enterprise transition, was ever in the cards.[13] None of the key participants wanted them enough or understood the problematic. They were drawn instead to the traditional Russian patrimonial pattern of "rent granting"; shifting administrative usage rights (*pomestie*, misleadingly called "property rights") from one group of servitors to another at the autocrat's discretion. Aspiring oligarchs and other favorites were granted indulgences to seize "prolonged warfighting material reserves," divert resources for their private use, and profit from foreign weapons sales. In astonishingly short order, they prevailed. Defense material reserves worth tens of billions of dollars were illegally sold abroad, a large portion to Asia, shipped

Table 4.1. *Real gross industrial output of the Russian federation*
1991–2000

	1991	1992	1993	1994	1995	1996	1997	1998	1999	2000
All industry	100	82.0	70.4	55.7	53.9	51.7	52.7	50.1	54.1	62.1
Defense (MIC)	100	84.4	64.6	39.2	31.2	22.7	19.7	19.2	25.5	32.0
Civilian	100	99.6	85.6	52.6	41.3	29.1	28.7	26.5	34.1	41.0
Military	100	49.5	32.5	19.9	16.6	12.8	9.4	9.9	13.5	17.5

Sources: All Industry: Economic Survey of Europe, United Nations, No.1, 2000, p. 227, table 13.4
Economic Survey of Europe, United Nations, No. 1, 2002, p. 232, table 8.4. *Defense Industry:* Julian
Cooper, "The Russian Military-Industrial Complex: Current Problems and Future Prospects," in Pentti
Forsstrom, ed., *Russia's Potential in the 21st Century*, National Defense College, Series 2, No. 14, Helsinki,
2001, p. 43. The underlying data are taken from VPK publications.

through ports on Japan's Nihon Kai, including Maizuru. Rosvooruzhenie (the Russian arms sales agency) became a lucrative sinecure, and control of the crown jewels (i.e., Russia's mineral wealth) was transferred from the VPK to Yeltsin's oligarchs.

Arms production plummeted roughly 90 percent in a couple of years. The production figures in Table 4.1 provide a clear impression of the debacle. Much of the deployed arsenal was decommissioned, dismantled, and sold for scrap. This would have had a devastating impact on the military balance had America not downsized reciprocally, as indicated in Table 4.2. Moreover, the VPK suffered a double blow because its civilian production was adversely affected by the diversion of previously subsidized resources to the oligarchs and by oligopolistic distribution practices that replaced Soviet era goods with expensive foreign imports. As a consequence, the majority of the VPK's production capacities, both military and civilian, are now drastically underutilized and are becoming increasingly obsolete.

The operational curtailment of the VPK, however, hasn't caused civilian industry to flourish. Russia's new oligarchic resource barons – with some exceptions, like Kakha Bendukidze – have preferred to confine their investment activities to purchasing real estate and transferring assets abroad. Where a proper structural demilitarization strategy would have preserved full employment and gradually brought general prosperity, Yeltsin's Muscovite rent granting plundered the military and caused mass unemployment, resource demobilization, and 3.4 million premature deaths for the sake of providing his servitors with a flamboyant lifestyle.[14]

Table 4.2. *Russian and U.S. military equipment arsenals, 1998*

Tanks	
Russia	16,210
USA	8,369
AFV/APC	
Russia	28,530
USA	27,627
Artillery/MRLS	
Russia	16,453
USA	7,225
Combat aircraft	
Russia	2,868
USA	4,475
Major surface warships	
Russia	44
USA	134
Attack submarines	
Russia	72
USA	66
Strategic submarines	
Russia	26
USA	18
Strategic ballistic missiles	
Russia	180 SS-18 (10 MIR V)
	188 SS-19 (6 MIR V)
	92 SS-24 (10 MIR V)
	360 SS-25 (1 WARHEAD)
USA	590 Minuteman III
	50 Peacekeeper MX
	115 Minuteman II SILOS (START Accountable)
Strategic bombers	
Russia	28 TU95H (WITH ALCM) plus 5 in Ukraine
	32 TU-95H16 (WITH ALCM) plus 20 in Ukraine
	6 TU-160 (WITH ALCM) plus 19 in Ukraine
USA	95 B-1B
	66 B-52H
	13 B-2

Source: International Institute for Strategic Studies, *The Military Balance 1998/99*, Oxford University Press, London, 1999, pp. 20–7, 108–112.

SUMMARY

- The Soviet Union wasn't an optimally microadministrated "command economy" designed to maximize socialist consumer welfare. It was instead a physical management system that mobilized and processed resources and engineered and fabricated goods using physical rather than competitive market value criteria.
- Managers, administrators, and workers were motivated by being offered traditional western bonuses, perks, career rewards, wages, and piecework incentives and by being threatened with a host of punitive sanctions. They were closely monitored and supervised. The fruits of their labor, however, were restricted by prohibitions against competitive market value-added maximizing.
- The substitution of physical for value-added production was the consequence of the Bolsheviks' comprehensive criminalization of private for-profit activities in mining, manufacturing, construction, utilities, commerce, banking, foreign trade, and business services, together with their prohibitions against entrepreneurship, private ownership of the means of production, and negotiated wage and price setting.
- Physical systems management was the principal cause of Soviet blight. As market theorists tirelessly insisted, the separation of demand from supply prevents consumers from receiving goods and services with the characteristics they desire and in their preferred assortments. It also prevents optimal investment and warps scientific and technological progress, transfer, and diffusion.
- However, physical systems management permitted the Kremlin to mobilize resources for defense without consumer or popular constraint. The use of these resources remained suboptimal, but the relatively small number of military products made it possible for the general staff to emulate foreign weapons characteristics, borrow (steal) technologies, and mass-produce weapons. Hence the Soviet Union was able to become a prodigal superpower.
- The Soviet elite gradually began to crave affluence and grew tired of martial regimentation. They could have executed an orderly transition, even under conditions of structural militarization, by preventing resources from falling into the wrong hands, redirecting physical systems management toward civilian needs, transforming physical into value-based systems management, adopting market-facilitating cultural

reforms, building market institutions, establishing the rule of contract law, initiating self-purchase privatization, providing lump-sum compensatory dividends for those unable to participate in self-purchase privatization, and creating competitive asset markets.

- They chose instead to revert to the traditional Russian patrimonial strategy of rent granting; reparceling administrative usage rights in the guise of property rights through "spontaneous privatization," unsupervised managerial acquirement of power over state assets, poaching and shock therapy (understood as the abolition of coercive state planning), and productive administration, together with the cancellation of all state contracts. Producers, distributors, and workers were left to fend for themselves and were given the opportunity to "legally" misappropriate state assets.

- Yeltsin could have done better but both didn't want to and was mislead by the advocates of shock therapy. As a consequence, important segments of Russia's economy remain in thrall to physical systems management. Structural militarization persists, and most of the population continues to be impoverished (by western standards). Shock therapy has created a parallel market, but it is dominated by a privileged minority and may prove to be little better for the majority than the physical management subsystems it has replaced.

5

MUSCOVITE METAMORPHOSIS

THE MUSCOVITE MODEL

Russia's postcommunist economic system has undergone a profound metamorphosis from a planned to a mixed-market authoritarian system with distinctive Russian characteristics traceable to the post-Mongol rise of Muscovy, including modernized forms of autocracy, sovereign authority over private property (patrimonialism), de facto tenure grants to servitors (*pomestie*), rent seeking (*kormlenie*), network mutual support (*krugovaya poruka*), plunder (*duvan*), protectionism (Slavophilism), subjugation, and extreme inequality – a system that can be concisely called the Muscovite model.[1] The Putin administration portrays the new regime as a transparent, consumer sovereign, laissez-faire system that includes private ownership of the means of production and operates under the rule of law. But in reality it is a "ruler sovereign" rent granting system in which alienable proprietary privileges masquerade as rights and in which the protean rule of men is organized to harness the nation's productive capacities to satisfy the autocrat's desires through state bureaucracy and tiers of powerful agents. The bureaucracy includes civil administration but most importantly the security services and the military. Powerful agents, typified by Putin's "oligarchs," oversee key productive activities on his behalf, collecting and remitting taxes and other payments as implicit asset usage fees.

As a Muscovite autocrat, Putin grants revokable charters or sinecures to lesser favorites, who are also required to serve the state. Bureaucrats, agents, and other supporters must be loyal to their liege – in particular, must work through insider networks to implement his commands – and are dismissible without cause. In return, they are given a relatively free hand in dealing with "outsiders," including an implicit license to plunder the administrative rights (formal ownership) of weaker parties and to exploit ordinary people. Like Mikhail Khodorkovsky, they may desire to plot an independent course, but they cannot do it because their properties and privileges aren't protected by the rule of law. They must play the Muscovite game or fall from grace.[2]

Throughout, Muscovite rent granting politics is in command, not the idea of the West. The system is free standing, requiring neither markets nor plans, but it is compatible with both. Its fundamental attributes are ruler sovereignty, rent granting, insider management and alienable formal ownership and entitlements that institutionalize moral hazard, and stultifying corruption under a facade of bravura. Conservative variants of the Muscovite model emphasize the role of the state bureaucracy; liberal variants empower autocratic agency. Putin's economy today is best described as liberal zigzagging toward the conservative side of the spectrum, not so much from the perspective of the market but in terms of expanding bureaucratic power, especially the influence of the security and military services.

His regime bears little overt similarity to Soviet administrative command planning. The old state monopoly of productive activity has been dissolved and replaced by new arrangements that purport to showcase private enterprise, personal ownership, and economic liberty. Individuals indeed are encouraged to utility maximize in choosing their training, education, and employment and managing their businesses, entrepreneurial ventures, investments, finances, consumption, and leisure activities. They are free to negotiate terms of exchange and contract for their own benefit rather than operating as civil servants. Consumer sovereignty seemingly has been restored and *Homo economicus* reenthroned.

But appearances are deceiving. The federation hasn't adopted competitive free enterprise, despite what the resurgence of private business might suggest. It has metamorphosed instead from a physical control into a mixed rent granting authoritarian system in which its rulers exert their economic sovereignty using a broad array of instruments ranging from state ownership, alienable private property, and revokable entitlements, (e.g., agent management of land, resources, and key industrial assets) to regulations, rules, incentives, largesses, and exclusionary markets.[3] For those who believe that Putin's mixed-market/rent-granting/physical management regime is a way station on the road to democratic free enterprise this is a distinction without a difference, but at least six hundred years of Russian economic authoritarianism augurs otherwise.

The best way to grasp the reality behind the facade is by recognizing the protean historical character of Russian authoritarian economic arrangements, which relied on rent granting and physical controls during the epoch of Czarist serf-slavery and Soviet administrative command planning, and on rent granting and market regulation after the abolition of serfdom in 1861, during early NEP, and briefly under Gorbachev.[4] The movement from a physically controlled economy to a mixed or even a purely value regulated system doesn't guarantee the establishment of democracy and consumer sovereignty any more than the introduction of wartime controls in the West necessitates a transition to authoritarianism. The litmus test consists not of abstract declarations of liberal intent but the realities of coercive political and economic power.

The distinguishing feature of Russian economic history has been pendulum swings between conservative and liberal authoritarianism, not a linear movement from slavery to freedom or from capitalism to social democracy. The disintegration of the Soviet Union has intensified a liberal authoritarian wave that began with Nikita Khrushchev's denunciation of the crimes of Stalin's past and has yet to run its course. It is easy to see why many construe it as a paradigm shift, but internal evidence demonstrates that Russia still hasn't westernized and suggests that in the fullness of time it will once again become illiberal.

SPECTRUM OF MUSCOVITE MANAGEMENT

The emergence of private business has significantly altered Russia's productive terrain by providing individuals with an array of new utility-seeking options. Under communism, people were permitted many kinds of personal choice. They could

- craft their leisure time,
- shop at state fixed prices or negotiate terms of exchange in collective farm markets,
- barter and pay for services in the informal (second) economy,
- save in the state bank and invest in their dachas,
- choose their education and training,

- choose their place of residence and jobs, and
- exercise limited discretion in performing their duties.

Boris Yeltsin's reforms expanded these rights to include private business ownership, entrepreneurship, and investment and improved the quality of established rights by making supply more responsive to purchaser demand. But this doesn't mean that competitive markets have triumphed or that the nation is better off. Microeconomic efficiency continues to be impaired by remnants of Soviet era physical controls, rent granting, and serious flaws in its market institutions. Russia's macroeconomy is severely dysfunctional. Unemployment and inflation are in double digits, GDP is only three-quarters the Soviet level, and new capital formation is a mere 20 percent of what it was in 1989.[5]

Russia's disappointing microeconomic performance reflects Muscovite autocracy, rent granting, the residual power of state ownership, physical controls, the misconstruction of Russia's markets, their mismanagement, and motivational dysfunction.[6] The macroeconomic catastrophe is attributable to Yeltsin's and Putin's resource demobilization and transfer strategy, on one hand,[7] and to the erection of exclusionary barriers to enterprise profit seeking, on the other. Virtuous aspects of the old regime have been discarded, inefficient elements retained, new mechanisms misdesigned, and old Muscovite demons unleashed. Russia's future, therefore, depends not simply on further enlightening and empowering individuals, a liberalization strategy inconsistent with the regime's real agenda, but on how the leadership deals with rent granting, residual state ownership, the physical control mechanism, misconstructed markets, institutionalized misregulation, resource demobilization, and destructive motivational disorders, given oligarchic entitlements and ruler sovereignty.

SEVERING THE VISIBLE HAND

The contemporary Muscovite economic control mechanism has severed many ligaments of the Soviet "visible" hand,[8] potentially empowering free enterprise. In 1991, Mikhail Gorbachev freed enterprises from their obligation to comply with Gosplan directives, shifting productive responsibility from the central planners to managers and their supervising ministries (Gosplan still exists, but its role is advisory). Ministerial microsupervision outside the military-industrial complex (VPK) withered soon thereafter. By the end of 1993, managers had assumed virtual control over enterprise production. The erosion of ministerial authority within the VPK was more gradual, but it too was substantially reduced by the start of the new millennium. Structural militarization remains, but for the moment the VPK, recently renamed the defense-industrial complex (OPK), including Minatom, isn't lashed to a military agenda.[9] The decontrol of Soviet era state fixed wages and prices followed the same pattern, with nonessential prices freed immediately and the rest, with the exception of prices for basic services like electricity, rent, public transportation, and education, being quickly liberalized. The state monopoly of foreign trade was rescinded and capital flight was permitted. More subtlety, the state ceased operating in the capacity of purchaser of last recourse. Under administrative command planning, the state agreed to purchase as many defect-free products as enterprises produced, backed by formal contracts. Managers bore no market risk and overproduced, judged on the basis of competitive standards. But this control mechanism too was terminated, in the spring of 1992, when Yeltsin unilaterally abrogated most state contracts. And as the last straw, most enterprises, including those in the military-industrial complex, were partly or wholly privatized in various strange ways, severing the ownership rights of the visible hand. In the process, managers obtained not only revokable, Muscovite-style proprietary authority over enterprise production but the right to dispose of former state assets,[10] and proprietors were free to switch from physical norms to competitive market profit seeking or any other principle that advanced their self-interest.[11]

NETWORK TIES THAT BIND

Some managers immediately seized the opportunity to profit seek that was thrust upon them, some were driven to follow suit, while others succumbed to moral hazard. Most managers, however, continued to operate reflexively. Military-industrial firms, many of which remain state owned, produced weapons without orders, fully expecting the state to buy them. Capital durable enterprises did the same. When this strategy failed, they turned to their established supply, production, and distribution networks, including regional and local governments, for support. Some surrogate orders were issued, and goods were accepted in lieu of cash tax payments.[12] Enterprises bartered among themselves, and workers received promissory notes or goods instead of money wages. George Kleiner and Valerii Makarov estimated that 80 percent of the retail and wholesale industrial goods trade in the late 1990s was in the form of barter, and workers often waited more than a year to be paid.[13] Products and technologies were also adjusted within these physical constraints. Thus, the response of Russian industry to the mass cancellation of plans and contracts was to operate within the parameters of the physical system, relying on the principle of mutual network support (*krugovaya poruka*) instead of capitalizing on the opportunities implicit in their expanded economic liberty.[14]

The old order was preserved in other subtle ways. Soviet era technologies were infungible. It was difficult and expensive to introduce new product lines, binding enterprises technologically to the communist past. This applied to multiproduct industrial enterprises as well as other important activities, like natural resource extraction and distribution. Transportation, communications, agriculture, and government services, including education, followed the same pattern, so while managers in these areas were free to respond to market signals and incentives by improving product characteristics, altering output mixes, modernizing, and expanding market scope, their actions were constrained by the limitations of the physical management mechanism. Enterprises produced for compartmentalized subnetworks and their barter circles or for export, with little concern for prices or costs just as they had under administrative command planning.

These behaviors reflected a continuation of managerial and worker mental frameworks from the Soviet period. As a consequence, supply wasn't significantly more responsive to demand, but physical productivity declined. Decontrol, without compensatory marketization, narrowed the "division of labor" and idled resources.[15] Central planning, ministerial direction, guaranteed state purchase, state bank credit, and the material technical supply system had provided a mechanism for linking local and regional production networks across the USSR, thus facilitating specialization, with its well-known productivity benefits, during the Soviet period. When these features and institutions vanished, interrepublican and interregional coordination disintegrated, compelling local and regional activity clusters to inefficiently produce intermediate inputs and final goods for their own use at higher cost. Despecialization, as Adam

Smith explained long ago, reduces productivity and national income, and so it did in the case of Russia.

Similarly, the old integrated network had mobilized resources. Factors and assets had been fully harnessed. The new regime by contrast immobilized resources that previously had been assigned throughout the integrated network, further exacerbating the decline in aggregate production potential. The survival of physical suballocational, interindustrial production and distribution elements of the Soviet control system thus was doubly disadvantageous. It allowed opportunities afforded by economic liberalization to go unutilized and caused Russia's economic potential to revert to levels not far above those of its "rude" natural economy.[16]

SUBSISTENCE MARKETS

These sustained losses weren't anticipated by those who thought that the market would spontaneously fill the vacuum left when the state coordinative network was decommissioned or who assumed that diminished productivity in the physically controlled sectors would be more than offset by improved efficiency in marketized activities. They missupposed that participants in post-Soviet Muscovite markets would maximize their incomes and make suppliers responsive to consumer demand. This was a plausible scenario, but few suppliers were in a position to improve supply or efficiently negotiate terms of exchange. Ordinary buyers and sellers frequently found themselves in "subsistence" markets.[17] Workers couldn't afford to purchase the western goods that flooded the retail shelves in affluent urban areas and were intended for the "new Russians," a small segment of society that prospered from asset transfers, rent seeking, and occasionally productive entrepreneurship. Further, producers didn't have the resources to modify characteristics and technology to satisfy impoverished local consumers.

Nominal empowerment had little beneficial impact on productivity or on the welfare of the majority because they were prisoners of postcommunist circumstances and their rent granting rulers were unconcerned with their plight. Those ensnared in subsistence markets were also dependent in other senses. Mass involuntary unemployment drove down wages below the poverty line for more than 40 million.[18] Workers had the right to negotiate better terms but couldn't do it, nor could they find alternative jobs outside their professions or in other regions. Rust-belt manufacturers were crowded out of the credit market by the new insiders and were denied shelf space in prosperous locales by oligarchic importers of western consumer goods.[19] Managers were able to pay some heed to the forces of supply and demand even under these adverse conditions, but their dependency tightly circumscribed their gains. Collective farmers were hemmed in by the monopolistic Soviet era food storage and distribution network, lack of credit, and distrust of outsiders, who they rightly believed wanted to filch their land. State employees were forced to work for a pittance, as government jobs were cut and the private sector fell into deep depression. And "outsider" entrepreneurs were discouraged by the mafia, which invariably preyed on successful businesses.

EXCLUSIONARY MARKETS

Lucrative businesses, by contrast, were set aside as preserves for Moscow's favorite agents, oligarchs who were sheltered from competition and displayed little interest in efficiency and optimization.[20] Their privileged status enables them to collect excess profits, but exclusion rather than monopolistic profit maximizing is their primary goal. They act like rent seekers. Their attention is focused on suppressing domestic rivals and on privileged contracting and asset poaching. Russian manufacturers, for example, are deterred from providing cheap substitutes for foreign consumer goods by the import divisions of oligarchic natural resource exporters and their banking affiliates, who control retail shelf space and deny credit to domestic suppliers. The collapse of the ruble in 1998, which increased import costs and ruined many new Russians, weakened these exclusionary barriers, but their effects remain significant.

The government is the primary feeding ground for the oligarchs, who receive exclusive rights to provide insurance and financing; broadcast TV and radio programs; transport, import, and export goods; operate utilities; and acquire cheap resources directly and indirectly through the liquidation of the military-industrial complex's prolonged war fighting reserves.[21] They are recipients of Muscovite state charters intended to stifle rather than facilitate Pareto market building, and they have indeed succeeded in shifting it. Activities of the mafia complement and compound this suppression of free enterprise. Small commercial proprietorships (including beggars) must pay to play, and competitive threats are ruth-lessly suppressed.

MOTIVATIONALLY DISORDERED MARKETS

Russian productive activities are marred further by culturally condi-tioned "motivational disorders": unscrupulous, inappropriate, and irra-tional behaviors, and neurotic syndromes that supplant rational utility maximizing.[22] These are usually treated as peripheral aspects of bounded rationality in western societies, but they deserve special mention here because much of what passes for conventional Russian corporate "gov-ernance" and "entrepreneurship" is motivated by psychological factors incompatible with the rationality postulates of Pareto optimality. Russian managers and entrepreneurs often feign competence but awe and intimi-date associates with rash criminal gestures that subvert rational economic calculations. They indulge in games of "blindman's bluff" and other forms of theater that caricature responsible decision making, promote moral hazard, and impede self-improvement. These disorders might only be ephemeral manifestations of transition shock, but they appear to reflect aspects of the Muscovite mentality that cannot be easily alleviated.[23]

RULE OF LAW

The picture is bleak. Much productive activity is still physically deter-mined (including state ownership), and economic efficiency is severely constrained by the existence of subsistence, exclusionary, and motivation-ally disordered markets. The only hope radiates from the initiative of some entrepreneurs providing customized goods and services to the new Rus-sians, including mansions, private education, state-of-the-art medicine, and other luxuries, and more recently from "progressive" oligarchs like Mikhail Khodorkovsky.[24] These entrepreneurs are the darlings of the transitologists, who believe that their energy will allow them to gradually marketize the physical management subnetworks, liberate subsistence markets, overcome private and state exclusionary barriers – rent seek-ing and motivational disorders – if Vladimir Putin establishes the rule of law.[25] Russia's entrepreneurs are handicapped in the Muscovite system because economic opportunities are restricted by closed subnetworks, exclusionary markets, state favoritism,[26] government misregulation, mafia extortion, and moral hazard. Most of these barriers are permissible under existing law, and the rest are honored in the breech.

The establishment of the rule of law, therefore, means not just more laws or more compliance but also the eradication of Muscovy by repealing rent granting and agent privilege and promulgating new legislation that makes Pareto-efficient contracting possible.[27] It requires that the parliament and the president repeal oligarchic entitlements and strip agents of their ill-gotten assets; and it necessitates a legal code assuring everyone full-fledged property rights and equal economic opportunity free from moral hazard; a set of guidelines that permit judges to fairly adjudicate contract disputes in the same spirit, and an ironclad executive mechanism to enforce judicial verdicts. Once this is accomplished, entrepreneurs should have no trouble competitively seizing profit opportunities wherever they might lie, secure in the knowledge that protectionism, favoritism, and extortion won't subvert their efforts.

Most other recommended reforms are subcases of this general principle. The rationalization of land ownership; the development of property rights; corporate governance; market structure; and the reforms in military-industrial complex, state programs, governance, fiscal federalism, and the banking, credit, tariff, tax, and regulatory systems are all intended to assure equal opportunity, and consumer sovereignty. Insofar as current arrangements in all these areas are noncompetitive, anticompetitive, or encourage adverse selection, the economy is incompletely governed by the rule of law, and reforms could be Pareto improving. The same reasoning can also be applied to social welfare, where democratically approved state transfers and regulations provide superior outcomes to those of free enterprise.

Clearly, Russia is technically capable of extricating itself from the Muscovite model – the dead hand of its Czarist and Soviet past. Putin, moreover, is cognizant of what needs to be done. He has endorsed the "dictatorship of law" and championed land, tax, credit, banking, trade, and regulatory reforms. He has called for improved corporate governance, antitrust legislation, and fiscal federalism.[28] These efforts have had some benefit and offer the prospect of further gains. But the persistence of Muscovite rent granting authoritarianism and revokable "property" rights, physical management subnetworks, subsistence and exclusionary markets, pervasive discrimination, and acute depression implies that an enormous gap will remain between Russia's economic potential and its actual performance.

RULER SOVEREIGNTY

Effective postcommunist liberalization has proceeded slowly because Kremlin leaders desire the benefits of general competition on their terms. Putin, his oligarchs, the security services, the mafia, and the new Russians refuse to forgo ruler sovereignty and their agent privileges, including rent granting, rent seeking, asset seizing, and asset stripping.[29] They are prepared to promote equal economic opportunity under the rule of law to improve micro- and macroeconomic efficiency in activities outside their control, and they endorse land reforms that enable them to add vast estates to their portfolios. But they are unwilling to accept any major change in the distribution of wealth and power achieved at their expense. Putin has refrained from curbing rent granting, vigorously enforcing antitrust laws against his favorites, upholding the law of contract against his cronies, progressively taxing the affluent, restricting capital flight, rescinding Yeltsin's corrupt privatization of the state's assets (despite the Yukos affair), and requiring oligarchs to pay the full unsubsidized price for their state resource purchases.[30] He has also failed to provide credit to assist the technological transformation of rust-belt enterprises, has resisted decollectivization, and continues to tolerate the mafia.

The benefits of the rule of law and related technical reforms in contemporary Russia therefore are narrowly circumscribed. Opportunity in markets serving new Russians is gradually becoming equalized, increasing productivity and welfare, but it would be rash to expect radical change elsewhere in physical management subnetworks, subsistence and exclusionary markets, government, oligarchic enterprises, and foreign direct investment. Russia's Muscovite system is severely underproductive and inegalitarian and is likely to remain so for the foreseeable future. It lacks sufficient grass-roots initiative to mobilize and revitalize itself and cannot integrate into the global economy as an exporter of high value added products.[31]

RESOURCE DEMOBILIZATION

Most of the microdeficiencies of Russia's economy fall beneath the perceptual threshold of the average foreign observer. Urban centers, especially Moscow, have been refurbished; stores on Tverskaya Street are crammed with western imports; prices rival those in Europe for upscale lodging and dining and tourist and business services; and traffic is astonishingly congested. Few non-Russians appreciate the extent to which forced substitution caused by physical management, subsistence and exclusionary markets, corruption, and motivationally disordered business practices diminishes the utility options of ordinary people.

If it weren't for massive involuntary unemployment, hyperdepression, rampant inflation, a shriveled capital stock, capital flight, unexportable manufactures, the financial crisis of 1998, and more than 3.4 million premature deaths,[32] most specialists wouldn't care that the Russian system had metamorphosed into a new type of rent-granting Muscovite system rather than into a competitive, profit driven market economy. Despite all the happy talk, Russia's fifteen-year-long depression remained deeper in 2003 than the America's Great Depression at its nadir in 1933 (Fig. 5.1). It is therefore important, in appraising the comparative merits and potential of Russia's postcommunist economy, to appreciate that its depression is endogenous – that it isn't the inevitable consequence of transition, as the successful parallel Chinese experience demonstrates, but was caused by Yeltsin's Muscovite agenda.[33]

Resource demobilization developed in two phases. The initial impetus was Gorbachev's promotion of managerial independence, bare-knuckled entrepreneurship, and "spontaneous" privatization.[34] This was followed by Yeltsin's decision at the onset of his rule to cancel most contracts with state enterprises, rescinding the government's longstanding commitment to purchase all flawless products, without simultaneously compelling or inducing managers to maintain production at full employment levels with directives or market stimulants. Just as mass contract cancellation diminishes aggregate effective demand in the West, it immediately triggered an acute Russian depression. "Shock therapists" applauded Yeltsin's decisiveness, believing that the dire consequences would force managers to adjust their supply to satisfy market demand, and they predicted a full recovery in 500 days.[35] But this optimistic forecast was dashed, because no steps were taken to replace the visible hand with the rule of law.

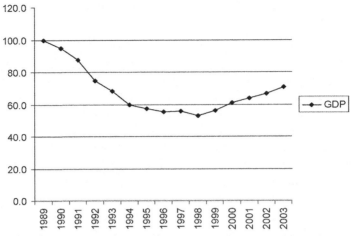

Figure 5.1. Russia's Hyperdepression in the years 1989–2002.
Sources: Data for 1989 and 1990 are from Table 1 column 3, p; 94; data for 1991–
2001 are from *Economic Survey of Europe*, 2002, United Nations, No. 2, Table B.1,
p. 162; Evgeny Gavrilenkov data for 2002 are from Steven Rosefielde and Masaaki
Kuboniwa, "Russian Growth Retardation Then and Now," *Eurasian Geography and
Economics*, Vol. 44, No. 2, 2003, pp. 87–101. "After Russia's Financial Crisis: Structural
and Institutional Changes in an Era of Globalization," paper presented at the Allied
Social Science Associations meeting, Washington, DC, January 5, 2003; data for 2003
were estimated by Iliaronov (July 18, 2003).

Managers of state property, who previously had been red directors subject to stringent fiduciary and operational controls, suddenly were given a
free hand over employment, production, marketing, finance, investment,
mergers, acquisitions, and divestitures. They were permitted to divert their
firms' revenue streams for personal use, which led to a rash of spending
on luxury cars, apartments, lavish dining, and foreign travel and to capital
flight, even if wages were unpaid and the enterprises were bankrupted.
They were allowed to asset strip, that is, sell lucrative enterprise assets to
themselves for a pittance, leaving their firms with the debt, and to acquire
other properties for a fraction of their worth through the collusion of
government officials.[36] The best connected obtained generous state contracts, which often were disguised transfers from the state coffers. And
nascent oligarchs were allowed to buy valuable natural resources at low
fixed prices for profitable resale.[37]

The sum and substance of these various swindles was the fostering of a
get-rich-quick mentality that subordinated competitive profit maximizing

to rent seeking, asset stripping, and asset grabbing. Managers discovered that it was much more "rational" to succumb to moral hazard by stealing wealth and living parasitically off rents with the Muscovite state's tacit approval than to fret about supplying a disordered productive mechanism.

These destructive tendencies, which can be collectively called the "Muscovite disease," were exacerbated by the government's subsequent scheme for "privatizing" industrial assets that hadn't already been stripped or seized. Four basic classes of shares were authorized, one each for workers, managers, the state, and outside shareholders. Insiders, that is, workers and managers, received approximately half the shares. Workers were allotted 80 percent and managers 20 percent of these inside holdings, but operational control was retained by managers, including the right to fix compensation, subject to an annual insider shareholders meeting, where workers could theoretically dismiss managers, and impose new rules. This arrangement pitted the workers and managers against each other, encouraging the managers to bleed their firms dry and strip the assets before the workers had them preemptorially removed.[38] The traditional principle of *krugovaya poruka* (mutual support) often placed limits on these demobilizing incentives, but the adversarial character of Anatoly Chubais's Muscovite privatization program nonetheless strongly deterred effort, production, and investment.

And if this weren't bad enough, the exclusionary tactics of the oligarchs used against erstwhile competitors in the old Soviet industrial sector prevented improvment-minded rust-belt managers from receiving the credit and market access they needed to modernize and recover. The same policy that created the oligarchs and their business school–trained successors carried with it the seeds of chronic resource demobilization.[39] In the twinkling of an eye, Russia went from a sixty-two-year strategy of resource mobilization to one of demobilization, which now cannot be cured unless the government adopts the rule of law empowering Pareto-efficient competition or intervenes to bolster aggregate effective demand using Keynesian, Schachtian, or Soviet methods.[40]

DISEMPOWERMENT

Moreover, even if Putin's economy was in full-employment, generally competitive, Keynesian equilibrium, the productive system would still flunk two crucial tests; as choice remains circumscribed and income and wealth are extremely inegalitarian. Workers and ordinary consumers in Russia today can take or leave what they are offered (forced substitution) and in some instances achieve negotiated Walrasian equilibrium within the limits of the nation's physical management subsystems and its subsistence, exclusionary, and motivationally disordered markets. But they aren't consumer sovereign. Their demands only weakly influence supply, and transactors cannot count on Marshallian profit maximizing to satisfy preferences.[41] Nor should anyone have any illusion that social justice will be improved by a radical redistribution of income, wealth, and power any time soon. Perfunctory chatter of liberalization, privatization, stabilization, and globalization under the rule of law only fosters the illusion that these failings can be easily remedied by simple appeals to reason.

LIBERAL AUTHORITARIAN REFORM

The peculiarities of Russia's post-Soviet productive system are consistent with its liberal authoritarian Muscovite tradition. Whenever Kremlin autocrats grew weary of creating workfare programs for their servitors, they assigned them supplementary jobs as state tax collectors empowered to exploit the peasantry for their own benefit and that of the crown.[42] In turn, those peasants who couldn't subsist on their residuals resorted to foraging and brigandry or perished. Everyone more or less grasped the basics. They understood the injustice, brutishness, excess, and inefficiency, but each estate or stratum acquiesced in its own fashion. Russia's oligarchs are Putin's servitors and tax collectors in the natural resources, utilities, and media sectors. Industrial workers, collective farmers, and civil servants are the state's forgotten people, reduced to poverty, or driven into crime. And the new Russians consititute a fluid stratum providing useful services to the oligarchs and the state. They are allied with privilege but could mature into a western-oriented middle class.

The system is liberal compared with the conservative or despotic alternatives, but it isn't benevolent. Moreover, it could endure unless there is a cultural transformation that completes the march toward democracy and the rule of law begun by Pyotr Chaadaev at the start of the nineteenth century. Its malign attributes include severe microlevel forced substitution, underproductivity, inefficiency, disorder, macroeconomic dysfunction, growth retardation, isolation from the global economy, pronounced income inequality, and social injustice.

Benevolent reform is possible in all these regards within the core authoritarian, ruler sovereign system. Macroeconomic activity in the market segment of the regime can be increased through Keynesian fiscal policies, especially financial incentives for modernizing private investment. The civilian component of the moribund rust belt can be revived through government contracts, the military-industrial complex sector can be revived through rearmament, and the dispossessed can be employed in government public works programs.[43] Growth can be stimulated by curbing moral hazard to encourage investment and by transferring and diffusing superior technologies from abroad. Inflation can be curbed through monetary discipline. None of these initiatives will alter the fundamental inferiority and inequity of the rent-granting Muscovite system, but each could help mitigate its harshest flaws.

Should these reforms come to pass, and should Russia recover to the Soviet level, further progress toward the western norm will be arduous, because the benefits to be gained by Putin will be small compared with the resistance of those with an interest in the status quo. It will take a leader with vision and courage to push liberal authoritarian reform to its benevolent limits or press beyond this threshold to democratic consumer sovereignty.[44]

THE THIRD WAVE

This view isn't universally shared. The Washington consensus continues to believe that markets have achieved critical mass in Russia, vouchsafing a generally competitive transition.[45] Some neoinstitutional globalists see Russia following the same path, based on different principles,[46] while others envision Russia's structural (institutional) problems being solved by a new wave of audacious domestic entrepreneurs like Oleg Deripaska, Roman Abramovich, Alexei Mordashov, and Andrei Melnichenko,[47] who in addition to grabbing stakes in natural resources and utilities are venturing into rust-belt industries and agriculture.[48] They are said to be concentrating resource and industrial activity, "cherry-picking" the best assets, and rationalizing them with the aid of western consultants to build a "clan" market economy that capitalizes on economies of scale. Unlike

Poland, which has focused on small-scale entrepreneurship, Russia, it is claimed, will revive its heavy industrial base and keep foreign investors out. Perhaps one of these visions will be realized, but it remains difficult to see how Pareto optimality can be achieved without the rule of law; how globalization can overcome the determined resistance of physical management subnetworks, oligarchs, and authoritarian bureaucrats;[49] or why the third wave should be as efficient as general competition.[50]

REVIVAL OF SUPERPOWERDOM

Benevolent reform in Russia may also be subverted by resurgent militarization. Kremlin autocrats are accustomed to thinking of their nation as a superpower. Even after the Soviet Union's collapse, when Moscow relinquished control over more than 30 percent of its communist domains, its economy was prostrate, and its military-industrial complex was in disarray, Yeltsin insisted that the G7 expand to include Russia in a G8. It seems reasonable, therefore, to expect that the allure of vast power will intensify as the post-Soviet Muscovite system consolidates. The signs of a militaristic reversion, like Putin's defense modernization program scheduled for 2006, are mounting, and such a reversion appears to be gathering momentum.[51]

SUMMARY

- Russia's economy has not transitioned in accordance with the idea of the West; instead, it has undergone a Muscovite metamorphosis (within the liberal authoritarian paradigm).
- The new regime is best conceived as a Muscovite economic system, with the word "Muscovite" intended to conjure up historical images of autocratic privilege, rent granting, servitor rent-seeking, rapacity, subjugation, inequity, and social injustice. Above all, authoritarian politics, not free enterprise, is in command, and the closed, opaque character of the system fosters moral hazard and stultifying corruption.
- The key features of Putin's Muscovite economy are resource demobilization manifested in mass involuntary unemployment and underutilization of capacity, mesoeconomic disorganization, structural

segmentation separating insiders (the president, his administration, the upper echelon of the security community and the state bureaucracy, the oligarchs, the mafia and the new Russians) from the vast majority stuck in the physical management system (Gaddy's virtual economy), subsistence markets, and the lower echelons of the state apparatus; and extreme inequality. It is a system founded on administrator privilege revokable at the sovereign's discretion, despite the formalities of nominal private property rights.

- These pathologies are caused by the state's authoritarian approach to productive management. Russia has shunned Pareto-efficient markets, preferring to let the president preside over a patchwork of allocational, productive, financial, and distributive mechanisms. The government has the power to distribute assets, and exclusive contracts. It tightly regulates regional authorities (fiscal federalism); collects taxes; and manages the monetary system, foreign exchange rates, and international trade. It has legalized markets but conferred exclusionary privileges that discourage efficiency in high value added activities while effectively locking the majority of the population in a Soviet era physical management system and subsistence markets.

- The Muscovite system is ruler sovereign. The preferences of the majority of consumers don't govern supply, and democratic representation doesn't determine the provision of government (dis)services.

- The Muscovite system is gravely microeconomically inefficient. It cannot compete in the global marketplace. As in the Soviet era, GDP growth statistics must therefore be discounted.

- The Muscovite system can achieve full employment despite its microeconomic inefficiency. But achieving this would require a strong assault on rent granting and exclusionary privilege or military rearmament, which would eliminate idle capacity in the VPK and encourage the reemergence of Russia as a prodigal superpower.

6

MILITARY-INDUSTRIAL REFORM

The contours of Russia's emerging Muscovite economic system are coming increasingly into focus, but the details remain unsettled. Whether the Kremlin tilts toward liberal or conservative authoritarianism will depend importantly on Putin's handling of military-industrial reform. A decision to build full-spectrum, fifth-generation armed forces at Soviet procurement levels without competitively transforming Russia's economic base would surely mean a return to the conservative past. It would entail a restructuring of the oligarchy, with those in a position to gain from rearmament benefiting most. Alternatively, downscaling production capacities to current levels of arms delivery would strengthen the resource tycoons, while a full transition to consumer sovereign free enterprise would expand possibilities, permitting more efficient conservative and liberal variants.

The last option would be superior from the standpoints of Paretian economic efficiency and international security, but for the moment it appears only a remote possibility because the leadership is wedded to full-spectrum Soviet-type armed forces, despite Putin's call for a professional military by 2010,[1] and is gradually subordinating Yeltsin's oligarchic priorities to its great latent superpower concerns. The rationale for full-spectrum armed forces is geostrategic. Russsia is a Eurasian continental power with blue water naval capabilities in the Baltic Sea and Pacific Ocean. It relies on space-assisted nuclear strategic deterrence and an extensive conventional border defense. Although large anti-NATO dedicated forces are no longer essential either to the west or southwest – indeed, Russia is even contemplating joining the European Union[2] – its Eurasian borders warrant attention. These theaters (*teatry voennykh destvii*) are protected primarily by conventional land, air, and sea power and provide a platform for extensive operations in the Asian Pacific, South Asia, and the Middle East, where advanced conventional forces, some armed with tactical nuclear weapons with potential "strategic" impact, are becoming more prominent. Russia doesn't presently need the accouterments of RMA (revolution in military affairs), including plasma technologies and "information warfare" (IW) to secure these ends but probably will require significant capabilities as China modernizes its forces and for more remote contingencies involving the United States and Western Europe.

The United States is the world's only active superpower because it has full-spectrum capabilities, flexible surge capacity, and superior RMA. A return to the Soviet past for Russia would entail matching the United States' military scope while quantitatively compensating for its technological inferiorities with a larger arsenal. As before, it will be relegated to a junior status unless it greatly improves its technological prowess, and it may still never be more than a subpower if the present RMA gap widens.[3]

This is why many western defense analysts question the rationality of Russian remilitarization. They simply don't believe that the effort is justified unless the Kremlin can devise an economic system that allows the federation to compete effectively in RMA. Similar reservations apply to a no-frills variant of the full-spectrum approach emphasizing RMA because Russia lacks an innovative commercial base to support the effort.

Either way, if the Kremlin opts for a great-power military, the undertaking will be costly. Military reform thus is more than a matter of deciding whether to maintain large or small armed forces configured in this or that fashion; it involves reconciling aspirations with the possibilities of alternative productive systems. Russia can preserve the status quo with a small military, idling its defense-industrial complex (OPK); return back to the future; or move forward with an effective RMA program best accomplished through free enterprise.

It is important to grasp that the Muscovite model permits Putin to preserve structural militarization or abandon it as he prefers, despite a considerable volume of literature claiming that a full-spectrum Soviet-type defense is unattainable. The Soviet era military-industrial capital stock exists, and the costs of remanning it are hardly prohibitive, given low industrial wages and persistent mass unemployment.[4] Although the OPK physical management system is no longer freestanding, missing components can be revamped and enhanced by market outsourcing. And market barriers can be surmounted by requisitioning and price fixing where required. The decision to reform, therefore, is discretionary, not mandatory, from a supply-side perspective.

The contrary view is predicated on the assumption that the OPK will be compelled to competitively bid for resources from oligarchs and new Russians and pay top dollar for state-of-the-art military technologies purchased abroad. But this assumption is not valid. The state can brush oligarchs aside and commandeer resources internally, and it can pirate much of what it needs from the West. As a reported specialist in industrial espionage, Vladimir Putin doesn't require coaching, and the OPK has a wealth of experience in replicating foreign defense technologies and adapting them to Russian conditions.

The OPK's reliance on arms export sales,[5] foreign coproduction, and other assistance to finance substantial portions of its activities doesn't contradict this assessment. While it may be true that Sino-Russian military technology exchanges will come close to averaging $5 billion annually in the period 1999–2004, this sum and all other arms sales are peanuts compared with Russia's hard currency resource and metals export receipts, which equaled $72 billion in 2000, for example.[6] With petroleum production surging to 8 million barrels per day in 2002 and heading toward 10 million barrels (eclipsing Saudi Arabian production), the OPK doesn't have to sell nuclear technology to Iran and China, participate in European Union national missile defense, be self-financing (*khozraschyot*), or depend on the "kindness of strangers."[7] The government merely has to match its defense priorities with a willingness to prevent capital flight and tax the natural resource base.[8]

The Putin administration has been reluctant to grasp this nettle. It has chosen to broadly endorse the aspirations of the general staff (genshtab), including its desire to expand its role in the civilian economy,[9] while pretending that full-spectrum programs can be self-financing through military arms sales. Critics justifiably insist that something has to give. The genshtab's wish list includes nuclear modernization; dual-use information systems; precision guided munitions; advanced conventional weapons; anti-stealth radar; indigenously stealthy air-launched cruise missiles; the S-400 antiaircraft/antiballistic missile; plasma coating to make fifth-generation aircraft invisible; information warfare tools; chemical and biogenetic weapons; and directed-energy weapons, including lasers, microwave radiation emitters, particle-beam generators, use of subatomic particles to destroy targets at the speed of light, and a new plasma weapon that could ionize the atmosphere and destroy incoming missiles.[10] It is moving in the direction of high-tech combat aircraft, electronic control and information systems, weapons based on new physical principles, tactical nuclear weapons to be used in conventional conflicts to achieve strategic impact, and reconnaissance-fire (or strike) systems (proposed by Ogarkov) that can make a strategic difference in large theater wars.[11] Topol-M ICBMs (intercontinental ballistic missiles) are replacing older land-based missiles for use as first- and second-strike weapons at a rate of 10 per year, and Moscow has threatened to transform them into MIRVs (multiple independently targeted reentry vehicles) if the United States goes forward with its national missile defense program.[12] New conventional but highly informationalized weapons coming on line include the Shkval torpedo missile; the M-55 reconnaissance plane, the Kh-31 supersonic antiship missile, the X-101 and X-555 strategic (cruise) missiles, the Iskander antiaircraft missile, and unmanned aerial vehicles, all embodying large amounts of information, some upgradable to reconnaissance strike missions.[13] And of course, the genshtab is promoting antisatellite technologies for space wars.[14] Genshtab analysts say that Russia will still have 3,000 "nonstrategic" nuclear warheads and should be able to field 1,000 TNWs by 2020 (within the Strategic Offensive Arms Reduction Treaty) [SORT]. And if this isn't enough, former head of army procurement General Anatoly Sitnov stated in 2000 that Russia's army needs $16 billion annually to maintain its already obsolete weapons to keep pace with other armies. It requires 250–300 mobile artillery systems, 1,500 gun-tubes, 150–200 planes and helicopters, and 5–7 antiaircraft complexes a year, as well as 30,000 full ammunition trains.[15] The CINC of the navy, Admiral Vladimir Kuroyedov, stated that the navy should have 12–15 SSBNs, 50 SSNs, and 35 diesel submarines, plus 70 ocean-going surface combatants, in order to globally contest America, the post-9/11 rapprochement notwithstanding.[16]

These particulars add up to full-spectrum, fifth-generation armed forces significantly larger than America's in almost every category, including national missile defense, and indicate an aspiration to rival the United States' technological prowess. Soviet-style structural militarization assures that the goal is feasible because America's forces today and those envisioned by Donald Rumsfeld are a pale shadow of their size at the close of the

Cold War.[17] It is therefore ironic that, despite all of Russia's self-inflicted wounds, the preservation of structural militarization still permits the federation to be militarily competitive – and to some extent more potent through the assistance of complementary markets. The genshtab and the OPK have a wide range of opportunities for military and defense industry reform through selectively borrowing best western organizational practices, including modern corporate governance practices, and transferring appropriate technologies from abroad.

The alternative OPK reform strategy starts from the same foundation but forswears structural militarization, instead appropriately scaling force size and mobilization capacities to the magnitude of probable threats and rationalizing and optimizing defense activities. Structurally demilitarizing in part or in whole entails abandoning the idea of maintaining sufficient standing forces and mobilization capacities to defeat every imaginable threat and supporting additional reserves to cope with the unthinkable. It requires the subordination of the genshtab and the OPK to civilian control in theory and practice in order to prevent vested military interests from dictating defense policy. And it necessitates relinquishing insider-controlled physical systems management in favor of competitive demand-responsive supply, including market factor and product price setting and Paretian profit maximizing.

If these reforms are complemented by optimal policymaking, administration, and regulatory management, the composite defense-industrial reforms will be ideal. Achieving the best reforms will require policymakers to act in accordance with consumer sovereignty within the limitations imposed by Arrow's paradox, and consequently their specific characteristics cannot be deduced incontrovertibly, even if everyone shared the same assessment of the threat. All that can be reasonably inferred is that the size, composition, and efficiency characteristics of Russian military forces and mobilization capacities would much more closely resemble those of the European Union, America, and Japan than the full-spectrum Blochian defense the genshtab prefers and that social welfare would be immensely enhanced by the corresponding gain in Paretian economic efficiency.

Since policy choices even in the ideal case are constrained by factor endowments and accessibilities, this broad picture can be further refined by taking a variety of facts into account. Perhaps the most important involve demography and health. Russia's population is rapidly declining.

Immigration aside, deaths are exceeding births by approximately nine hundred thousand per year, and official forecasts envision the continuation of this trend to 2050 due to extraordinarily low fertility caused in part by the detrimental effects of excessive abortions and an emerging AIDS epidemic.[18] Although, population estimates for 2050 vary widely – from 70 to 110 million but in any case down from the total of 145 million in 2002[19] – it is obvious that prudent makers of defense policy should optimize at lower force levels given anticipated reductions in troop and worker cohorts. The same logic applies to the supply of scientists, engineers, and technicians as well as to the costs of repairing Russia's tattered health, education, social welfare, and mesoeconomic systems.[20] Even though the OPK's military-industrial capital stock may for the most part be in good repair, the productiveness of complementary inputs has been greatly diminished and may take decades to restore.

Where does Putin stand in this matrix of defense reform possibilities? Does he really support fundamental change, and if so, what kind? Is he leaning toward resuscitating and streamlining Soviet-type structural militarization or toward implementing a Paretian consumer sovereign defense? The Reform and Development of the Defense Industrial Complex Program 2002–2006, signed by Prime Minister Mikhail Kasyanov in October 2001, provides various clues. The document reveals that the Kremlin is moving toward reconsolidation of state authority, driven in part by the aging of the OPK's capital stock, underemployment, low pay, and poor enterprise finances.[21]

The plan envisions downsizing the OKP, which currently consists of 1,700 enterprises and organizations located in 72 regions, "officially" employs more than 2 million workers (more nearly 3.5 million), and produces 27 percent of the nation's machinery and 25 percent of its machinery exports.[22] Nineteen of these entities are "city building enterprises," that is, defense-industrial towns where the OPK is the sole employer.[23] The total number of OPK enterprises and organizations has been constant for a decade, but some liberalization has been achieved in ownership and managerial autonomy. At the start of the postcommunist epoch, the VPK was wholly state owned. Now 43 percent of its holdings remain government owned, 29 percent are mixed state–private stock companies, and 29 percent are fully privately owned. All serve the market in varying degrees but retain a collective interest in promoting government patronage and can be quickly commandeered if state procurement orders revive.

As during the Soviet period, the OPK's mission isn't confined solely to the Ministry of Defense (MOD). Its activities are overseen by the genshtab, which is responsible for provisioning both the uniformed military and the rest of the armed forces, including the MVD, FSB, and border troops.[24]

Kasyanov's proposal calls for civilianizing some 1,200 enterprises and institutions, stripping them of their military assets, including intellectual property, and transferring this capital to 500 amalgamated entities called "system-building integrated structures." This rearrangement will increase the military focus of the OPK by divesting it of its civilian activities, beneficially reducing structural militarization in this regard, but it will strengthen the defense lobby and augment state ownership. The program calls for the government to have controlling stock of the lead companies (design bureaus) of the system-building integrated structures. This will be accomplished by arbitrarily valuing the state's intellectual property at 100 percent of the lead companies' stock, a tactic that will terminate the traditional Soviet separation of design from production and create integrated entities capable of designing, producing, marketing (exporting), and servicing OPK products. State shares in nonlead companies will be put in trust with the design bureaus.

The Kremlin intends to use ownership as its primary control instrument, keeping its requisitioning powers in the background and minimizing budgetary subsidies at a time when state weapons procurement programs are small compared with those of the Soviet past. Ilya Klebanov, former deputy prime minister and now minister for industry, science and technology and the architect of the OPK reform program, hopes in this way to reestablish state administrative governance over domestic military-industrial activities while creating new entities that can seize a larger share of the global arms market.[25] He contends that this is unavoidable because private owners within the OPK prosper at the state's expense by exporting weapons and technologies they haven't created and neglect to reinvest the proceeds productively.[26]

To facilitate the development of fifth-generation weapon systems, the OPK reform program envisions a two-prong strategy. During the first phase, in the years 2002–4, the development of these systems will be assigned to lead companies and the integrated structures they oversee. But, thereafter, superior diversified research and production complexes capable of producing globally competitive military and consumer goods

Table 6.1. *Defense industrial organization: The scheme for 2005–6*

Type of equipment	Number of integrated structures
Aviation equipment	5–7
Missile and space equipment	9–10
Radio equipment and control systems	7–9
Communication and telecommunication	2–3
equipment	2–3
Electronic equipment	2
Precision guided munitions	2–3
Tanks and artillery	2–3
Optics and electronics (laser) equipment	1–3
Ammunition and special chemistry	6–8
Shipbuilding	3–5
Shipbuilding equipment	3–5
Total	42–58

Source: Vitaly Shlykov, "Russian Defense Industrial Complex after 9–11," paper presented at the conference on Russian Security Policy and the War on Terrorism, U.S. Naval Post-graduate School, Monterey, California, June 4–5, 2002, pp. 13–4.

will be developed, a strategy reminiscent of Gorbachev's schemes in the late 1980s. Table 6.1 provides a preliminary list of these new structures.

The specific tasks that will be assigned to these new integrated structures were formulated by the Security Council of the State Armaments Program for 2001–10 and were approved by President Vladimir Putin on January 20, 2002, but this forty-three–volume document, with twelve "approvable" subprograms, is classified. Colonel General Alexei Moskovsky provided a few glimpses into its contents in an interview published in *Krasnaya Zvezda*, February 19, 2002. The State Armaments Program covers nuclear forces, space systems, aviation and air defense, conventional armaments, command and control, basic military research, and equipment destined for other "power structures" (interior troops, border guards, FSB, etc.). Forty percent of budgeted funds are to be allocated to research and development during the years 2000–5, quadruple the share in the preceding plan. The actual figure for 2001 was 41 percent, with 48 percent of funding devoted to serial weapons production. After 2005, a tidal change is contemplated: R&D will drop to 15 percent and serial production will expand to 65–70 percent as Russia seriously turns its attention to military modernization.[27] A fifth-generation fighter under development at "Sukhoi" will be part of this expansion, with mass production commencing in 2009.[28]

As with all programmatic documents, the feasability of these schemes deserves to be regarded with skepticism. Vitaly Shlykov doubts that they can be achieved within the current fiscal framework, noting that the government implausibly expects 55–60 percent of the funding to be provided from OPK profits, although he understands that these goals could be easily reached if Putin returned to the Soviet era strategy of *pushek i masla* (guns and margarine).[29] Klebanov's demotion on February 18, 2002, likewise calls the Putin administration's commitment to the OPK reform program into question.[30]

But, more fundamentally, the approved reform fails to address the core issues of structural militarization and Pareto optimal design and efficiency. Obsolete civilian product lines are detached from the OPK, reducing structural militarization in the first phase, only to be replaced by high value-added, OPK-produced civilian exportables in the next stage. The melding of design and production makes the new consolidated OPK structures potentially more responsive to domestic and foreign weapons demand, but the genshtab's authority remains paramount,[31] and there is no hint of how corporate governance will be adjusted to create incentives that will make designers responsive to customer demand. Likewise, no thought appears to have been given to matching the structure of administrative and operational reforms to optimal future force configurations. If the Putin team was really serious about reforms, whether it harbored Soviet-style or liberal aspirations, pride of place would have been given to a plan showing how the OPK is supposed to get from here to there, but no guidance is provided. Consequently, Klebanov's scheme seems symptomatic of Russia's schizophrenia: leaders are simultaneously drawn to restoring the federation's power while resisting the requisite transfer of resources from the oligarchs to the OPK and optimally tailoring reforms to priority security needs. This tug of war almost certainly precludes structural demilitarization and Paretian optimal design and efficiency. Russia by default seems headed toward patchwork structural military reactivization along Soviet lines that will entrench full-spectrum militarization as the highest priority, maintain the inefficiencies of physical systems management, and restore state ownership rights through backdoor proprietary claims on military technology, bringing the nation full circle back to the future by giving it an economy and military that provide the illusion of comprehensive security while consigning the people to a living standard that falls further and further behind those of the developed West.

OPTIMAL REFORM: A WESTERN PERSPECTIVE

The global community can't compel Putin to discard structural remilitarization or choose Paretian optimal defense reforms, but western policymakers, as stakeholders in international security, can legitimately press for mutual accommodation and in so doing place constraints on the scope of Russian remilitarization. The Bush–Putin agreement pledging Washington and Moscow to reduce their strategic nuclear forces to 1,500–1,700 weapons not only pares their arsenals[32] but places caps on the scale of permissible nuclear modernization. Curbs on chemical and biological weapons and other weapons of mass destruction have a similar effect, as would efforts to establish ceilings on tactical nuclear weapons for conventional war fighting. The redeployment of conventional forces east of the Urals mandated by the conventional forces in Europe (CFE) agreement provides another disincentive to overbuilding because it implies that war with the West isn't imminent.

The principle can be leveraged further by restricting the scope of space-based offensive systems and, most critically, by badgering the Kremlin to cut the military manpower under the genshtab's aegis from 3 to 1 million. Drastic reductions, in addition to discouraging weapons overproduction, will pressure Moscow to seriously contemplate abandoning conscription in favor of a professional army dedicated more to peace making than Blochian mass war.[33] It would induce Moscow to concentrate on RMA and to field forces compatible with the West's for prosecuting the war on nonstate terrorism, thereby integrating Eurasia into the western security system instead of adopting an adversarial posture.

If the West had its druthers, it would also urge Moscow to unilaterally forswear widespread S-400 national missile defense deployment and limit the size of its blue water navy. Such initiatives could succeed with Putin's acquiescence, but restoring Russia's military power may require more than the bare-bones RMA strategy pressed by the West. The genshtab could suboptimize under western pressure by constructing a formidable military designed to defend its southern and Asian Pacific borders and by developing force projection capabilities to restore its presence in the Third World, supplementing a core professional RMA army.[34] Since the Russians aren't obligated to conform to the West's wish list, the Kremlin's ideal may not be entirely to America's or the European Union's liking and could retain a strong element of structural militarization, but mutual accommodation might be significant enough to make international security stronger than it was during the Cold War.

The preceding assessments of Russia's present and potential military power can be clarified further with the assistance of physical and economic comparisons. Readers unfamiliar with the difficulties inherent in compiling weapons inventories for and valuing the defense activities of authoritarian productive systems may feel that they have entered the twilight zone. Estimates at best can only be rough approximations. Comparative data on Russian and American physical deployments in 1998 taken from standard official sources have already been provided (see Table 4.2). They are sensitive to unexplained judgments about "decommissionings" and probably understate Russia's capabilities. Nonetheless, the figures show that Russia remains numerically superior to America in all categories other than naval forces. One implication is that if Russia successfully achieves full spectrum, fifth-generation military modernization its advantage will widen unless the United States reciprocally expands its deployments. Another is that Russia can pursue a defense policy that includes downsizing without jeopardizing numerical parity. As during the Cold War, these "bean counts" need to be discounted in light of Russia's technological shortcomings in some weapons systems, but this doesn't substantially alter the problematic.

The data on annual defense spending also show a high level of Russian defense activity but expose important vulnerabilities, especially in the areas of new arms procurement and military modernization, reflecting the negligible rate of new arms acquisitions in the period 1991–2002. Table 6.2 reports the official defense budgetary figures in rubles, corresponding burden estimates, and their composition. These figures continue to significantly understate defense activities for a variety of technical reasons, including the existence of extrabudgetary requisitioning, the exclusion of non-MOD military services under the genshtab's control, and the OPK's penchant for concealment. The burden figures are further impaired by the non-Paretian disequilibrium that distorts Russia's prices.

Table 6.2. *Official russian defense budgetary statistics, 1992–2001*

Panel I: Defense burden (Ruble defense share of GDP)

1992	1993	1994	1995	1996	1997	1998	1999	2000	2001
4.7	4.4	4.4	4.6	3.0	3.1	2.1	2.6	2.6	2.9

Note: Military pensions were moved to the Social Budget in 1998.

Panel II: Composition of the defense burden, 2000 (percent)

Personnel	35.6
Operations and maintenance	26.9
Procurement	19.4
R&D	11.1
Infrastructure	2.8
Nuclear	2.1
MOD	0.7
Other	1.4

Source: International Institute for Strategic Studies, *The Military Balance 2001–2002*, Oxford University Press, London, 2002, p. 110, tables 14 and 15.

For these reasons, the dollar estimates presented in Tables 6.3 and 6.4, based on the CIA's direct costing methodology, provide a more reliable impression of the comparative domestic and international level of the contemporary Russian defense effort. The figures in Table 6.3 extrapolate current military activities from the territorially adjusted Soviet era data and are expressed in the dollar prices of the year 2000. The nonweapons base used for these projections is the CIA's, but the weapons estimates are the author's. The alternative statistics presented in Table 6.4 are calculated identically, but CIA data are used throughout. The aggregate results for both measures are broadly alike. They indicate that the dollar value of Russia's defense activities (excluding paramilitary operations) is approximately half the dollar value of America's defense activities, but the procurement figures differ markedly due to the higher base of the author's series. The dollar burdens, reflecting the opportunity cost of producing Russian weapons in the United States, are both in the vicinity of 10 percent using the CIA's GNP purchasing power parities, quadruple the official ruble and double Christopher Hill's figures.[35] They rise several percentage points using the World Bank's GDP estimate and approach 20 percent when computed using the "market" exchange rate.[36] Allowance for the non-MOD component of the genshtab's domain requires further upward adjustment for all estimates, suggesting that, although the dollar value

Table 6.3. *Russian defense spending in 2000 (2000 dollars)*

	Total	Weapons	Nonweapons
Soviet Union			
1984	201.5	97.3	104.2
1991	252.3	135.2	117.1
2000	117.4	24.7	93.7
Territory adjustment	.7	.7	.7
Russia			
2000			
1978 prices	82	17.3	65.6
2000 prices	182	38.4	145.6
"Burden"			
CIA ppp	10.2		
SNA 99	14.6		

Method: Growth estimates for 1984–91 assume the trend during 1976–84 prevailed up to 1989 and was zero 1989–91. The rates for 1984–9 were 4.6, 6.8, and 2.3 for total defense, weapons, and nonweapons activities respectively. The nonweapons growth rate was computed by subtracting 1991 weapons from total defense activities and comparing this estimate with the figure for 1984. The 1991 weapons estimate is extrapolated to 2000 using the VPK's military-industrial production index. The figure is 0.175. Nonweapons are extrapolated at 0.8, a coefficient that subjectively balances the status quo in military manpower with declines in other categories.

"Burden" CIA ppp: The CIA's 1989 estimate of Russian GNP, $1.23 trillion, is deflated to 1978 prices and adjusted to the 2000 output level. See Steven Rosefielde, *Efficiency and Russia's Economic Recovery Potential*, p. xxii, table S1 (the index 1989 = 100 Russia 2000 is 64.1), and United Nations, *Economic Survey of Europe*, No. 1, 2002, p. 230, table B.1. *"Burden" SNA 99:* Adjusts the ppp in the numerator downward 30 percent but leaves the numerator unchanged on the assumption that the agency's defense dollar estimates were correct (except for learning curve misadjustment).

Assumption: Russia's military manpower was 3 million in 1984 and 2000, but military construction and operations and maintenance have fallen sharply.

Sources: False Science, tables R1, R4 Total excludes military pensions and RDT&E. Steven Rosefielde, *Back to the Future*, table 2, unpublished manuscript version, 2002. *Economic Report of the President*, Washington, DC, 2002, p. 324, table B-3. Steven Rosefielde, *Efficiency and Russia's Economic Recovery Potential to the Year 2000 and Beyond*, Ashgate, Aldershot, 1998, p. xxii.

of Russian defense activities has tumbled, the military burden remains onerous.

Without fretting about false precision, these various statistics reveal that Russia's defense activities remain extensive and continue to constitute a significant economic burden. The OPK is largely intact, and the Kremlin retains a military-industrial production capacity that permits Putin to rapidly increase weapons production severalfold. He therefore can return back to the future, reactivating structural militarization, with its colossal productive burden, but for reasons already examined he

Table 6.4. *Russian defense spending in 2000 (CIA, 1978 dollars)*

	Total	Weapons	Other
Soviet Union			
1984	141.5	32.2	109.3
1991	156.2	32.2	124.0
2000	104.8	5.6	99.2
Territory adjustment	.7	.7	.7
Russia			
2000			
1978 prices	73.4	3.9	69.4
2000 prices	162.9	8.7	154
"Burden"			
CIA ppp	9.2		
SNA 99	13.2		

Method: Growth estimates for 1984–91 assume the trend during 1976–84 prevailed up to 1989 and was zero 1989–91. The rates for 1984–9 were 2.0, 0, and 2.6 for total defense, weapons, and nonweapons activities respectively. The nonweapons growth rate was computed by subtracting 1991 weapons from total defense activities and comparing this estimate with the figure for 1984. The 1991 weapons estimate is extrapolated to 2000 using the VPK's military-industrial production index. The figure is 0.175. Nonweapons were extrapolated at 0.8, a coefficient that subjectively balances the status quo in military manpower with declines in other categories.
Sources: See Table 6.3.

would be better advised to embrace an optimal defense that increases the allocation of resources to the civilian sector and tilts Russia's evolutionary trajectory toward liberal authoritarianism or, better still, toward westernization.

SUMMARY

- Russia needs an optimal security strategy keyed to its economic potential.
- The potential of Russia's Muscovite economic system is large enough to support the full-spectrum, fifth-generation rearmament scheduled for 2005–10 if Putin restores the genshtab's control over the federation's natural resources, for the Soviet era military-industrial complex is largely intact and the missing pieces can be reassembled.
- As part of Russia's structural militarization, the genshtab wants to enlarge the armed forces beyond what is required for optimum security. The buildup desired will be sufficient to restore the federation's

undisputed status as a superpower, but only a junior one. In addition, it will provide little tangible benefit because the Muscovite model will prevent Russia from developing the commercial base to compete technologically with America in RMA. Moreover, full-spectrum rearmament will strengthen authoritarianism, nail the coffin shut on democratic free enterprise, starve civilian investment, hamper global integration, and bind Russia to Soviet-style impoverishment.

- The Putin administration shares the genshtab's misplaced ambition and is in denial regarding the long-term economic implications. It has approved Klebanov's military reform program, but it is reluctant to confiscate resources from the oligarchs and transfer them to the genshtab. Putin, like Yeltsin before him, has therefore promoted self-financing paper military reforms that, although clever in many respects, cannot be realized.
- High natural resource prices, particularly high petroleum prices, have allowed the Kremlin to temporize, hoping that full-spectrum rearmament can be painlessly achieved without shattering the status quo.
- As weapons production ramps up in 2006, however, Putin will be compelled to fish or cut bait.
- The recentralization of state authority over the regions and the oligarchs and the stacking of the bureaucracy and the Duma with high security service officials are a few of many indicators suggesting that when push comes to shove, Putin will gradually succumb to the poisonous lure of structural militarization.
- Western security analysts, largely under the influence of their public culture, don't believe that Russia will implement full-spectrum, fifth-generation rearmament by 2010 or immediately thereafter. They could be right, but they are blind to the unfolding drama and underestimating the risks.

7

NATIONAL VULNERABILITIES

Analysts who view the world through an idealistic prism have myriad reasons for disbelieving Russia was, is, or will ever be structurally militarized. They suppose that rational Kremlin leaders wouldn't overfund defense and will drastically reduce military outlays if they did because the risks of aggression under the new world order are small. They remind us that neither Russia nor its neighbors (excluding Japan) have explicit irredentist claims against each other, that Moscow's nuclear deterrent precludes conventional war, that the war on terrorism is being won, that democracies won't tolerate militarism, that the nascent middle class is commercially minded, that Russia is becoming a normal civil society that appreciates peace, that its elites want to be respected in Europe, and that Putin's reforms will assure national economic success. As proof, they note that the European Union (EU) and the United States recognize Russia as a market economy[1] and are encouraging it to join them in exploring ways of expanding economic ties, including possible accession to the EU and membership in the World Trade Organization (WTO).[2] They describe Moscow's relations with Teheran and Beijing as nonthreatening because Moscow had no qualms about selling advanced weapons and nuclear reactors to the mullahs and the Chinese People's Liberation Army (PLA).[3] And the Putin–Bush post-9/11 antiterrorist coalition makes a disarming first nuclear strike from Washington "unthinkable."[4] If Russia's leadership isn't worried about large-scale aggression from America, NATO, China, and Iran, why should it fret about attacks from its other neighbors? Nor does a resumption of Russian imperialism in the Baltic states, the rest of the former Soviet Union, Finland, Japan, or other targets of opportunity seem probable, implying that there are no objective grounds for national insecurity and full-spectrum rearmament.

All these various arguments are compelling if it is assumed that Russia's leaders feel economically and militarily secure enough to relinquish their ambitions and acquiesce to American hegemony. But none of these conditions are satisfied. Despite its bravado, the Putin administration knows that the verdict is out on the international competitiveness of the Muscovite economic system. It understands that Russia's demographic, health, and human capital woes, together with its continuing technological and material decline vis-à-vis China, the West, Japan, South Korea, and India, make it vulnerable to foreign pressures of diverse kinds, including migratory colonization. Its leaders understand that Russia needs to be protected against these threats, and they aren't ready yet to relinquish the option of countervailing American hegemony and seizing targets of opportunity. The globe is undergoing a profound reconfiguration of income, wealth, and power that provides Russia's security insiders (*siloviki*)[5] with ample reasons for rearmament.

ECONOMIC VULNERABILITIES

The root cause of Russia's dim comparative economic prospects was elaborated in chapter 5. It is Muscovite authoritarianism, which combines rent granting and physical systems management with adversely selective markets founded on alienable proprietary privileges instead of inviolable ownership rights, substitutes the rule of men for the rule of contract law, and enthrones insider privilege at the expense of efficiency and consumer sovereignty. In Russia, the powerful prosper at the people's expense by asset grabbing, asset stripping, and rent seeking, often oblivious of competitive profit and utility maximizing. The results include extreme under utilization of capacity, mass unemployment, factor misallocation, underinvestment and misinvestment, capital flight, feeble inflows of foreign direct investment, and nearly invisible domestic technological progress and diffusion. A system of this sort may give an illusion of growth by reactivating idle capacity[6] but cannot outperform more Pareto efficient rivals in the long run, qualitatively or quantitatively, even if its vast mineral wealth from time to time generates transient bonanzas. Accordingly, Russia must underperform as compared with the West, despite prattle about catching up with Portugal,[7] and it is likely to be outdistanced by China, undermining its national security.

Although too few appreciate the systemic basis of these vulnerabilities, there is a growing awareness among economists who rely on Paretian microconcepts and Keynesian microconcepts that the "right" conventional policy mix isn't enough to alter Russia's blighted prospects.[8] Adjusting the money supply, interest rates, foreign exchange rates, and tax rates and otherwise improving regulation is no more effective now than during the Soviet era. The problem is the system; all the rest is just damage control.

Evgeny Gavrilenkov, former director of Moscow's Higher School of Economics, echos this assessment by citing Ivan Aksakov, a mid-nineteenth century statesman who lamented, "Above all, it is the lack of common honesty in Russia, in its narrowest and most ordinary sense, which astounds. This fatal flaw in character deprives the government of the opportunity to wield any reliable executive power, by robbing it of a necessary number of honest, faithful lower-ranking officials."[9] Gavrilenkov finds that recent economic growth is attributable to natural resource investment and government featherbedding, with few spillovers into manufacturing. Even a modest decline in oil prices will sharply reduce growth, already under pressure from a state-manipulated appreciation of the foreign exchange rate. He complains about the fragile fiscal mechanism, the inexorable rise of noninterest federal expenditures as a share of GDP, feeble employment growth, capital flight, and "capitalism without capital" due to the bank sector's underdevelopment. The old Soviet savings bank, Sberbank, which remains state owned, controls around 70 percent of the retail market, prompting Gavrilenkov to observe that "one of the first decrees of Lenin's government was to nationalize banks and little has changed since then, despite the fact that Russia is now home to over 1,900 banks."[10] Arkady Dvorkovich, deputy economic development and trade minister, warns in the same vein that the economy will start shrinking in 2004 if the pace of reforms doesn't accelerate, and Andrei Illarionov, Putin's top economic advisor, insists that growth through 2015 will drop to 0.2 percent per annum if state spending rises to 40 percent of GDP from its current level of 35 percent.[11]

Even western economists who have little experience in Russia and interpret its behavior in textbook abstractions have started to grasp that the "tsars" viral strain plaguing the federation is immune to their prescriptions. The IMF still hopes to perfect its medicine, but its archcritic, the Nobel laureate Joseph Stiglitz, places the blame on permanent damage caused by the IMF's and the Gaidar government's malpractices. According to Stiglitz,

Theoretical and empirical research at the World Bank and elsewhere, including the examples of Poland and other countries that took different approaches, has shown that restructuring is possible before privatization; that how privatization occurs does make a difference, both in the short and long run. Privatization without good corporate governance typically does not lead to faster growth. It does, however, lead to a whole host of problems. In the long run, we should be concerned not just with the pace of economic growth but with the kind of society that is being created.[12]

There are those who dissent. Anders Aslund, former advisor to Yeltsin's government together with Andrei Shleifer and Daniel Treisman, is particularly optimistic about Russia's economic prospects. They contend that the economy is stable, dynamic, and wealth creating because the Kremlin, at their urging, embraced the Washington consensus program of stabilization, privatization, liberalization, and democratization. Contrary to Stiglitz's assessment, Russia neither has been "lost" nor has it been deformed. It has been won![13] Aslund concedes that the transformation was more protracted and traumatic than he had anticipated[14] but blames this on Yeltsin's cautious reforms and an excessive budget deficit of 8 percent, compounded by the EU's protectionism and by ill-advised obstructionism by "oligarchs, regional governors and the Communist Party."[15]

These obstacles, he claims, have now been overcome by the market. The financial crisis of 1998 bankrupted most oligarchs and transformed many others into progressive businessmen. The Communists entered the government, and the regional governors lost half their financial resources to the federal government. The parliament now has a solid reformist majority, public expenditures have been cut, barter has been tamed, a flat personal income tax of 13 percent and a corporate profit tax of 24 percent have been introduced, judicial reform has been undertaken, land has been privatized, banking laws have been improved, and a new labor code has been adopted. The overall result is an economic miracle. "In effect, the Kiriyenko-IMF program of July 1998 has been implemented ever since, and the results are impressive by any standard, showing that a market economy can work wonders in Russia, and that it doesn't matter how an enterprise is privatized because private property can be transferred through sales and bankruptcy."[16] Aslund doesn't forecast Russia's intermediate term rate of sustainable growth but clearly expects a surge of direct foreign investment that will propel a rapid catchup to the West's high per capita income frontier.

This is very good news. It not only implies better times for Russia and the world but should eliminate the vestiges of structural militarization. Stiglitz, however, contests all Aslund's assertions and accuses him of rewriting history to salvage the Washington consensus. His specific rebuttals have merit and provide a healthy antidote to the fable of how Russia was won.[17] For example, he observes that the financial crisis of 1998 was caused by the IMF's bad advice, not cured by it.[18] But this technical sparring on closer analysis is neither here nor there. The alternative policies Stiglitz recommends, like Aslund's, presume that Russia was and is a well-functioning Paretian market that can be turbocharged by technical fixes, whereas the reality is just the reverse. Russia's "transition" was stillborn. The Muscovite authoritarian model that has triumphed subordinates Paretian efficiency, productivity, technological progress, and social justice to power and privilege. Its performance can be enhanced by superior policies, but its potential is inherently inferior. It makes no fundamental difference in the long run whether Russia partially liberalizes, reduces extraneous bureaucratic interference, cuts taxes, devalues to discourage "hollowing out and the 'resource curse,'"[19] or even attracts massive foreign investment if it retains Muscovite authoritarian insider privilege seeking, which inevitably will pervert good intentions, just as it did under Soviet rule.[20]

MILITARY VULNERABILITIES

The genshtab's apprehensions about Russia's economic insecurity thus are entirely justified. Prospects for an improved living standard are bleak because the easy gains reaped by reactivating idle capacity will soon be exhausted and inegalitarianism is unlikely to decrease. The openness of Russia's economy, the decriminalization of business, the legalization of entrepreneurship, price decontrol, partial privatization, limited introduction of the rule of law, and democratization hold out hope that the rate and quality of growth could beat the Soviet standard, but these beneficial factors are countervailed by rent granting, resource demobilization, capital flight, moral hazard, the rule of men, high mortality, low fertility,

Table 7.1. *Growth projections 1995–2025*

	GDP 1995 ($ billions)	Population growth trend	GDP 2025	Index 1995	Index 2025
Great powers	21,534	0.7	70,703	100	100
America	7,100	0.8	14,095	33	20
Japan	2,714	0	2,741	13	4
Europe	7,437	0	9,445	35	13
Russia	675	−0.4	965	3	1
China	3,581	0.7	44,422	16	62

Note: Population projections are provided for 1995–2015 by the UNDP. These have been extended an additional ten years. China's per capita GDP growth is estimated at 8 percent, a figure corroborated by post-1995 official growth statistics. Russia's per capital GDP growth prospects have been upgraded to take account of the Putin bubble and are assumed to parallel Europe's.

Method: Projections are computed by multiplying the per capita growth rates in table 15.3 by the population growth rates in table 15.4, compounded 30 years from 1995 to 2025.

Sources: Steven Rosefielde, *Comparative Economic Systems: Culture, Wealth and Power in the 21st Century*, Blackwell, London, 2002, p. 213, table 15.3, p. 214, table 15.4. The underlying data are derived from United Nations, *Human Development Report 1995*, Oxford University Press, New York, 1995, p. 176, table 22, p. 200, table 41.

an explosion in birth abnormalities, an Aids pandemic, and diminished human capital.[21] As is widely understood, rapid growth and falling population are almost never associated with one another,[22] and so because of its decrease in population alone, Russia will be challenged to match the long-term Soviet rate of growth even if it fully harnesses its idle structurally militarized capacities.

Prudent Russian national security analysts therefore shouldn't expect Russia, with all its structural anomalies, to see a growth in GDP of more than 3 percent per annum in the period 2002–25 on a quality-adjusted (hidden inflation – adjusted) basis (see chap. 2). As Illarionov's forecast of 0.2 percent per annum suggests, Russia's economic performance could easily be much worse for a variety of reasons, including the possibility of resurgent civil discord.[23] Table 7.1 illustrates the danger from a global perspective.

Russia's per capita GDP growth may keep pace with Japan's and the EU's but not with the growth rates of the Anglo-American economies, China, South Korea, Taiwan, Malaysia, and India. The gap in living standards between the federation and its neighbors will widen, and China's living standard will overtake and then surpass Russia's. The absolute magnitudes, using United Nations data, are especially sobering, as are reasonable adjustments based on other standard series. Russian GDP will fall to less than a tenth of America's and China's, diminishing the Kremlin's clout in the global marketplace. And Russia's shrinking population will give these rivals similar advantages in manpower.

Material welfare will increase as Russia's productivity rises and its population thins, but its power will diminish. America will enjoy a military manpower pool three times larger than Russia's, and China will have one more than ten times larger. And their weapons production surge capacities will be correspondingly asymmetric.

During the Cold War, the Soviet Union, with its 290 million people and its structurally militarized economy, was able to field armed forces substantially greater than those of the United States, but Russia's population could well fall below 125 million by 2025, and its GDP, estimated by the CIA as 47 percent of America's in 1989, could decline to between 5 and 15 percent of America's 35 years later, depending on how rubles are converted to dollars. Even if Putin opts for full structural remilitarization, the correlation of forces won't be going the Kremlin's way, because a mere doubling of America's defense burden, to 6 percent of GDP, would place its military capacity beyond Russia's ability to compete. Worse still, the absolute size of China's GDP will reach or surpass America's, allowing its armed forces to dwarf Russia's too.

Beyond this speculative arithmetic, it should also be appreciated that, unless Putin drastically alters the Muscovite authoritarian production model, Russian won't be a significant player in the global industrial goods and high value added technology market. Its civilian manufactures will remain unexportable, and its weapons sales will slip as India and China not only become self-sufficient but compete toe to toe with Rosvooruzhenie (the Russian arms export agency). The Kremlin is about to be buffeted by "future shock," for the Indians and Chinese are becoming major beneficiaries of foreign industrial technologies acquired through learning by doing and prodigious direct foreign investment. This will not only provide a fillip to Indian and Chinese modernization and growth but could allow these countries to emerge as great powers more quickly, should they harness the technological knowledge they gain to their national missile defense and RMA programs.

For much of the past decade, Russia, because of the decline in its conventional capabilities, has relied on nuclear deterrence to fend off

potential threats. However, the implementation of a nuclear missile defense by the United States, China, or India, for example, could radically
alter Russia's security problematic, permitting these other countries to
use RMA and conventional forces without serious concern for Russian
nuclear retaliation.[24] Of course, such a change in the international security situation doesn't mean that opportunities will be seized, but it does
demonstrate the fallacy of appraising the federation's security from the
standpoint of the status quo. An ineffective economic system is a liability
that should not be cavalierly disregarded.

Westernization combined with an optimal security regime would
obviate these long-run perils. Russia's sustainable growth rate, given its
economic backwardness, low wages, geography, potential export competitiveness, and susceptibility to the "Dutch disease"[25] (overvaluation of the
foreign exchange rate associated with resource wealth), should be several
percentage points higher than the Muscovite rate. This would be enough
to allow Russia to stay abreast of China and gradually close the living
standard gap with America. Spreading the wealth should revive fertility
rates, while direct foreign investment would spur technological progress,
allowing the genshtab to harness the resulting know-how to deal with
American, Chinese, and perhaps Indian advances in RMA and national
missile defense. Russia's successful integration into the global market
would facilitate the allocation of investment to best use and diminish
the risks of armed conflict, as would its entry into the WTO, the EU,
and NATO as a full-fledged western society. Westernization from this
perspective is a win–win strategy that rescues Russia from foreseeable
perils and fosters the convergence of its living standard with the living
standard of Portugal and beyond.

Adverse selection by Putin, the oligarchy, the Yeltsin family, the genshtab, and elements of the inner circle cannot match this benefits package
and is apt to be destabilizing, especially if the Kremlin's international aspirations remain detached from reality. No one should be astounded if the
genshtab once again overestimates the utility of vast military power or
grotesquely exaggerates the forces needed to attain it. Vitaly Shlykov,
using previously unpublished data, revealed that the Soviet general
staff, in formulating its superpower force requirements, overestimated
American short-term tank production capacities by a ratio of more than
25 to 1 (Fig. 7.1).[26] Of course, there may have been some dissimulation
for political effect, but Shlykov argues that the genshtab is adroit at both
recognizing threats and exaggerating them. It appreciates America's

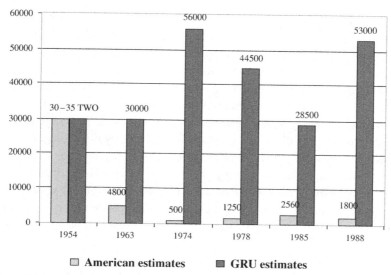

□ **American estimates**   ■ **GRU estimates**

Figure 7.1. American Mobilization Capacity: Tank Production 1954–88.
Source: Vitaly Shlykov, *Chto Pogubilo Sovetskii Soiuz? Genshtab i Ekonomika*, Moscow, "Voenny Vestnik MFIT," No. 9, Moscow, September 2002, p. 118. (Used by permission.)

military technological prowess and has fevered perceptions of what it might become. Likewise, Chinese military-industrial advances haven't been lost on Kremlin security professionals. They know that Beijing is testing a new series of vastly improved intercontinental ballistic missiles and is on the cusp of crossing the threshold to high-tech self-sufficiency.[27]

Their response, detailed in chapter 6, has been reflexive; they have pressed for the procurement of fifth-generation technologies at Soviet era levels, which should be best construed as a holding operation from the standpoint of Table 7.1. The genshtab may wish that Putin's Muscovite market model will make structural militarization more competitive for the duration, but their ingrained skepticism and the postcommunist record suggest that they know better. Structural remilitarization is a default option, absent westernization, given the unfolding reconfiguration of global power together with valid Kremlin fears and complexes.[28]

It can be combined on a tactical basis with membership in the WTO, affiliation with NATO and the EU, a Russo-Franco-German entente, participation in the war on terrorism, arms control and disarmament, and a balancing strategy of aligning with the Third World against America. And it should suffice to preserve hegemony along the southern flank and in the region of Caspian Sea, despite sales of nuclear technology to Iran. But it cannot turn the tide for the sick Eurasian superpower.[29] It cannot transform the Kremlin's Muscovite economy into an engine of prosperity.

The course of least resistance for a genshtab that fears the worst but cannot change the system is to urge reinvigorated structural militarization and hope that the leadership discovers a path that combines civilian economic efficiency with a defense-focused Muscovite productive mechanism. Suspended disbelief, however, entails its own set of perils. The leadership and the genshtab could lose sight of Russia's long-term systemic vulnerabilities, adopting policies with unintended consequences. Instead of using arms control treaties to constrain Chinese capabilities, Russia, by rearming to Soviet levels, could precipitate an arms race it is bound to lose and encourage aggressive engagement that puts the world at risk in the period 2010–25 without solving its long-term security problem thereafter.

Whereas the United States winked at Soviet ballistic missile reloads and a multitude of other treaty violations, Beijing could respond tit for tat, drawing India, Pakistan, and the United States into the steeplechase. Blustering in Central Asia, the Middle East, or the Asian Pacific could have a similarly adverse outcome. Unable to confront the new reality, Moscow is likely to find itself contradictorily striving to reattain past superpower glories through intimidation – out of resentment of American strategic independence (the Bush Doctrine)[30] – while seeking the indulgence of powerful strangers. "Doublethink" often served Moscow well during the Cold War, when the West thought it wise to appease Moscow, but now that Russia is at risk of becoming a "paper tiger," strong nations are going to exploit its weaknesses – a dynamic that is bad for Russia and global stability. Whether resurgent structural militarization precipitates a catastrophic arms race after 2010 or Russia eventually is overwhelmed in whole or part by foreign settlers, dismembered, disempowered, subjugated, or destroyed by war cannot be foretold, but some unhappy ending is in the cards unless it repudiates its baneful Muscovite legacy.[31]

SUMMARY

- Western public culture provides a long list of cogent economic and political reasons for believing Russia will jettison structural militarization.

- These reasons are invalidated by the counterlogic of the Muscovite economic system and the Kremlin's unwillingness to relinquish the options of seizing targets of opportunity or countervailing American hegemony. A variety of other security concerns, including the potential Chinese threat, further diminish the likelihood that Russia will abandon structural militarization.

- The ceaseless effort to portray the Muscovite economy as self-healing – that is, self-transforming into a democratic free enterprise system – is unconvincing. Joseph Stiglitz is right: The Muscovite model is path dependent.

- Likewise, the reconfiguration of global wealth and power is making Russia more and more vulnerable. Its GDP will probably be only 1 percent of the global total by 2025, leaving it in the dust behind America, China, the EU, and Japan.

- Russia's declining population will sharply curtail the Kremlin's ability to field the armed forces needed to defend its borders, and a parallel fall in the number of scientists and engineers will hamper its economic and military potential.

- The genshtab response to these concerns, given past precedent, is likely to include an exaggerated perception of the threat (e.g., American tank production capacity was overestimated during the Cold War by a factor of 25) and massive production of arms to make up for Russia's manpower and technological deficiencies.

- Although democratic free enterprise and an optimal security approach are Russia's best options, the Kremlin doesn't have the insight or the resolve to extricate itself from structural militarization.

8

THE MIASMA OF GLOBAL ENGAGEMENT

The diplomatic miasma created by 9/11, the Iraq war, and President George Bush's discovery that Vladimir Putin is a man who can be trusted is making it more difficult for analysts to come to grips with the fatal consequences of the Muscovite syndrome. The Bush administration until recently has been content to portray Putin as an enlightened westernizer even though he stacked regional governorships, the Duma, and his administration with KGB and military officers, placed control over the balloting apparatus solely in the hands of the federal security bureau (FSB), and repressed independent television.[1] It has emphasized his credentials as an economic liberal pressing fiscal federalism, business, tax, and judicial reforms, overlooking the growing power of the central state apparatus and Russia's plutocrats. Further, it praised the Kremlin as a stalwart ally in the battle against nonstate terrorism[2] and the struggle against weapons of mass destruction (WMD) proliferation and as a champion of global arms control and disarmament, turning a blind eye to the Chechen war, "reform" plans for full-spectrum, fifth-generation rearmament, and proscribed weapons sales to Iraq.[3] Just as before, Russian policies were criticized here and there, but the money kept flowing for cooperative space exploration, the dismantling of nuclear weapons[4] (which often meant no more than the removal of replaceable nuclear triggers), the construction of nuclear fuel reprocessing plants (which were then used for other purposes), and joint antiballistic missile defense, along with myriad other thinly veiled "goodwill" handouts, on the false premise that the Kremlin had been redeemed. And Russia was further rewarded by being mislabeled a "market" economy for tariff purposes and was assisted in pursuing admission to the WTO.

Perhaps America was adequately compensated by Russian assistance in Afghanistan, Putin's tolerance of the Bush administration's withdrawal from the 1972 ABM treaty, and his toothless agreement to cut Russian nuclear forces, which assuaged EU misgivings about the United States' increasing ability and willingness to go it alone. But beyond this, the sound and fury signified nothing, because American indulgence couldn't make Russia's Muscovite economy significantly more competitive than its Soviet predecessor, and the genshtab could hardly be impressed by Bush's hugs and kisses.

The demonization of America in the wake of the Iraq war is also masking Russia's drift toward prodigal superpowerdom. America is being caricatured as a rogue superpower bent on world domination, willing to intimidate, subdue, and occupy as conditions warrant.[5] Instead of spreading the gospel of westernizing democracy, economic freedom, and social justice through institutions of global governance like the United Nations, the United States, according to the accusations, is practicing "Pax Americana" and reviving the Cold War.[6] The war on terrorism and the repression of WMD programs in the Third World are, from this perspective, merely pretexts for neo-imperialism, which should be opposed by forming coalitions at home and abroad. Progressives are exhorted to organize, protest, press for political change, invoke the law, educate, step up agitation for arms control and disarmament, and encourage civil disobedience. Nonsuperpowers everywhere are expected to forge new international alliances and obtain control of multinational institutions like the IMF, the World Bank, and the WTO. The United Nations is called upon to condemn American transgressions and support just causes, including increased financial support for developing countries and more generous North-South transfers of wealth.

In this scenario, Russia, as a born-again progressive, peaceful, economic liberty–loving democracy, was scripted to align with France and Germany in staunchly combating the United States with every diplomatic tool in its arsenal.[7] Some even foresee Russia joining forces with the EU to form a military counterweight to American imperial ambitions.[8]

But, when the dust settled, Russia emerged on its steady course back to prodigal superpower. Despite the obligatory equivocations, the Kremlin has neither forged an EU entente against America nor widened its "partnership for peace" with Washington.[9] Instead, it has demanded concessions for the accession of former Soviet bloc nations into the European Union,[10] sniped at the West for NATO expansion,[11] conducted a mammoth nuclear exercise,[12] announced the successful development of a new *ICBM* to defeat America's national missile defense,[13] and vigorously sought to carve out "imperial" spheres of influence in Moldova, Georgia, and the *CIS*.[14] On the domestic front, it has continued to spin grandiose schemes for market liberalization[15] and economic justice,[16] promising to secure property rights and coopting the liberal agenda[17] while persevering in its criminal prosecution of Khodorkovsky and other oligarchs,[18] and clearly signaling that rent seekers should not confuse their caretaking with inalienable gifts of sinecure and property. The staffing of the bureaucracy and government with security and military personnel has proceeded apace[19] and embers of democracy have been all but extinguished in two "managed" elections that eliminated the liberal parties from the Duma[20] and elected Vladimir Putin president for life in fact, if not de jure. And last but not least, martial rhetoric has escalated to the Soviet level.[21] A recent article by the Mikhail Yuriev, former deputy chairman of the Duma and liberal Yabloko party member, entitled "Fortress Russia" conveys the mood some at least believe is being cultivated by the siloviki in the White House, with Putin's tacit approval.[22]

Yuriev blames "normalization" for impoverishing Russia and dangerously reducing its material capacities. He contends that G-7 policies have been maliciously designed to subjugate the Kremlin and will succeed unless Putin abandons Yeltsin's course. "If we do not close this gap or at least reduce it substantially, we are certain to lose our status as an independent country and separate civilization in the foreseeable future." Salvation requires Moscow to turn its back on an "open" economy and its face toward a "closed" one. This doesn't mean repressing domestic markets. Yuriev explains that expelling foreigners and confiscating their assets under the banner of a Russia first ideology will be sufficient to make the superiority of the Russian way of life transparent. Accordingly, Russia should withdraw from all multilateral international relations and base its bilateral relations on the "rejection of common human values, and in general, of everything but our own interest." The sum of these policies "will be known as the Fortress Russia strategy." Isolationism need not be permanent. It can be dispensed with in several decades. But in the interim, it will allow Russia "to win the next cold war and, if necessary, hot war." If this ranting is even remotely indicative of the shape of things to come, then Russia will not be anything like a "normal country" on a meandering path toward democratic free enterprise, global integration, and, as some believe, a salubrious counterweight to the America "mono-pole."

The Bush administration finally got the message in the spring of 2004, albeit equivocally, judging from CIA director George Tenet's recent testimony to the U.S. Congress.[23] American officials have expressed alarm over Russian press censorship, the demise of democracy, veiled attacks on private property, the economic inefficiency of oligarchy,[24] the martialization of the government and society, the excessive powers of the FSB and siloviki, interventionism in Moldova, Georgia and the CIS, a new "European divide,"[25] and the general rise of authoritarianism.[26] Uncharacteristically, the Bush administration expressed its displeasure substantively by unilaterally repudiating the SORT agreement,[27] threatening Russia's suspension from the Group of Eight, and more subtly upgrading the Federation to a "developing nation" status and thereby downgrading its preferential access to the G-7 as a "transition" state.[28] Perhaps, this is only a zig or a zag in Russian–American relations.[29] Perhaps the liberal democratic Putin will ultimately defeat his FSB alter ego. But he doesn't have much time.

The clock will be ticking on the Muscovite economy and rearmament. Whether or not Goskomstat chooses to camouflage the truth, Putin's Muscovite economic system won't support the creation of a middle-class mass consumption society or lead to adequate growth, causing Russia to lose ground vis-à-vis the West and its emerging neighbors, China and India. Its domestic legitimacy will wither as the inferiority of the Muscovite model sinks in, prodding leaders to embrace heightened military power as a political option.[30] A concomitant deterioration in its defensive posture and its power projection capabilities due to further advances in the West and among the countries on its borders will intensify the pressure to rearm.

Russia's antipathy toward economic liberty, democracy and social justice (an antipathy inherent in the Muscovite economic system) and its penchant for structural militarization cannot be dispelled by public relations and western solicitude. Russia is captive to a legacy of poisonous authoritarianism. Although France and Germany want to believe that Russia will become a militarily benign social democracy like them, and although America hopes Moscow will once again be a strategical partner, all will be disappointed unless Putin is pressed harder to change.[31] The federation will gradually devote more and more resources to building a full-spectrum, fifth-generation arsenal that will provide a credible challenge to the West.

The result need not be a renewal of the Cold War, but structural remilitarization to the Soviet level does contain the seeds of global destabilization. Even if Russia refrains from provocative behavior, the risks of bi- and multipolar arms races are high because the Kremlin cannot resist a futile regime threatening arms competition.

SUMMARY

- Russia's drift back toward prodigal superpower status is being abetted by wishful thinking in the West and Moscow.
- The West's public culture strongly inclines it toward nonconfrontational engagement in which democratic free enterprise is promoted through economic assistance and sanctions.
- There was a brief moment after Russia's financial crisis of 1998 when it appeared that Washington had learned the importance of candor in dealing with the Kremlin, but it didn't last. The tragedy of 9/11, the subsequent war on terrorism, and the Iraq war in their various ways have widened the gap between illusion and reality.
- Putin's increasing authoritarianism set off alarm bells in Washington during the spring of 2004, but the new resolve is unlikely to last.
- Rapid-fire shifts in Putin's foreign policy, together with the usual chatter about prosperity being just around the corner, are keeping Russian eyes equally blinkered.

9

PUTIN'S CHOICE

Vladimir Putin doesn't know whether Russian "civilization" is compatible with the enlightenment precepts of economic liberty, democracy, and social justice – precepts that, according to Samuel Huntington, are founded on rational individual utility seeking, guided by the Golden Rule, and implemented through the rule of contract. Putin cannot be sure that Russian culture is any more compatible with the EU social democratic welfare state or that Russia can survive with its Muscovite economy, representational authoritarianism, and structural militarization. But he must somehow decide whether to preserve the status quo, tilt to the American or Franco-German dream, or chart some other course, cognizant that the "rest" cannot be best.

There are numerous "third paths" other than the Muscovite model that might be considered. The Kremlin could look to the past for inspiration, resurrecting Soviet administrative command planning, East European market communism, or Yugoslav worker management, but these options seem political and economic dead ends. It could survey the orient. The closest fit would be China. Until recently China, like the Soviet Union, had a one-party communist government and an economy featuring state ownership of the means of production, central planning, and physical systems management. The path of Russia and China diverged, however, following the dissolution of the Soviet Union. Where the Russians opted for a "demobilization model," showcasing oligarchic privatization and relatively unrestricted capital flows, the Chinese preserved their resource "mobilization strategy," retained state ownership in core enterprises, invested heavily in public works, gradually privatized without severe oligarchic distortions, maintained strict financial controls, and adopted a vigorous manufacturing export-oriented strategy, integrating it into the global economy. The differences in the impact of these institutional and policy reforms could not have been starker. The Russian economy went south, the Chinese north.

Putin can and probably should experiment with Deng Xiaoping's methods. It wouldn't take much. He could reimpose stern restrictions on capital outflows, fix the foreign exchange rate, expropriate oligarchic assets, initiate public works programs to reemploy the population, and revive the moribund machine-building sector with an export-led strategy propelled by secure direct foreign investment. If Russia were westernizing, this would be bad advice. The strategy substitutes the visible for the invisible hand and constitutes a partial restoration of physical systems management. But it might be markedly better than the Moscovite alternative. Although capital restrictions in principle should deter foreign investment, China is the world's largest recipient of foreign direct investment. Domestic capital isn't fleeing the mainland for havens in the West, and controls allowed Beijing to avoid the Asian financial crisis of 1998. Russia's enormous natural resource revenues also mean that the strategy is financially feasible. All that is required is (1) the diversion of funds that used to nourish the VPK and now feed the oligarchs to the task of modernizing the country's dilapidated infrastructure, (2) the strengthening of private property rights thereafter, (3) introducing capital controls and high tariffs, and (4) fostering Russia's manufacturing export integration into the global economy.

Success isn't guaranteed. Capital controls work in China in tandem with high tariffs and an undervalued currency because foreign investors believe that the Communist Party will allow them to recoup their capital derivatively as excess export profits (owing to the low labor costs) and build bridgeheads for their brands. What is required is that the investors have faith that the government won't soon overvalue the foreign exchange rate and tolerate wage inflation, preventing them from earning handsome profits to compensate for restricted asset repatriation. What is also required is that the government institute measures to foster competition allowing foreign direct investors to operate on an equal footing, offsetting the adverse effects of protectionism associated with capital controls, tariffs, quotas, foreign exchange rate fixing, and managed wages. Putin can't have it both ways. He cannot attract foreign investment and foster competitiveness ("a democratization of income and wealth") while retaining Muscovite oligarchic rent granting and state-assisted predation. This is probably why Moscow isn't seriously contemplating the Chinese model, although cultural incompatibility may be another important factor.[1]

A Germanic version of Deng Xiaoping's control regime – like the one devised by Hitler's finance minister, Hjalmar Schacht, which combined markets, resource mobilization, and privilege with authoritarianism and strategic state controls – might prove more serviceable. The Nazis devised a resource-mobilizing market system that was characterized by strong private property rights and the selected rule of law, that relied heavily on public works and military expenditures, and that was stabilized by tariffs, quotas, external financial controls, and foreign exchange rate fixing. It didn't attract much direct foreign investment, a cardinal feature of Beijing's model, but it did allow cartels and privileged individuals to prosper at the workers' expense. Perhaps Putin will muddle through to a Schachtian economy, not unlike the one urged by Yuriev, strengthening the rule of contract law, paring his oligarchs' privileges, taking back a large portion of their wealth, but enhancing their property rights over the remaining assets to revive industry while preserving (or jettisoning) the goal of rearmament.[2] Should he do so, Russia will enjoy full employment, higher utilization of productive capacity, reduced capital flight, an improved living standard, and faster intermediate-term growth, but Russian Schachtianism cannot excel. Its Golden Age growth trajectory would almost certainly be less than the West's precisely because it impedes direct foreign investment and consumer sovereign technology transfer.

Nonetheless, the Kremlin should prefer a Schachtian system over the Muscovite model if it desires a full-spectrum, fifth-generation defense of maximum size because such a system has a higher mobilization potential. The resource entitlements of oligarchs are much smaller and the property rights better in a Schachtian system than in the Muscovite model, and thus genshtab would be allowed to operate at higher capacities. It follows directly that Putin's Muscovite model is inferior to a wide array of feasible substitutes, whether the leadership stresses prosperity or military preparedness. And of course from a western perspective the Muscovite model is worse than EU social democracy and American democratic free enterprise. The only justification for sticking with it is to rule by rent granting in a tried and failed Russian tradition.

Rational expectationists, assuming that Putin is a reasonable man, would be inclined to conclude that he will move forward to a Schachtian and ultimately a Paretian system, gradually subduing and reducing the scope of Russia's oligarchs and transforming these agents into western corporate directors. Even Alexei Mordashov, the oligarchic CEO of Severstal (Northern Steel Company), decried the gulf between the country's rich and poor: "Generally speaking it's bad for the economy because of the high concentration of wealth in the hands of just several groups."[3] A shift from a parasitic to a competitive business form of Muscovite authoritarianism would greatly improve the federation's prospects. Transitologists like Anders Aslund periodically make the claim that such a shift has already been accomplished, but his plea for oligarchic amnesty belies this position.[4] Insincere assertions of enlightened reform are a Muscovite cultural reflex and shouldn't be taken seriously. Small groups of "progressive businessmen" continue to gobble ever larger chunks of Russia's asset base, with no sign of an early reversal,[5] defying rational expectations. If change is coming, the pace is likely to be glacial, or as Putin's assault on Yukos suggests, it won't involve a movement toward Pareto.[6]

This means that Putin won't be able to construct economic, political, and social institutions that optimize the potential of his foreign and security policies. He may perceive numerous strategic possibilities for advancing Russia's interests and defending the nation in the wake of the Iraq War, but he is apt to overestimate their economic feasibility. Hope notwithstanding, Russia cannot become the centerpiece of an ideological bloc. It cannot compete with China as the leader of the developing world, nor be a hegemon in South Asia or the Middle East. It cannot be a dominant force inside the EU or NATO, nor oppose the United States anywhere. Having acquiesced to EU and NATO expansion, the only thing the Kremlin can accomplish with a Muscovite (or Schactian) economy is to remilitarize as a temporary deterrent to potential aggressors like China, with no other rational strategic purpose. This seems to be a meager reward compared with the risk of precipitating a renewed arms race with America and causing a destabilizing escalation in the production of WMDs by China, India, Pakistan, North Korea, and Japan, but Putin's judgment may be impaired by the delusion that his authoritarian regime can be made globally competitive. It is essential, therefore, that the West refrain from nurturing the illusion that Russia has or can soon construct a Muscovite political economy that will provide the Kremlin with worthwhile options. Putin can restore the federation's vast military power, but he needs to know that its economic and security costs make this an irrational choice.

This will be a daunting task because the double-speak of international persuasion practiced today on both sides of the Atlantic which officially describes Russia's Muscovite economy as a "normal" market system puts a gloss on reality and abets denial.[7] The West doesn't want to be the bearer of sad tidings, and Putin doesn't want to hear the message.

SUMMARY

- Russia can continue trodding its chosen path back to prodigal super-powerdom or change course in a few culturally viable ways.
- It can improve the macroeconomic performance of the Muscovite model by launching large-scale public works projects of the sort recommended during the 1930s by John Maynard Keynes. This won't remedy the system's microeconomic deficiencies but will greatly reduce the extent of involuntary unemployment.
- In searching for alternatives to the Muscovite model, the Kremlin could consider the usual suspects. It could try socialist models from the Cold War era, like those of East Europe and the Yugoslavian labor managed system, though Russians have lost faith in utopia.
- The success of Deng Xiaoping's Chinese "socialist" model should make it a contender, but with its focus on competitiveness, servicing western consumers, and attracting foreign capital, this model would threaten Putin's rent-granting style of Muscovite rule.
- The South Korean and Japanese models have sometimes been touted, but Russian economists are keenly aware of their cultural incompatibilities.
- A controlled disequilibrium model of the type devised by Hilter's finance minister, Hjalmar Schacht, in line with Yuriev's "Fortress Russia" concept might be more to Putin's liking. It features strong state financial controls, including strict barriers to capital flight, while excluding foreign firms that might threaten Russia's oligarchs and Kremlin rent-granting rule.
- Putin could choose between a military- or a civilian-focused version of this strong property rights corporatist model.
- An American free enterprise model or a European social democratic model would yield better results, but these are only remote possibilities because they entail scuttling authoritarian privilege.

- With the Muscovite and Schactian models, Putin can have both prosperity and security but only in the short run. Neither model can turn Russia into a prosperous superpower in the long run and Putin cannot expect to compensate for the shortcomings of the model with conquest and plunder.
- Putin probably won't choose. His authoritarian instincts will lead him to gradually ally with the forces of structural militarization.

10

CANDOR

The terrorist attacks on 9/11 and the Iraq war provide an invaluable opportunity to reassess prevailing strategies of global engagement. Throughout the Cold War and the first phase of the "end of history," great powers and superpowers sought advantage by filtering reality through the lenses of their public cultures while searching for pragmatic compromises. American free enterprisers and European social democrats trumpeted the idea of the West, each with their special spin, the Soviets propounded Marxist-Leninism, but the subtext in the East and West was usually about conflict management on terms everyone could abide. This is why there was no third world war. Crises tended to erupt only when targets of opportunity like postwar Eastern Europe or missile bases in Cuba proved too tempting.

This fragmented engagement required an artfulness that was sometimes lacking, and it often spawned confusion because the criteria of success were fuzzy. Just as individuals disguise their hidden agendas from themselves and others by espousing lofty ideals, makers of foreign policy aren't always guided by their declared principles. During the Cold War, it was never clear whether advancing ideals, pursuing hidden agendas, or avoiding conflict was primary or whether declaratory goals were desirable or realistic. Idols of perception, as Francis Bacon observed in the sixteenth century, blur objectivity and warp policy. Americans, Europeans, and the Soviets had panaceas that were trotted out on all occasions (free enterprise, corporatism, and central planning) even though many knew that no economic system was universally applicable. The resulting dissonance made it difficult for senior officials to "think outside the box," objectively perform routine analysis, and optimize national welfare. For example, several former CIA directors acknowledged[1] that they knew their subordinates underestimated Soviet defense activities but didn't rectify the problem because the facts clashed with liberal preconceptions and the unwritten rules of diplomatic engagement. Because of the public culture in the West, western leaders held that the Kremlin wasn't conducting an arms buildup and that, even if it was, they should look the other way in order to coax Soviet leaders into westernizing. It was better to misinform the public than to risk putting Moscow on the defensive.[2]

Events subsequently justified this rationalist gambit. Gorbachev may have been critically influenced by it, saving the West hundreds of billions of dollars on defense. But the same cannot be said for the campaign of the Washington consensus favoring shock therapy, for it has set the stage for Russia's reemergence as a prodigal superpower.

Objective national security analysis is clouded further by partisanship. Domestic and foreign interest groups discovered long ago that their causes can be advanced by cherry-picking ideals and lobbying for their adoption as the guiding principles of national policy. Islamists insist that America should be constrained by their interpretation of international law, pacifists argue that war is never an option, foes of uni- or bipolar superpowerdom contend that it is unfair to deny Kim Il Jong weapons of mass destruction, and even activists who oppose Pax Americana, or Russia or European Union versions urge Washington, Moscow, and Brussels to intervene here, there, and everywhere on their behalf.[3]

Further, the shadow culture of any given society cannot be overlooked. Human behavior isn't governed solely by idealism, pragmatism, and partisan interest. It is also influenced by conflicting subliminal values that societies publically disavow. Pareto-efficient markets, for example, assume that participants adhere to the Golden Rule and eschew deceptive practices. Yet the same western tradition applauds W. C. Fields's adage "Never give a sucker an even break," which contradicts the founding principles of free enterprise. Similarly, while enlightenment reason, which informs American public culture, presumes that people of goodwill can always peacefully resolve their grievances, western shadow culture also sometimes applauds preemption. This ambivalence is why many Britains and Americans who opposed to the Iraq war before the event switched to supporting it shortly thereafter. Shadow values matter because they provide a psychological basis for escaping the constraints of declaratory norms and purposively pursuing partially or wholly conflicting objectives. Such values represent aspects of reality that people wish to conceal, that they may prefer not to see, but that profoundly influence policymaking and partly determine what policies can be implemented. Moreover, the involvement of shadow values is the rule rather than the exception. It isn't an accident that Japan's cultural symbols are the sword and the chrysanthemum and that America's are the olive branch and the arrow-wielding eagle.

Rational expectionalists in America, Europe, and Russia who firmly believe Putin will cleanse the federation of authoritarianism, Muscovite economic management, and structural militarization deny that complexity, partisanship, and shadow cultural values often trump enlightened rationality, but the evidence doesn't bear them out anywhere, including America. Despite the cumulative expenditure of hundreds of billions of dollars, the CIA and most Sovietologists, blinkered by western public culture, never managed to get the Soviet Union right. Their appraisals of aggregate Soviet economic growth, improvements in per capita income, structural militarization, and systemic convergence were all wrong, and the environment of misguided idealism and partisan pleading made it exceedingly difficult for better informed insiders to think dispassionately about security and to act pragmatically.

Things aren't likely to be better this time around unless Putin and counselors east and west face up to the realities of Muscovite economics and structural militarization. Paying lip service to free enterprise, democracy, social justice, or social democracy isn't enough. Western policymakers need to disabuse themselves of their unfounded belief that chanting mantras, lavishing gifts (assistance), and threatening economic sanctions will persuade the Kremlin to kick its authoritarian habits. This strategy may play well in Washington, Paris, and Frankfurt but will fall on deaf ears in Moscow. It won't serve as a source of inspiration, nor as a tool of influence and persuasion. Putin (supported by the majority of the electorate), his inner circle, the FSB, the genshtab, the bureaucracy, the oligarchs, the new Russians, and the mafia like things just the way they are. Nor are they concerned that Washington will turn off the spigot. Kremlin leaders know that America's public culture approves governmental efforts to buy influence even if recipients only pretend to comply.[4] They will bleat the credo, whine for gifts, and protest the injustice of sanctions, but they won't relinquish their privileges.

Putin and his team are equally in denial. They cannot admit to themselves or others that insincere adherence to western values is unlikely to bring prosperity or enhance national security. They cannot legitimate

Muscovite rule by lauding the merits of authoritarian privilege. And they dare not implement effective representative democracy,[5] the rule of contract, unabridged market competition, and social justice or curtail the power of the security services without toppling their house of cards. They are stymied at every level and seem confused by the swirl of partisan intrigue.

The only alternative for those who prefer not to leave "bad enough" alone is to shed "tried and false" tactics requiring players to pretend that idealism, pragmatism, partisan duplicity, and dubious shadow values will assure good results. Rational expectations theories that presume behavior is automatically governed by the idea of the West must be discarded, the limits of assistance and economic sanctions acknowledged, the distortive effect of partisan advocacy recognized, and the volatile potential of shadow values borne firmly in mind.

Starting with the issue of public culture, the West needs to tweak its ideology by softening claims of universality and historical necessity. The principles of economic liberty, democracy, social justice, and the welfare state are logically sound and ethically appealing. They command widespread respect and don't have to be reinforced with dubious claims of transcultural superiority and historical inevitability. They can exert a powerful attraction without the denigration of well-functioning communalist societies like that of Japan[6] and without the pretense that "inferior" social systems are on the brink of being swept into the "dustbin of history."

Eliminating untenable claims to universality and historical necessity may have some tactical disadvantages and irritate those who need to believe destiny is on the West's side, but these disadvantages will be outweighed by the benefits of making diplomatic engagement more realistic and less provocative. Instead of hypocritically congratulating Putin for successfully building a just, democratic, free enterprise society while chiding him for failing to finish the job, western leaders will find that more candid engagement will improve accommodation. They should concede the possibility that Russia might construct a social system better culturally suited to its needs than the American or EU model, gaining in return the ability to characterize the federation's productive arrangements, political governance, and society more objectively. Putin, under this new protocol, could be congratulated for some aspects of privatization, liberalization, market competition, and entrepreneurship, as well as balloting, legal, penal, and civil rights reforms, while being cautioned that these accomplishments don't come to the same thing as democratic free enterprise. He could be told without equivocation that Russia is on the path back to the future in that it is restoring the Muscovite economic mechanism, structural militarization, authoritarian governance, and social inequality. And most important of all, he could be advised that Russia's material and security potential will be severely impaired unless remedial action is promptly undertaken. It could be explained to one and all without cultural filtration that, unless the Kremlin alters its course, the federation will once again become a prodigal superpower and be afflicted with nuclear insecurity. These insights might jar the Kremlin to its senses and have the further benefit of placing other international security matters in proper perspective and creating a superior framework for informed dialogue.

Instead of bribes (assistance) and economic sanctions being disingenuously linked to economic liberty, democracy, and social justice, carrots and sticks should be precision guided toward ridding Russia of Muscovite economic governance and structural militarization. Policymakers should insist that Russia adhere to international property right norms and provide equal market access to all, including foreigners, under a Paretian rule of law. And they should press Russia to repudiate rent granting, democratize, suppress oligarchy, redistribute wealth, and reduce physical systems management to prevent the kind of selective market liberalization that strengthens the Muscovite economic stranglehold. Likewise, they should aim security assistance and sanctions at eliminating structural militarization in all its hydra-headed forms rather than restricting them to a few politically visible programs. Although the Nunn-Lugar nuclear control and antiproliferation objectives and Russia's antiterrorist cooperation are worthy of continued support[7] – but only if pursued in conjunction with scrupulous monitoring and enforcement – they should not be conflated with the higher aim of reducing structural militarization, which above all else means downsizing the VPK. And of course no one should harbor any illusion that assistance and sanctions will make Putin do anything fundamental unless he is persuaded that the changes are in his interest.

Clarity of purpose also provides a defense against the distortive influence of partisan advocacy by separating high-priority national security objectives from selling chickens, allowing policymakers east and west to optimize joint outcomes without distraction.[8] And it heightens awareness of the possibility of shadow cultural surprise. Western leaders need to appreciate that, while Washington, Brussels, and Moscow share a common public culture descended from the Enlightenment, their shadow cultures differ. Muscovite values determine Russian behavior more pervasively than counterpart shadow values affect the West. Rent granting, intrigue and duplicity are the norm, often without rational purpose, and as Yeltsin's shock therapeutic policies demonstrate, leaders are impetuous. The Kremlin cannot resist saying one thing and doing another or perpetually reversing its policies in a zigzag fashion. It habitually probes the gray areas of its accords and views treaties and contracts as tactics: one-way commitments only binding on other parties. And of course when confronted, Russians either resort to brazen denial or disingenuously promise reform. This package of shadow culture–sanctioned behaviors constitutes a syndrome that must be factored into rational western engagement strategy in order for western leaders to better anticipate and manage the shape of things to come.

Likewise, Moscow would be well advised to appraise American motives more dispassionately. The vigorous exercise of power to suppress nonstate aggressors possessing WMD and stabilize the European heartland on pre-Soviet lines isn't a "neo-imperialist" expression of the United States' shadow culture.[9] The Kremlin is justified in complaining that aspects of the foreign policy of the United States are discordant with its founding principles, but the Kremlin still doesn't comprehend the deeper dynamics.

Switching to a more sophisticated strategy of international security conceptualization and engagement would help here and with the larger task of crafting a safer and more prosperous global future. Although Andrei Kokoshin, former senior deputy chairman of the Russian Defense Council, fails to grasp this, the major lesson from the Iraq war and its aftermath is that the United States is no longer a "paper tiger" and is unlikely to face a serious challenge from "out-of-theater" land powers.[10] Even if Moscow succeeds in constructing a full-spectrum, fifth-generation military force capable of deterring a nonexistent American threat on its western front, manpower deficiencies will prevent it from projecting its military power to theaters that matter.[11] Full-scale rearmament therefore is trebly fatuous. There is no American or NATO threat to the Russian motherland. Russia will never develop the sea power required to effectively counter the United States outside Eurasia. And any such effort will needlessly provoke a multilateral arms race involving unstable players, including China, India, and Pakistan.

Confronting these truths is critical for Russia. The post–Iraq war world order doesn't require the Kremlin to suboptimize its defense or become an American dependency. The Putin administration has the ability to improve its security and economic prospects in a wide spectrum of areas by realistically assessing its options and shedding self-imposed constraints. It doesn't have to shoot itself in the foot by forming anti-American coalitions or precipitating a renewed arms race, and with sufficient resolve it can eradicate authoritarianism, the Muscovite economic system, and structural militarization.[12]

Kremlin insiders often speak as if they understand this, but they don't seem to grasp that the logos of Muscovy is driving them in the opposite direction. They pretend that "democratic authoritarianism" is democracy, "insider free enterprise" is laissez-faire, "Paretian rule of men" is the rule of law, and "optimal structural militarization" is optimal national defense. They act like Muscovites and insist that their behavior strictly conforms to the idea of the West. This isn't good enough. Oxymorons are no defense against prodigal superpowerdom and social injustice. Russia's leaders must candidly face up to the social consequences of Muscovy and westernize for the greater good.

The West can help Putin do the right thing by setting a good example. It too needs to candidly admit that what it calls pragmatic engagement often is melange of special interest politics and public culture placebos. Pretending that Russia has transitioned to democratic free enterprise and extirpated structural militarization may be comforting, but it is also irresponsible. The West needs to coolly assess the Muscovite threat, to help itself and Russia avert unpleasant outcomes. Both sides have ample latitude for constructive dialogue and shouldn't allow Baconian idols to deter them from seizing the initiative.

SUMMARY

- The strategy and tactics of global engagement, like those of personal relations, are shaped by complex psychocultural forces. They aren't governed one-dimensionally by reason, ideology, ideals, consistent values, or hidden agendas.
- Although it is often supposed that diplomacy seeks to advance national interests through the artful use of engagement strategies and by

employing public cultural values, persuasion, enticement, punishment, and manipulation, policymakers seldom operate on the basis of well-defined objectives or lucidly perceive reality. They are enthralled by ideals and bewildered by institutional expediency, partisan advocacy, and countervalues.

- This is why "rational expectations" models are naive. Reason can be used to articulate, analyze, and solve problems, but it isn't self-fulfilling. It, like fate (the "end of history"), doesn't assure happy endings.
- The threat posed to Russia and global stability by authoritarianism, Muscovite economics, and structural militarization and by Russia's potential to reemerge as a prodigal superpower has been hidden beneath the threshhold of public perception in Moscow and the West by the miasma of eclectic discourse.
- This has prevented both parties from grasping the dangers, sorting out options, and taking appropriate countermeasures.
- The first imperative for successfully resolving the Muscovite challenge is unvarnished realism. Moscow and the West must come to terms with Russia's tendency toward prodigal superpowerdom and work cooperatively to overcome it.
- This is all the West can do. It cannot beguile Moscow into purging Russia's poisoned authoritarian cultural legacy.
- If Putin or his successors fail to acknowledge or meet the challenge, then the West can only limit the damage.

CONCLUSION

It isn't easy to ferret out the truth. If nothing else, Sigmund Freud has taught us that human behavior cannot be reliably grasped using rationalist or positivist methods. The mind operates consciously and subliminally on multiple levels, possesses inconsistent motives, and employs complex rules. Perceptions are often filtered inaccurately by convictions and cultural cues, and people don't easily acknowledge error. No one therefore should be surprised that most Sovietologists failed to accurately comprehend Soviet reality. Western public cultural values like tolerance, diversity, and conflict avoidance, combined with sympathy for socialist ideals, sanitized otherwise informed perceptions of the Kremlin's economic accomplishments and military aspirations. And the complexities of soft sciences like economics compounded the problem.

Had the USSR endured for another sixty-nine years, as it well might have, the majority of Sovietologists would still be unable to accept the truth about its physical management system and structural militarization. The USSR would have continued to be characterized as a rational, centrally planned, communist superpower that after the tumultuous Stalin years was gradually liberalizing, improving its living standard, and westernizing.

Communism's *Götterdämmerung* and a wealth of incriminating post-Cold War evidence, however, have cracked this facade and provided the foundation for a more objective assessment. The research in this volume, informed by new evidence, demonstrates that the USSR's postwar economic performance was substantially inferior to America's. Contrary to the estimates of the CIA, the USSR's GNP and its per capita consumption growth both lagged well behind western norms. Its microeconomic performance – as reflected in educational choice, job choice, factor allocation, conditions of labor, innovation, technological progress and diffusion, wholesale and retail distribution, transfers, leisure, and personal freedom – was also inferior, but this had always been the mainstream view. The sum and substance of the old and new evidence, therefore, is that the Soviet Union was blighted but not destitute. Its population was equipped with basic necessities. It had food, clothing, shelter, mass transportation, and an ample supply of books on Marx and Lenin.

But the quality of most things public and private was low, and the ambit of choice was minuscule (utility was impaired by forced substitution). Instead of the USSR's 1989 per capita consumption (computed in dollars) being 60 percent of America's, as the CIA reported in 1991, the properly calculated purchasing power parity figure was closer to 20 percent. Despite decades of prodigious investment, typically equal to 35 percent of GNP, and massive expenditure on RDT&E (including technology transfers from the West obtained through industrial espionage), Soviet consumers found themselves continuously falling behind the developed West under the banner of "scientific" communist central planning. Gorbachev said it: The Soviet Union was in the grip of stagnation (*zastoi*), and every Russian knew it was true, even though the Cambridge School, the CIA, European social democrats, and convergence theorists insisted it couldn't be so.

This volume also challenges another sacred cow, the belief that, while the Soviet Union was a superpower, it wasn't structurally militarized. When this possibility wasn't being rejected out of hand, it was said that the VPK and the genshtab didn't demand ever more resources to cope with foreign threats, didn't have an institutional inside track to acquire them, nor had a rapid mobilization capacity. The approved Sovietological view was carefully nuanced. Both the CIA and Franklin Holzman (the leading liberal Cambridge School opponent of the agency), mimicking the official Soviet handbook *Narodnoe Khoziaistvo SSSR*, argued that the share of GNP devoted to defense, with minor exceptions, had been declining steadily after 1969 (for the arcane details, see chap. 3). This trend implied that the Soviet Union wasn't structurally militarized, because either defense spending was too low, as Holzman maintained based on an estimate of 3–5 percent of GNP, or because enlightened leaders were in command, as the CIA's 12- to 15-percent figure suggested. Although both the CIA and Holzman acknowledged that the Soviet Union was a superpower, they heatedly denied that Moscow had embarked on a rapid arms buildup or was endeavoring to achieve arms superiority.

The new evidence demonstrates that the CIA and the Cambridge School were wrong across the spectrum. Not only was Soviet defense spending in the vicinity of 30 percent of GNP, close to the figure conjectured by the Office of the Secretary of Defense in 1990, but the rate of real weapons growth had been high throughout the entire period. Although Holzman and the CIA had claimed defense spending was declining as a share of GNP, the genshtab and the VPK clearly were having their way, building the full-spectrum, prolonged war fighting capital stock stipulated in their military doctrine and obtaining the resources for mass weapons production, with or without the blessing of the political authorities.

The combination of a failed consumer economy and a hypertrophic defense sector made the USSR a prodigal superpower. Even when this was recountenanced, it was given a benevolent spin, either by claiming that the USSR could prosper if it disarmed or could not prevail in a protracted Cold War because it lacked economic staying power. The new evidence indicates that both propositions were wrong. The deficiencies of the Kremlin's physical management system meant that no productive system constructed on Soviet principles could incorporate consumer sovereignty or be microeconomically efficient. Even if the USSR completely disarmed, its economy could not escape the squalor. Likewise, the success of the VPK over decades showed that, if the leadership remained united behind its Blochian agenda, structural militarization could perpetuate itself indefinitely, growing as rapidly as Moscow's enormous investment in military RDT&E allowed, while forcing the population at large to content itself with a Spartan regimen.

Had the West been weaker after Stalin died, the Kremlin could have used its military power to material advantage, as it had earlier in Eastern and Central Europe, exacting tribute to compensate for its consumerist failings. But when NATO foreclosed this option, its vast power became a dead end. Although no external power could have imposed regime change, Soviet leaders gradually came to realize that maintaining Russia's status as a prodigal superpower was foolish. For the nation and for themselves, the only return on a lifetime of military investment, other than the preservation of Communist power, was dreariness.

Gorbachev's doomed experiment with *glasnost'* (candor), *perestroika* (radical economic reform), *uskorenie* (acceleration), *demokratizatsia* (democratization), and *novoe myshlenie* (new security thinking) can be interpreted as a half-hearted, venal attempt to break out of the dual-sided trap of material squalor and structural militarization by building markets to provide the privileged with both guns and *la dolce vita*.

His leasing reform *arenda* and his encouragement of "spontaneous" privatization, managerial independence, and entrepreneurial opportunism, together with the abolition of Gosplan's directive authority, have been widely viewed as precursors to Yeltsin's and Putin's more ambitious efforts at liberalizing, democratizing, and westernizing Russia, which culminated in a huge reduction of up to 90 percent in weapons production and a lesser but substantial paring of Russia's armed forces.[1] The Washington consensus has seized upon these leaders' statements of intent to declare that the federation is well on the road to becoming a normal, liberal, democratic market system, and the majority of credulous security analysts have misinferred from contemporary defense spending data that the VPK has shrunk proportionally, closing the book on structural militarization.

The central thesis of this book is that the change that has actually occurred is far less than meets the eye. The Russian economy hasn't transitioned to democratic free enterprise, and structural militarization is alive and stirring. Soviet physical systems management has metamorphosed into a Muscovite model that combines authoritarian market direction, rent granting, and revokable proprietary privileges and has residual aspects of physical systems management, including VPK structural militarization. As in the Soviet days, Russians have the right of the ballot, but this doesn't make the regime democratic, despite the emergence of political parties, because the people aren't sovereign. It is the president and his administration who rule, independent of parties and the people's will.[2] And while weapons production remains a pale shadow of what it was in the communist past, not only is the genshtab in control of an intact military-industrial complex, but the Putin administration has signed off on an ambitious full-spectrum, fifth-generation rearmament plan scheduled to be in peak operation by 2010.[3] Structural militarization hasn't withered, it just went into low gear, to remain there until the genshtab and the Kremlin leadership decide to restore the status quo ante.

Thus, despite all the imagery of radical change, Russia hasn't been genetically recoded. It remains trapped in a Muscovite authoritarian mold, and its heavy-handed, albeit more liberalized, central economic management and its military aspirations are gradually leading it to resume its status as a prodigal superpower.

This disturbing tendency has gone largely unnoticed in the West and Russia itself, for the same reason that physical systems management and structural militarization weren't given their due during the Cold War. The leaders of both systems are in denial. The ideals of western public culture, which are now espoused by the Putin administration, incline politicians, scholars, and publicists to portray reality as they wish it to be, even though they perceive the dissonance. This proclivity is reinforced by standard fragmented diplomatic engagement, which supposedly will result in benign, enlightened authoritarians (of the same type as Catherine the Great) being persuaded to change their stripes by philosophers bandying ideals and appealing to reason and history and by western leaders tying economic assistance and sanctions to diverse targets and threatening regime change.

Diplomatic engagement of this kind abets Russia's slide into prodigal superpowerdom and must be discarded because it has a tried and proven record of failure. The problem seems to lie not in such engagement itself but in a confusion of ends and means. Western practitioners seem lulled into complacency by a belief that reason or history is on their side,[4] have too high a regard for the efficacy of economic assistance and sanctions, or find it in their institutional interest to engage in the diplomatic process for its own sake. "Calling things by their right names," as Leninists liked to say, may seem unimportant, but it is not. Present dangers cannot be accurately diagnosed and appropriate policies devised openly (or behind executive curtains) without an objective perception of reality, and Putin cannot be alerted to the peril if we don't recognize it ourselves. It is still an open question whether the Kremlin can be persuaded to abandon Muscovite economics, and forsake structural militarization even if it recognizes the risk it runs of turning Russia into a prodigal superpower once again and the dangerous consequences of the multilateral arms race likely to result. But this shouldn't deter the West from trying.[5]

GLOSSARY

ACW Advanced conventional weapon.

adjusted factor cost A technique for adjusting fiat unit production cost prices (fiat value added) to conform with western price formation principles. Soviet ruble prices (fiat values) were factor cost adjusted by stripping nonwage components (retail turnover taxes and profits) and adding imputed interest charges. The resulting adjusted ruble prices had the form of properly constructed value-added prices but not the content because neither wages nor imputed interest charges were competitively determined.

ALCM Air-launched cruise missile.

approved contradiction A logical, behavioral, or policy contradiction that a society chooses to disregard because it raises doubts about the integrity of the society's public culture.

authoritarian economic sovereignty Control over micro-, meso-, and macoeconomic supply is governed by "authorities" instead of individuals. The people serve the authorities, primarily for the authorities' benefit.

authoritarianism Political rule by an individual (autocracy) or a coterie. More generally, any system of rule where individual autonomy is subordinated or tightly constrained by coercion, administration, management, dictates, and rules.

Balkan wars Wars between Serbia and its neighbors, ended by NATO intervention in the late 1990s.

barracks socialism Derisory Marxist term for Spartan forms of socialism that prevent people from realizing their full human potential.

Blochian war Machine-age type of war supported by structurally militarized economies. In Blochian war, entire societies are mobilized for the purpose of war preparedness and war fighting. The concept is ascribed to Ivan Bloch, a nineteen-century advisor to Czar Nicholas II.

137

Bolshevik revolution A coup d'etat led by Vladimir Lenin, head of the Bolshevik Party, which deposed Czar Nicholas II in 1917 and installed a "Communist Party" dictatorship as well as a physical management system in lieu of markets.

Cambridge School A group of distinguished Sovietologists residing in Cambridge, Massachusetts, and their affiliates. The Cambridge School authoritatively applied adjusted factor costing to the measurement and analysis of Soviet economic performance.

CBW Chemical biological warfare.

CER Cost-estimating relationship.

CFE Treaty on conventional forces in Europe.

chain index A statistical index composed of multiple segments, each with its own base, that are "chained" together into a single series.

CIA Central Intelligence Agency.

city-building enterprises Defense-industrial towns controlled by the defense-industrial complex (OPK).

command economy Popular term for a Soviet-type physical management system in which planning directives and incentives play an especially large role. Command economies, like military organizations, are hierarchical, there is strict subordination by rank, and direct orders cannot be disobeyed.

consumer sovereignty Pareto requirement that micro-, meso-, and macroeconomic supply be determined solely by competitive consumer demand.

cost of Soviet empire Phrase suggesting that structural militarization and the burden of Soviet occupation in Eastern Europe were onerous and encouraged Communist accommodation with the West.

counsel of despair High-risk policy recommendation offered when other options are precluded by moral hazard or hard reality.

defense-industrial complex (OPK) New name for the Russia military-industrial complex (VPK). It is unclear whether it will stick or disappear.

DIA Defense Intelligence Agency.

DOD U.S. Department of Defense.

dual-track engagement Strategy of employing two different means or simultaneously pursuing inconsistent policy objectives that preserve multiple options. The term is used here to distinguish declaratory policy guided by the ideals of the public culture from pragmatic bargaining sometimes governed by the principles of the shadow culture.

Dutch disease Loss of export manufacturing competitiveness when foreign exchange rates appreciate in response to petroleum windfalls.

economic liberty Individual right to seek and maximize utility, constrained only by the rule of contract law and the Golden Rule of moral conduct. It is the right to Pareto optimize.

economy of shortage Shorthand for a resource-mobilizing, physically managed economic system (a Soviet-type economy) in which military and investment incentives induce a perpetual shortage of consumer goods.

end of history The Hegelian concept that when God dialectically actualizes himself, creation will be perfect and will never change thereafter. Hence the end of history. Marx secularized the concept by claiming that history would culminate in the establishment of perfect communism. Fukuyama believes that the motor of history since the French Revolution has been democratization, which will culminate in democratic free enterprise.

Euler's theorem A mathematical theorem stating the conditions under which the value of an outcome is equal to the value added of it parts. The theorem is used in economics to specify the relationship between the market value of goods and the corresponding value added of capital, labor, and land.

evil empire A term coined by the Reagan administration to express the accusation that the Soviet Union was imperialistic and despotic.

exceptionalism An antiglobalist viewpoint that holds that for each country there is a unique political and economic system that best promotes its national welfare.

exclusionary market A market with narrow scope intended to preserve the income, rents, and wealth of insiders to the exclusion of would-be competitors. Exclusionary markets may be oligopolistic or monopolistic, but profits need not be maximized by producing to the point where marginal cost equals marginal revenue. The term encompasses a wide variety of suboptimizing possibilities.

fiat prices Prices fixed by authorities on any arbitrary basis that does not accurately replicate competitive equilibrium values.

Fisher ideal The geometric mean of two indexes, the Laspeyres and the Paasche. Fisher ideals overweight the slower growing index, a result justified by utility theory on some interpretations.

general staff (genshtab) The supreme uniformed Russian military authority responsible for all civil defense, defense-industrial, preparedness, readiness, military mobilization, security, and war-fighting activities.

globalism A term used to express the claim that all nations are or will be governed by the same political and economic principles. It is frequently assumed that the globe is democratizing and adopting free enterprise, but some offer opposing visions. Hence there can be a "clash of globalizations."

golden age growth rate Optimal sustainable rate of long-term growth for an advanced Pareto-efficient economy.

Golden Rule The principle of doing unto others as you would have them do unto you (fair play). Important for assuring the efficient operation of the rule of contract law.

Goskomstat The Soviet state statistical agency. The acronym is still used in the postcommunist period, together with the alternative Roskomstat (Russian statistical agency).

Gosplan The Soviet state central planning agency. The institution survives but no longer has directive responsibilities.

Gossnabsbyt' The Soviet state wholesale allocation system.

gross domestic product (GDP) The aggregate value of all marketable goods and services computed at market or official state prices. This measure of aggregate activity excludes income derived from assets held abroad. GDP is only economically meaningful when prices are competitive (or are shadow equivalents). Otherwise prices are weak indicators of utilities and opportunity costs.

gross national income The income paid to primary factors of production for their services computed at market or official prices. Gross national income is only economically meaningful when prices are competitive (or are shadow equivalents).

growth retardation Diminishing economic growth attributed in the Soviet case to flagging technological progress and a low elasticity of capital labor substitution, both caused by the defects of physical systems management.

GRU Glavnoe Razvedovatel'noe Upravlenie: Main Intelligence Administration, the foreign intelligence organ of the Russian Ministry of Defense.

hedonic Relating to or characterized by pleasure or satisfaction. Hedonic indicators try to quantify the psychological benefit of consumption.

hyperdepression Extreme economic depression, defined here as substantially deeper than the American Great Depression, which caused a 27.5 percent fall in GNP between 1929 and 1933.

idea of the West An array of ideals, inventoried by Samuel Huntington, that epitomize western values. The core economic subset of these ideals (motives) are economic freedom, democracy, social justice, tolerance, diversity, and conflict avoidance. The interpretation of these ideals in practice is often contextual, subject to dispute, and qualified by subcultural shadow cultural, and countercultural values.

impoverished superpower A term popularized by Charles Wolf, Jr., and Henry Rowan suggesting that the defining characteristic of the USSR was the disparity between its living standard and its military might. The concept implied that the USSR's threat potential was constrained by its impoverishment.

IW Information warfare aimed at influencing enemy perceptions and at attitude management.

Iraq war The Anglo-American–Iraqi war of 2003.

KGB Komitet gosudarstvennoy bezoparnosti (Soviet Committee on State Security), the USSR's foreign intelligence service. Renamed FSB (Federal Security Bureau) after 1991.

khozraschyot **(economic cost accounting)** Principle of Soviet enterprise self-sufficiency according to which revenues from operations must equal or exceed costs. *Khozraschyot* served as a microeconomic control mechanism preventing enterprises from producing at a loss unless expressly authorized by their ministerial supervisors.

krugovaya poruka Principle of mutual support or collusion between entities of the same or differing ranks, often referred to as a "family circle."

laissez-faire Eighteenth-century term for free enterprise, which during the Enlightenment implied morally disciplined, unfettered commercial activity. The term has a pejorative connotation for those who view capitalism as a depraved system of worker and peasant exploitation.

Laspeyres index An index that uses base-year weights. Laspeyres indexes are commonly used in economics to measure growth and inflation. They usually generate higher growth rates than indexes that employ final-year weights.

Lockean social contract Enlightenment notion that the harmony observed in human relations reflects the existence of an implicit social contract mandating that people refrain from preying on each other and act instead in accordance with ethical principles like the Golden Rule. The contract is the result of rational choice rather than a manifestation of genetically encoded behavior.

mafia Term used in contemporary Russia for organized crime.

mastering new technology A phase of the technological improvement process during which enterprises learn how to realize the productivity potential of new and improved technologies.

MBMW Machine building and metalworking.

MEAC Military-Economic Analysis Center (contained within the CIA).

MEAP Military-Economic Analysis Panel.

mesoeconomics A branch of economic theory concerned with the institutions connecting microeconomic and macroeconomic processes.

military-industrial complex (VPK) *Voennyi-promyshlennyi kompleks* is a formal institutional network connecting the Soviet (and now Russian) genshtab, Ministry of Defense, military enterprises, civilian firms, and construction, communications, planning, civil defense, military intelligence, and other security organizations into a cohesive structurally militarized entity. The integration of the VPK is higher than its American counterpart, which is based on a loose community of interest. The VPK recently has been renamed the *oboronnyi-promyshennyi kompleks* (OPK; defense-industrial complex).

Minatom Ministry of Atomic Energy, responsible for Russian nuclear weapons and civilian nuclear activities.

MIRV A multiple independently targetable reentry vehicle is a pod of nuclear weapons that can be directed at more than one target.

MOD Russian Ministry of Defense.

modernization Process through which less developed nations attain the techno-logical sophistication of advanced countries. Since technology is separable from culture, societies can modernize without westernizing. The idea of the West im-plies that nonwesternizing modernization will be less effective and provide lower welfare than Pareto-efficient westernization.

Muscovite economic system An authoritarian productive system based on what Stefan Hedlund calls mental frames dating to the post-Mongal rise of Mus-covy. This system, which includes autocracy, rent granting, patrimonialism (the view that all assets ultimately belong to the sovereign), *pomestie* (tenure land grants given to supporters, not unlike the revokable property rights of today's oligarchs), *kormlenie* (tax "farming" and rent seeking), *krugovaya poruka* (net-work mutual support), *divan* (plunder), and Slavophilism (nationalistic prefer-ences), results in subjugation and extreme inequality. Liberal variants provide transactors with a significant degree of economic and political autonomy.

MVD Ministry of Internal Affairs (Ministerstvo Vnutrennikh Del). Soviet and Russian domestic intelligence service. The same acronym also applies to the Ministry of Foreign Affairs, which causes confusion.

NATO North Atlantic Treaty Organization.

new Russians Term for Russia's nouveaux riches, relatively affluent business-men, administrators, luxury service workers, and criminals, many of whom are purveyers to oligarchs and their circles.

9/11 Date of Osama Bin Laden's aerial attacks on the New York World Trade Center and the Pentagon (2001). It marks a tidal shift in American attitudes toward domestic security and political military strategy as well as the end of the post-Cold War "end of history."

NMD National missile defense. This is the current term for the American anti-ballistic missile defense program that abrogated the Soviet–American ABM Treaty of 1972 (a treaty that was flouted by the USSR but continued to be honored by the United States).

nuclear proliferation The spread of nuclear weapons production capabilities and nuclear weapons.

oligarchs Colloquial term for a small number of superrich businessmen who dom-inate Russia's exclusionary markets and acquired their wealth undeservingly through spontaneous privatization, other forms of asset seizing, asset stripping, presidential largesse, rent seeking, and a host of criminal activities. They tend to live nonproductively off their assets, transferring their money to safe havens abroad, underproducing, underinvesting, and suppressing competitive access to their preserves.

OKP *Oboronnyi-promyshennyi kompleks* (defense-industrial complex) is Russia's renamed military-industrial complex.

OSD Office of the Secretary of Defense.

overfull employment Excess employment, where the labor supplied is greater than the Pareto optimum, which means that some workers could increase their utility by substituting leisure for wages. Overfull employment in the West is caused by speculative booms; in the Soviet Union it was caused by various kinds of forced labor.

Paasche index An index that utilizes final-year weights. Paasche indexes are commonly used in economics to measure growth and inflation. They usually generate lower growth rates than indexes constructed with early-year weights.

Pareto efficiency Realization of the full economic potential of competitive, individual utility-maximizing economic activity.

peaceful coexistence Khrushchev-era Soviet term for a situation in which Cold War adversaries respect each other's territorial sovereignty and interests. The concept implied lower intensity engagement and the renunciation of military force as a means of resolving conflicts between ideological rivals.

PGM Precision guided munitions.

physical systems management A nonmarket approach to production, factor allocation, and goods distribution based on physical rather than market value criteria. Associated in the Soviet case with Gosplan, Gossnabsbyt', Goskomtsen, the supervisory ministerial apparatus, and enterprise bonus incentivization.

positivist A scientific evaluation standard stressing objectivity and uncontamination by normative judgments.

premature deaths Deaths occurring before their actuarially expected date. The concept provides a benchmark for assessing whether discontinuities in mortality trends are attributable to natural or political causes.

production potential A term coined by Abram Bergson to distinguish technically from economically efficient production. Production potential is a supply-side optimum disconnected from consumer utility and demand.

psychocultural A term drawing attention to the fact that productive and consumer choice making isn't always rational in a strict economic sense, as people's behavior is influenced by diverse neuroses, psychoses, institutions, and cultural rules.

purchasing power parity A measure of worth computed by valuing goods produced and sold in a foreign nation at home country prices.

rational expectations A term reflecting the Enlightenment view that behavior can be accurately deduced from the principles of morally disciplined rational choice-making. The assumption of moral discipline makes the construct idealistic.

RDT&E Research, development, testing, and evaluation. These are the four core elements of the technological adoption process. Mastering new technology is an additional phase in which acquirers learn how to utilitize the technology's full potential.

realization crisis A crisis that erupts when latent policy contradictions are realized. The Soviet Union's collapse, for example, was precipitated by the realization that its physical production management system was unreformable.

reconnaisance-fire (strike) systems Weapons systems capable of simultaneously identifying unanticipated threats and attacking them.

red directors Soviet era term for enterprise managers who supervised and commanded instead of responding to market signals and attempting to maximize profits.

RMA Revolution in military affairs. The term stresses the disjuncture between traditional concepts of war fighting and new ones based on advanced technologies, such as those exemplified in the Iraq war.

Rosvooruzhenie The Russian arms export agency.

ruler sovereignty Type of effective demand in which goods and services are supplied to satisfy some powerful entity or ruler rather than individual consumers.

Russian disease Massive corrupt transfers of state property to a small number of powerful individuals who repress competition and live passively off their preserves, causing severe resource demobilization.

Schactian system An economic control regime of the type devised by Hitler's financial advisor Hjalmar Schacht. In this system, private property is preserved but business autonomy is greatly restricted.

sebestoimost' Prime cost; the labor, capital, and rental cost of production.

security services All branches of the Russian security community.

servitors Nobles who, under Tsar Peter the Great, were required to provide twenty-five years of state service.

shock therapy Radical institutional or systemic change undertaken to revitalize the economy. Often used as a term of derision for radical policies that have catastrophic consequences.

siloviki A shadowy power clique that has been active in the past two or three years and has influenced Putin's personnel appointments.

social democracy A variant of the idea of the West. In this variant, a socially concerned state manages an otherwise free economy through democratic means to promote social justice. The model is often referred to as the welfare state.

SORT Strategic Offensive Arms Reduction Treaty.

Sovietologist Scholar specializing in Soviet studies. The term is broader than *Kremlinologist*, which refers to specialists who focus on Soviet domestic and international politics.

spurious innovation Development of products and process that have new or altered characteristics and are assigned higher prices but do not possess increased value.

START Strategic Arms Reduction Talks.

Stolper–Samuelson theory Application of general competitive theory to international trade, given factor immobility; it explains why relative prices should become globally proportional and living standards converge toward a common high frontier.

structural militarization Term used to describe a productive system with a large embedded military-industrial sector capable of persuading government leaders to provide sufficient resources to deal with worst-case security threats in the long run. Structural militarization can be thought of as chronic Blochian war preparedness.

subsistence market A low-productivity, low-value-added market developing out of physical management networks barred from pursuing profitable opportunities in exclusionary markets.

superpower A nation with a potentially dominating superiority, especially but not exclusively military. The criteria for military superpowerdom today, exemplified by the United States, are full-spectrum capabilities, flexible surge capacity, and superior RMA.

System of National Accounts (SNA) Standardized system of national income accounting devised by the United Nations and other international institutions.

systems-building integrated structures Proposed military-industrial production conglomerates headed by former Soviet design bureaus (now Russian state-owned companies) vested with controlling shares of systems-building integrated structures. Key element of Klebanov's military reform program.

systems directors Highest decision-making authorities presiding over the physical management system.

technical efficiency The supply-side potential of a productive system. Technically efficient points lie on the production possibilities frontier everywhere including the economically efficient Pareto ideal, given prevailing equilibrium prices.

TNC Tactical nuclear weapon intended for conventional war fighting.

TNW Tactical nuclear weapon.

tolkachi **(pushers)** Soviet sales and acquisition enterprise personnel responsible for trading capital and intermediate goods to overcome shortages resulting from supply misallocation by Gossnabsbyt'.

transformational depression Economic depression caused by the disruption of shifting from one system to another.

TVD *Teatry voennykh destvii* (theaters of military operations).

UAV Unmanned aerial vehicle.

value added Market value contributed by primary factors of production in extracting raw materials, fabricating them, and providing services. Value added is economic when factor prices are competitively determined. Fiat value added has no obvious utilitarian meaning.

value subtracted Market value diminished by primary factors of production in fabricating raw material or providing disservices. Spoiling otherwise useful things.

virtuality A term coined by Clifford Gaddy and Barry Ickes to convey the idea that physical productive management remains the predominant principle governing Russian productive activity despite the emergence of subsistence and exclusionary markets.

VPK *Voennyi promyshlennyi kompleks* (military-industrial complex).

Washington consensus A term coined by John Williamson to describe a set of micro- and macroeconomic principles that leading international institutions in Washington, D.C., like the IMF and World Bank, believe best serve the cause of economic development and global prosperity. The key elements are free enterprise, financial discipline, and democracy. The Washington consensus champions liberal globalization, opposes systemic diversity, and believes that only liberal principles are universally applicable regardless of culture or system.

westernization The adoption of western ideals, including economic liberty, democracy, social justice, tolerance, diversity, and conflict avoidance, by developing and transitioning economies. Westernization is a more demanding concept than modernization, which merely involves the adoption of western technologies.

NOTES

PREFACE

1. *Johnson's Russia List*, no. 6541, November 7, 2002.
2. See Steven Rosefielde and R.W. Pfouts, "The Mis-specification of Soviet Produc-tion Potential: Adjusting Factor Costing and Bergson's Efficiency Standard," in Steven Rosefielde, ed., *Efficiency and Russias Economic Recovery Potential to the Year 2000 and Beyond* (Aldershot, England: Ashgate, 1998), 11–21.

INTRODUCTION

1. Francis Fukuyama, *The End of History and the Last Man* (New York: The Free Press, 1992). Cf. Stanley Hoffman, "Clash of Globalizations," *Foreign Affairs* 81, no. 4 (2002): 104–15. Francis Fukuyama's "end of history" refers to the ideals of the French Revolution, not Karl Marx's full communism. He argues in his seminal 1989 *National Interest* article that mankind's future was fixed by 1806 and that all the rest was just the dialectical unfolding of the ideals of democracy, fraternity, and equality. History didn't end with communism, as many western intellectuals anticipated, because Hegel, was right and Marx wrong. The motor of history was the French Revolutionary credo, not the more illiberal universal regime socialists imagined. Absent Hegel, Fukuyama's thesis is an expression of faith in the superi-ority and staying power of liberal democracy. The concept is the political subset of the "Washington consensus." It implies that liberal democracy never will be dis-placed again by authoritarianism. Fukuyama ascribes his thesis to Sergei Kozhev (Kozhevnikov), a Russian Stalinist (and alleged agent provocateur) who taught at the Sorbonne in the 1960s. It should be noted, however, that Fukuyama now acknowledges that history did not end as initially claimed, because technological progress continues unabated, increasing productivity and reshaping human po-tential (lecture series delivered at the Hopkins Nanjing Center, Nanjing, China, March 11–13, 2003). Fukuyama, like Marx, sees his writing as an totality. Readers interested in his concept of the end of history therefore should also consult *Trust: The Social Virtues and the Creation of Prosperity* (New York: The Free Press, 1995), *The Great Disruption: Human Nature and the Reconstitution of Social Or-der* (New York: The Free Press, 1999), and *Our Posthuman Future: Consequences*

147

of the Biotechnology Revolution (New York: Farrar, Strauss & Giroux, 2002). Cf. Shlomo Avineri, "The End of the Soviet Union and the Return to History," in Michael Keren and Gur Ofer, eds., *Trials of Transition: Economic Reform in the Former Communist Bloc* (Boulder, CO: Westview Press, 1992), 11–18.

2. Samuel Huntington, "The West: Unique, Not Universal," *Foreign Affairs* 75, no. 6 (1996): 28–46.

3. As explained in chapter 5, Russian authoritarianism has many unique characteristics traceable to the post-Mongol Muscovy consolidation. For a full exposition of this thesis, see Stefan Hedlund, *Russian Path Dependence*, pt. 3, London, Routledge, 2005.

4. Karl Marx, *The Economic and Philosophic Manuscripts of 1844* (New York: International Publishers, 1964).

5. *Russia's Uncertain Economic Future* (Washington, DC: Joint Economic Committee of Congress, June 28, 2002). Available at http://www.access.gpo.gov/congress/joint/sjoint02.html.

6. Christopher Hill, "Russian Defense Spending," in *Russia's Uncertain Economic Future*, 161–82. But cf. Christopher Davis, *Defense Sector in the Economy of a Declining Superpower: Soviet Union and Russia, 1965–2001* (Amsterdam: Defense and Peace Economics, Overseas Publishers Association, 2001), and Jeremy Bransten, "Russia: Foreign Minister Ivanov Emphasizes Moscow's Pro-Western Orientation," *Johnson's Russia List*, July 11, 2002. Ivanov said, "Moscow's priorities are firmly anchored in the West. Russia knows it cannot resuscitate the bipolar world of the Cold War era.... Moscow will not try to compete with the world's lone remaining superpower."

7. This is probable despite the G8's pledge to provide Russia with $20 billion for downsizing, disposing of, and decontaminating its nuclear forces and facilities. See Nicholas George, "Soviet Nuclear Legacy Seen as a Global Threat," *Financial Times*, June 29, 2002; "Russia Ending Involvement in Iranian Reactor," Stratfor.com, June 29, 2002; Nick Paton Walsh, "Terror Fear over Lost Nuclear Parts," *Observer*, June 30, 2002; David Filipov, "Nations Pledge $20 Billion to Secure Russian Arms," *Boston Globe*, June 29, 2002.

8. Lennart Samuelson, *Rod koloss pa larvfotter, Rysslands Ekonomi i Skuggan av 1900 Talskrigen* (Stockhom: SNS Forlag, 1999). Anders Aslund and John Hewko attribute Russia's blighted transformation to the destructive effect of Soviet entitlements and dependency. See Aslund and Hewko, "Reality to Clash with Idealism When Communism Collapses," *Washington Times*, July 2, 2002.

9. Steven Rosefielde, *Comparative Economic Systems: Culture, Wealth and Power in the 21st Century* (Oxford: Blackwell, 2002), chap. 16, 237–48.

10. Samuel Huntington, *The Clash of Civilizations and the Remaking of World Order* (New York: Simon & Schuster, 1996). See also Peter Murrell, ed., *Assessing the Value of Law in Transition Economics* (Ann Arbor: University of Michigan Press, 2001).

11. Strobe Talbott, *The Russia Hand: A Memoir of Presidential Diplomacy* (New York: Random House, 2002). There has been a lively debate about whether turning a blind eye to the abuses of Russia's systemic transformation was brilliant statesmanship or perverse and counterproductive. Lilia Shevtsova (Moscow

Carnegie Center) argues that Clinton's handling of Russia should be viewed pragmatically, not humanistically. She claims that on this ground he was successful because Clinton made Russia more pro-western while compelling Yeltsin to abandon the Baltics and accept the incorporation of many Eastern European states into NATO. Moreover, according to her, the Chechen war, the abuses of privatization ("loans for shares"), and liberalization were determined internally, and therefore Clinton is not responsible for "losing Russia." Likewise, she praises him for "superpower decline control." She also contends that a tougher line, "surgery without anesthesia," wouldn't have worked. Coddling provided "substance for symbolism," and Clinton was right to see terminating the Soviet system as his principal goal rather than promoting democracy and Pareto-efficient markets (the idea of the West). See Lilia Shevtsova, "Is America Responsible for Russia's Fate? Once More on the 'Russia Hand,'" *Johnson's Russia List*, June 26, 2002. Others argue that the same policies that succeeded in facilitating Russia's de-Sovietization could have yielded much better results without the squandering of tens of billions of dollars. See Gordon Hahn, *Johnson's Russia List*, June 29, 2002; Paul Starobin, "Did Bill Forgive Boris Too Much?" *Business Week*, July 8, 2002; Christian Caryl, "Giving the Russians Their Spinach," *New York Review of Books*, July 18, 2002; Celeste Wallander, "A Review of the Review of 'The Russian Hand'," *Johnson's Russia List*, July 2, 2002; Stanislav Menshikov, "Putin as Seen by Talbott," *Moscow Tribune*, July 4, 2002.

12. Rosefielde, *Comparative Economic Systems*, chaps. 5 and 6, 81–122.
13. Harry Broadman, ed., *Unleashing Russia's Business Potential: Lessons from the Regions for Building Market Institutions* (Washington, DC: World Bank, April 2002).
14. This cultural proclivity, together with an affinity for authoritarianism and privilege, is a constant amid the particularities of history and other aspects of cultural change. See, for example, Oleg Lurie, "The IMF Loan That Vanished Has Been Found in Abramovich's Swiss Company," *Johnson's Russian List*, no. 7096, art. 11, March 10, 2003:

Remember how a few years ago all sorts of government officials and associated media were all claiming in unison that the $4.8 billion IMF loan installment received just before the crisis of August 1998 had been used in full and for the intended purpose? That may well be true, but the term "for the intended purpose" is interpreted somewhat differently by the IMF and Russian officials. Thus, the naive IMF views "for the intended purpose" as referring to stabilization of the ruble; but Russian players seem to interpret it as the hasty distribution of foreign billions into the pockets of all and sundry. Thus, 100% of the 1998 IMF loan was transferred by an order from Mikhail Kasyanov. The first $4.8 billion IMF loan was formed at the account No. 999091 at the US Federal Reserve Bank on August 14, 1998. It was transferred not to the Central Bank of Russia, but for some reason to the Republic National Bank of New York, owned by Edmond Safra, suspected by the FBI of laundering Russia's criminal money. Further on, according to the Swiss scheme, mysterious things started happening to the IMF money. Instead of transferring $4.8 billion to Russia, the Republic National Bank of New York transferred the money through its Swiss Creditanstalt Bankverein branch to several directions which have nothing to do with the Russian budget. First, $2.35 billion were transferred to the Bank of Sydney (allegedly situated in Australia). However, the Swiss police found out that the Bank of Sydney had nothing to do with Australia but was registered in an offshore area and functioned from July 1996 to September 1998. Thus, a month after the loan was transferred, it disappeared. According to our Italian and Russian colleagues, part of the money transferred to the Bank of Sydney was placed in an account of a company which was 25% owned by a daughter of President Boris Yeltsin. Second, $2,115 million was converted into pounds sterling and transferred to the National Westminster Bank – here the trace of the money disappears. Third, $780 million and $270 million was transferred on August 14 and August 18 respectively to the Credit Suisse bank. These two transfers attracted the attention of Swiss investigator Loran Casper-Anserme in 1998, who together with Geneva prosecutor Bertrossa instigated the IMF loan investigation. At present, the Swiss Prosecutor's Office has the fullest data on this part of the loan. Forth, the most interesting and most thoroughly scrutinized transfer: $1.4 billion were transferred to the notorious Bank of New York and further to its Geneva branch, Bank of New York–Intermaritime. The money entered the account of a Russian "United Bank" owned by Roman Abramovich and Boris Berezovsky. At that time, there were no conflicts between the two tycoons. Subsequent events were very rapid. The IMF money was immediately transferred to the account of the Swiss RUNICOM company, owned by Roman Abramovich. Turning back the 1998 IMF loan, after the $1.4 billion were transferred to RUNICOM owned by Abramovich nothing special happened beside the economic crisis in Russia. However, soon after the crisis some people started asking "unnecessary" questions: how did the money get to Abramovich? Why was the fuss concerning "Kasyanov's" IMF loan gone so soon? Why did the Russian investigation come to a dead end and the Swiss police know much more? That is when troubles started happening to the excessively curious people. Investigator Nikolai Volkov, who joined the Swiss investigation concerning the loan was immediately dismissed from the Prosecutor General's Office with a blacklist. Everyone is familiar with the sad story of Prosecutor General Yuri Skuratov, who instigated the case on criminal misappropriation. Some excessively curious journalists had their bones broken. As for western bankers who decided to report to the FBI on loan swindling, it was even simpler with them – they were killed. The most famous example was Edmond Safra founder of Republic National Bank of New York December 1999. Almost five years have passed since the notorious IMF loan. Kasianov has become the prime minister, Abramovich is the Chukotka governor, Berezovsky has been exiled. For a long time, Russians in both the Prosecutor General's Office and the Kremlin did not remember about the disappeared loan. However, things are changing – lately, the Russian law enforcement bodies have also changed. For instance, the Prosecutor General's Office has withdrawn the criminal case No. 18/221050-98 "On misappropriation of the IMF loan" and started scrutinizing it. There is a new president in Russia, and I think it is more important for him to find the truth than to keep any old promises to the "Family". Moreover, as far as I can recall, Putin promised immunity only to Yeltsin himself, not to his Family and close associates.

(Translated by Arina Yevtikhova.)

15. The misappropriation of American transition assistance has been scandalous, with the Clinton and Bush administrations doing little more than slapping the Kremlin on the wrist. In the latest episode of the saga, the Pentagon was told that $95.5 million it spent on a facility to convert liquid rocket propellent for commercial use won't be needed because the propellant has been used in Russia's space program. See Rowan Scarborough, "Russia Diverted U.S. Aid on Arms, Inspector Reports," *Washington Times*, 2002. Cf. Peter Eisler, "Plan to Destroy Russian Weapons Nears Collapse," *USA Today*, October 1, 2002.

16. Alexander Yakovlev, *A Century of Violence in Soviet Russia* (New Haven, CT: Yale University Press, 2002):

The land of Rus accepted Christianity from Constantinople in A.D. 988. Characteristics of Byzantine rule of that era – baseness, cowardliness, venality, treachery, over centralization, apotheosis of the ruler's personality – dominate in Russia's social and political life to this day. In the twelfth century the various fragmented Russian principalities... were conquered by the Mongols, Asian traditions and customs, with their disregard for the individual and for human rights and their cult of might, violence, despotic power, and lawlessness, became part of the Russian people's way of life. The tragedy of Russia lay first and foremost in this: that for a thousand years it was ruled by men and not by laws.... They ruled ineptly, bloodily. The people existed for the government, not the government for the people. Russia avoided classical slavery. But it has not yet emerged from feudalism; it is still enslaved by an official imperial ideology, the essence of which is that the state is everything and the individual nothing. (pp. x–xi)

17. Anders Aslund, "The Drama Is Putin, But So Are the Results," *Moscow Times*, July 25, 2003: "Since July 2, a campaign has been pursued against Yukos.... It is a concerted, long-planned action... undertaken with the President's consent" that jeopardizes Russia's market transition. Cf. Marshall Goldman, "Russia Will Pay Twice for the Fortunes of Its Oligarchs," *Financial Times*, July 26, 2003, reprinted in *Johnson's Russia List*, no. 7266, art. 1, July 26, 2003. In "Problems of the Unstable Privatization Edifice," *Moscow Times*, July 31, 2003, reprinted in *Johnson's Russia List*, no. 7270, art. 8, July 31, 2003, Goldman wrote as follows:

Give Anders Aslund credit – he has no shame. After all the misleading advice he offered before the Aug. 17, 1998 crash ("How Russia Became a Market Economy"), he apparently has no hesitation in urging Western investors again to plunge into the Russian market.... That 17 oligarchs should emerge as dollar billionaires simply because they managed to gain control of already existing state property while at the same time, one-quarter of the population has fallen below the poverty line does not seem to concern him.... No wonder more than 70 percent of those polled in Russia are critical of the oligarchs and the privatization process. After the lamentable voucher and subsequent loans-for-shares programs, the owners of these privatized enterprises lack legitimacy... to call a three-year statute of limitation on claims against privatization a "sensible suggestion," as Anders does, ignores the terrible way the reforms were implemented and the just anger the public has toward what they see as massive theft. Perhaps the most unfortunate part of this sorry episode is that now that the damage has been done, there seem to be few remedies available except to undo the whole experiment and, of course, that would be just as disruptive.

CHAPTER 1

1. Abram Bergson, *Soviet National Income of and Product in 1937* (New York: Columbia University Press, 1953); idem, *The Real National Income of Soviet Russia since 1928* (Cambridge, MA: Harvard University Press, 1961); Abram Bergson and Simon Kuznets, *Economic Trends in the Soviet Union* (Cambridge, MA: Harvard University Press, 1963); Joseph Berliner, *Factory and Manager in the USSR* (Cambridge, MA: Harvard University Press, 1957); Evsei Domar, "A Soviet Model of Growth," in *Essays in the Theory of Economic Growth* (New York: Oxford University Press, 1957); Alexander Gerschenkron, "The Soviet Indices of Industrial Production," *Review of Economic Statistics* 29, no. 4 (1947): 217–26. Other important American contributors include Naum Jasny, *The Soviet*

Economy during the Plan Era (Stanford, CA: Stanford University, Food Research Institute, 1951); idem, *Soviet Industrialization, 1928–1952* (Chicago: University of Chicago Press, 1961); Donald Hodgman, *Soviet Industrial Production, 1928–51* (Cambridge, MA: Harvard University Press, 1954); Norman Kaplan and Richard Moorsteen, "Indexes of Soviet Industrial Output," 2 vols., Research Memorandum RM-2495 (Santa Monica, CA: Rand Corporation, 1960); Richard Moorsteen, *Prices and Production of Machinery in the Soviet Union, 1928–1958* (Cambridge, MA: Harvard University Press, 1962); Richard Moorsteen and Raymond Powell, *The Soviet Capital Stock, 1928–1962* (Homewood, IL: Irwin, 1966); Warren Nutter, *The Growth of Industrial Production in the Soviet Union* (Princeton, New Jersey, National Bureau of Economic Research, 1962). The British school on balance took a more charitable attitude toward Soviet economic performance. Some contributors here include Colin Clark, *A Critique of Soviet Statistics* (London: Macmillan, 1939); idem, *The Conditions of Economic Progress* (London: Macmillan, 1957); Robert Davies, *Soviet Industrial Production 1928–1937: The Rival Estimates*, Soviet Industrialization Project Series no. 18 (Birmingham, England: University of Birmingham, Center for Russian and East European Studies, 1978); idem, "Industry," in Robert Davies, Mark Harrison, and Stephen Wheatcroft, eds., *The Economic Transformation of the USSR, 1913–1945* (Cambridge: Cambridge University Press, 1994), 131–57; idem, *The Industrialization of Soviet Russia*, vol. 4, *Crisis and Progress in the Soviet Economy, 1931–33* (Basingstoke and London: Macmillan, 1996); Maurice Dobb, "Further Appraisals of Russian Economic Statistics," *Review of Economic Statistics* 29, no. 1 (1948): 34–8; Michael Kaser, "Le Debat sur la Loi de la Valeur en URSS: *Etude Retrospective 1941–1953*," *Annuaire de l'URSS*, CNFS, Paris, 1965; Alec Nove, "'1926/7' and All That," *Soviet Studies* 9, no. 2 (1957): 117–30; idem, *An Economic History of the USSR* (Harmondsworth, England: Penguin, 1972); Francis Seton, "Pre-War Soviet Prices in the Light of the 1941 Plan," *Soviet Studies* 3, no. 4 (1952): 345–64; Peter Wiles, *The Political Economy of Communism* (Oxford: Blackwell, 1962).

2. Slyvia Naser, "'John Maynard Keynes': A Man of Action as Well as Ideas," *New York Times*, January 20, 2002; Robert Skidelsky, *John Maynard Keynes*, vol. 3, *Fighting for Freedom, 1937–1946* (Penguin USA, New York, 2002); Steven Rosefielde, "Knowledge and Socialism: Deciphering the Soviet Experience," in Steven Rosefielde, ed., *Economic Welfare and the Economics of Soviet Socialism* (Cambridge: Cambridge University Press, 1981), 5–23.

3. Paul Krugman, "The Myth of Asia's Miracle," *Foreign Affairs* 73, no. 1 (1994): 62–78; idem, "What Ever Happened to the Asian Miracle?" http://web.mit.edu/krugman/www/perspire.htm (1997). Some series show the Soviets outstripping the Americans in per capita consumption, but even if the statistics are correct, the goods that Soviet consumers were allowed to purchase weren't responsive to their desires.

4. Vitaly Shlykov, *Chto Pogubilo Sovetskii Soiuz? Amerikanskaia Razvedka o Sovetskikh Voennykh Raskhodakh* (Who Destroyed the Soviet Union? American Intelligence Estimates of Soviet Military Expenditures), Voennyi Vestnik, no. 8 (Moscow, April 2001), 38. Shlykov uses the genitive case, and this usage is retained throughout this text.

5. For a detailed account of the formation, evolution, and impact of Abram Bergson's theories, estimates, and evaluations of Soviet economic performance, see Steven Rosefielde, "'Tea Leaves' and Productivity: Bergsonian Norms for Gauging the Soviet Union," paper presented at the Bergson Memorial Conference, Harvard University, November 24–5, 2003. Also see chapter 2 of this volume and Abram Bergson, "The U.S.S.R. before the Fall: How Poor and Why?" *Journal of Economic Perspectives* 5, no. 4 (1991): 29–44; idem, "Neoclassical Norms and the Valuation of National Product in the Soviet Union and Its Postcommunist Successor States: Comment," *Journal of Comparative Economics* 21, no. 3 (1995): 390–3. Cf. Daniel Berkowitz, Joseph Berliner, Susan Gregory, and James Millar, "An Evaluation of the CIA's Analysis of Soviet Economic Performance," *Comparative Economic Studies* 35, no. 2 (1993): 33–48.

6. Noel Firth and James Noren, *Soviet Defense Spending: A History of CIA Estimates, 1950–1990* (College Station: University of Texas Press, 1998); Abraham Becker, "Intelligence Fiasco or Reasoned Accounting? CIA Estimates of Soviet GNP," *Post-Soviet Affairs* 10, no. 4 (1994): 291–329; Gertrude Schroeder, "Reflections on Economic Sovietology," *Post-Soviet Affairs* 11, no. 3 (1995): 197–234.

7. John Williamson, "Democracy and the 'Washington Consensus,'" *World Development* 21, no. 8 (1993): 1329–36.

8. Cf. Fukuyama, *The End of History and the Last Man.*

9. Huntington, "The West: Unique, Not Universal." Cf. Mikhail Gorbachev, *Perestroika i Novoe Myshlenie* (Moscow: Politicheskie Literatury, 1987).

10. Gary North, *The Coase Theorem: A Study in Economic Epistemology* (Tyler, TX: Institute for Christian Economies, 1992). Ronald Coase explains how redistributive issues and externalities can be treated without state intervention in "The Problem of Social Cost," *Journal of Law and Economics* 3 (October 1960): 1–44.

11. Pareto efficiency refers to any set of bi- or multilateral transactions that allows every participant to optimize utility in the sense that no one can discover an additional opportunity that makes any transactor better off without diminishing the utility of another. The principle can be applied to factors, products, distribution, and transfers, hence the entire economy. It is an ideal case of neoclassical economics and general competition, but not the set of all possible systems. Pareto-efficient economies are compatible with many kinds of physical, psychological, and informational constraints. They need not be perfectly or generally competitive with symmetric information but are individualistically best under prevailing restrictions. These nuances should be borne in mind when judging the merits of the economic idea of the West.

For a further discussion of these technicalities, see Steven Rosefielde, *Comparative Economic Systems: Culture, Wealth and Power in the 21st Century* (Oxford: Blackwell, 2002), chaps. 2, 5, and 6. As explained in this text, Pareto-efficient economies are classifiable as category A ideal systems, while the American and Continental European economies fall into category B because aspects of their public cultures, together with their shadow cultures, contradict the "Golden Rule" axiom of economic liberty. Specifically, transactors in these economies often violate the rule of contract and seek market power. Strictly speaking, the public culture of category A systems must generate Pareto-efficient solutions and cannot have shadow cultures that impair this efficiency. The only exception is trivial. If the public values that people in a society profess cannot yield Pareto outcomes but the shadow values that govern their behavior do, then the ideal results are attributable not to Pareto-incompatible public values but to a virtuous shadow culture. It should also be observed that category A isn't uniquely associated with the idea of the West. It is possible to have a category A, Pareto-efficient economic system without markets, democracy, and social justice if it is perfectly planned and accurately reflects the people's will.

12. Rosefielde, *Comparative Economic Systems*, chap. 2.
13. Prime Minister Tony Blair's decision to declare war on Iraq despite majority popular opposition provides a good example of this possibility.
14. R. W. Pfouts, "The Theory of Individual and Family Demand: An Application of Bounded Rationality" (unpublished manuscript, spring 2002).
15. Kenneth Arrow, *Social Choice and Individual Values*, 2nd ed. (New York: Wiley, 1963).
16. Abram Bergson, "Social Choice and Welfare Economics under Representative Government," *Journal of Public Economics* 6 (1976): 171–90.
17. Paul Samuelson, "International Trade and the Equalization of Factor Prices," *Economic Journal*, June 1948, 181–97; idem, "International Factor-Price Equalization Once Again," *Economic Journal*, June 1949, 181–97; Wassily Leontief, "Domestic Production and Foreign Trade: The American Capital Position Reexamined," *Proceedings of the American Philosophical Society*, September 1953, 332–49; idem, "Factor Proportions and the Structure of American Trade: Further Theoretical and Empirical Analysis," *Review of Economics and Statistics*, November 1956, 386–407; Robert Solow, "Technical Change and the Aggregate Production Function," *Review of Economics and Statistics* 39, no. (1957): 312–20.
18. Samuel Huntington likens this eventuality, excluding world government, to the European Westphalian system of 1648. See Samuel Huntington, "The Lonely Superpower," *Foreign Affairs* 78, no. 2 (1999): 35–50.
19. Krugman, "The Myth of Asia's Miracle"; Krugman, "What Ever Happened to the Asian Miracle?" Abram Bergson, "Socialist Calculation: A Further Word," in *Essays in Normative Economics* (Cambridge, MA: Harvard University Press, 1966), 237–42, where he arrives at a similar conclusion for the Soviet Union.
20. Rosefielde, *Comparative Economic Systems*, chap. 15, 207–33. Cf. David Dollar and Aart Kraay, *Foreign Affairs* 81, no. 1 (2002): 120–33; James Galbraith, Joe Pitts, and Andrew Wells-Dang, "Is Inequality Decreasing?" *Foreign Affairs* 81, no. 4 (2002): 178–83.
21. Nikolai Bukharin and Evgeny Preobrazhensky, *The ABC's of Communism* (Baltimore: Penguin, 1969).
22. S. A. Karagonov, V. A Nikonov, and V. L Inozemtsev, "Russia and Globalization Trends: What Needs to Be Done?" Theses by the Council on Foreign and Defense Policy, November 2001. Even Joseph Stiglitz, a staunch critic of the Washington consensus, seems to believe that flawed systems can compensate significantly for their defects by adopting the right macroeconomic policies. See Joseph Stiglitz, "The Ruin of Russia," *The Guardian*, April 9, 2003, reprinted in *Johnson's Russia List*, no. 7138, art. 1, April 9, 2003.

23. According to Gertrude Schroeder and Imogene Edwards, the inefficient and undercapitalized Soviet consumption sector outstripped America's and the United Kingdom's during the period 1961–78, while weapons growth, which enjoyed the lion's share of R&D, was stagnant. See Gertrude Schroeder and Imogene Edwards, *Consumption in the USSR: An International Comparison* (Washington, DC: Joint Economic Committee of Congress, 1981), 25, table 14. On aggregate growth, see CIA, *USSR: Measures of Economic Growth and Development, 1950–1980* (Washington, DC: Joint Economic Committee of Congress, 1982). Data on Soviet weapons growth are provided in *Allocation of Resources in the Soviet Union and China – 1983* measured in 1970 prices. *Allocation of Resources in the Soviet Union and China* (Washington, DC: Joint Economic Committee of Congress, April 20, 1990), 40, fig. 4, shows procurement valued in 1982 rubles unchanged for 1980–89. On R&D outlays, see William Lee, *The Estimation of Soviet Defense Expenditures for 1955–1975: An Unconventional Approach* (New York: Praeger, 1977), 49–51.
24. Anders Aslund, *Building Capitalism: The Transformation of the Former Soviet Bloc* (Cambridge: Cambridge University Press, 2002).
25. The importance of cultural and institutional factors in explaining the inferior potential of eastern economic systems is elaborated in Lawrence Harrison and Samuel Huntington, eds., *Culture Matters: How Values Shape Human Progress* (New York: Basic Books 2000); Moses Abramowitz, "Catching up, Forging ahead, and Falling Behind," *Journal of Economic History* 46 (1986): 385–406; David Landes, *The Wealth and Poverty of Nations: Why Some Are So Rich and Some So Poor* (New York: Norton, 1998); Douglass North and Robert Thomas, *The Rise of the Western World* (London: Cambridge University Press, 1972).

CHAPTER 2

1. The Bolshevik revolution triggered a decades-long debate on the feasiblity of socialism. The main protagonists were Ludwig von Mises, Frederick Hayek, Lionel Robbins, and Oskar Lange. Two questions were at issue: (1) Must a system that criminalizes business, entrepreneurship, and private property collapse? (2) Can such a system be as efficient as market economies? Bergson concluded in a highly influential 1948 article (based partly on the survival of the USSR) that the answer to the first question was no. He waffled on the second question, erroneously arguing that a board of supermen could allocate resources rationally without markets (agreeing with Lange that they could solve Walras's general equilibrium equations) and on a less ethereal plane explaining that it was premature to judge the comparative merits of real as distinct from textbook socialism and capitalism. This judgment meant that there was no compelling reason to expect the Soviet Union to self-destruct even though it outlawed markets and flouted the principles of Pareto efficiency. See Abram Bergson, "Socialist Economics," in Bergson, *Essays in Normative Economics*, 234–36. Cf. Oskar Lange and Fred M. Taylor, *On the Economic Theory of Socialism*, University of Minnesota Press, Minneopolis, 1938. The fallacy in his supermen argument lies in the absence of a mechanism to reconcile their conflicting preferences, elucidated later by Kenneth Arrow in

Social Choice and Individual Values. Cf. Kenneth Arrow, "Optimal and Voluntary Income Distribution," in Rosefielde, *Economic Welfare and the Economics of Soviet Socialism,* 167–88, and Joseph Stiglitz, *Whither Socialism?* The MIT Press, Cambridge, MA, 1993. Then in a follow-up essay published seventeen years later, "Socialist Calculation: A Further Word," Bergson stated that

in view of the experience with socialism to date, the critics of this system have turned out to be nearer the mark than its proponents. At any rate, if we may judge from the experience of the USSR, there are reasons to doubt that socialism is especially efficient economically . . . , where reference is to the output of labor and capital together, factor productivity is not the same thing as economic efficiency, but if it is at all indicative of the latter, economic waste in the USSR probably much exceeds any recently experienced in the United States. Factor productivity in the USSR has been calculated to be far below that in the USA. (p. 238)

Somewhere along the way, Bergson concluded that the Soviet system in practice was comparatively inefficient because he discovered that combined factor productivity growth since 1928, computed at 1937 ruble factor cost, was negative. But this didn't lead him to infer that the system couldn't grow. "Efficiency surely should rise in the course of time, but it is difficult to gauge how much." For a more complete account of Bergson's shifting outlook, see Rosefielde, "'Tea Leaves' and Productivity"; Mark Harrison, "Postwar Soviet Economic Growth: Not a Riddle," *Europe-Asia Studies,* vol. 55, no. 8, December 2003, pp 1323–29; Steven Rosefielde, "Post-War Russian Economic Growth: Not a Riddle – A Reply," *Europe-Asia Studies,* vol. 56, no. 3, May 2004, pp. 463–66. Cf. Frederich Hayek, *Collectivist Economic Planning Critical Studies on the Possibilities of Socialism,* George Routledge & Sons (London: 1935); Frederich Hayek, "Socialist Calculation: The Competitive Solution," *Economica,* vol. 7, May 1940, pp. 125–149; idem, "The Use of Knowledge in Society," *American Economic Review,* September 1945; Ludwig von Mises, *Socialism* (Johnathan Cope, London: 1936); Lionel Robbins, *Nature and Significance of Economic Science* (London: 1935); Bergson and Kuznets, *Economic Trends in the Soviet Union*; Abram Bergson, "Technological Progress," in Abram Bergson and Herbert Levine, eds., *The Soviet Economy: Toward the Year 2000* (London: Allen & Unwin, 1983); CIA, *USSR: Measures of Economic Growth and Development*; Padma Desai, "The Production Function and Technical Change in Postwar Soviet Industry: A Reexamination," *American Economic Review* 66, no. 3 (1976): 372–81; Evsey Domar, "A Soviet Model of Growth," in *Essays in the Theory of Economic Growth* (New York: Oxford University Press, 1957); Gur Ofer, "Soviet Economic Growth: 1928–85," *Journal of Economic Literature* 25, no. 4 (1987): 1767–833; Martin Weitzman, "Industrial Production," in Bergson and Levine, *The Soviet Economy*; Angus Maddison, "Measuring the Performance of a Communist Command Economy: An Assessment of the CIA Estimates for the USSR," *Review of Income and Wealth* 44, no. 3 (1998): 307–23; William Easterly and Stanley Fischer, "The Soviet Economic Decline," *World Bank Economic Review* 9, no. 3 (1990): 341–71; CIA, *Measures of Soviet GNP in 1982 Prices* (Washington, DC: Joint Economic Committee of Congress, November 1990); Bergson and Levine, *The Soviet Economy: Toward the Year 2000.*

2. CIA, *USSR: Measures of Economic Growth and Development 1950–80*, 20, table 1, 22 table 2; idem, *Measures of Soviet Gross National Product in 1982 Prices*; Firth and Noren, *Soviet Defense Spending*, 129, table 5.10, 176, fig. 6.5. Also see Table 3.1 of this volume; the annual defense budget statistics in *Narodnoe khoziaistvo SSSR*; and Rosefielde, *Comparative Economic Systems*, 226, table A15.3, 210, table 15.2. The figures in these tables are on a per capita basis. Data for converting these statistics to GDP growth rates are provided in the corresponding UN source. See United Nations, *Human Development Report 1998* (New York: Oxford University Press, 1998).

3. This is inferred from the exact correspondence between the Kuboniwa-Ponomarenko GDP estimates for Russia described in the text and the CIA's GNP estimates for the Soviet Union for 1961–80 compared in Steven Rosefielde and Maasaki Kuboniwa, "Russian Growth Retardation Then and Now," *Eurasian Geography and Economics* 44, no. 2 (2003): 97, and the close correspondence with the two industrial series reported in the same article on p. 96, table 2 (Variant D and CIA). Since the "hidden inflation"–adjusted industrial statistics in the Kuboniwa-Ponomarenko series account for half the disparity between the Variant D rate and the official growth rate, it follows that this distribution also holds approximately for the CIA's estimates.

4. Franklyn Holzman, "Are the Soviets Really Outspending the U.S. on Defense?" *International Security* 4, no. 4 (1980): 86–104; idem, "Soviet Military Spending: Assessing the Numbers Game," *International Security* 6, no. 4 (1982): 78–101; idem, "Politics and Guesswork: CIA and DIA Estimates of Soviet Military Spending," *International Security* 14, no. 2 (1989): 101–31; idem, "Politics, Military Spending, and the National Welfare," *Comparative Economic Studies* 36, no. 3 (1994): 1–4.

5. Lee, *The Estimation of Soviet Defense Expenditures*; Statement of William T. Lee, Defense Intelligence Agency, "Estimating the Size and Growth of the Soviet Economy," hearing before the Committee on Foreign Relations of the United States, Senate, 101st Congress, 2nd session, July 16, 1990.

6. Firth and Noren, *Soviet Defense Spending*, 107, fig. 5.4. Procurement computed in 1982 ruble prices falls from 55.2 percent in 1951–59 to 40.5 percent in 1988–90. Also see p. 129, table 5.10.

7. CIA, "The Soviet Economy Stumbles Badly in 1989," in *Allocation of Resources in the Soviet Union and China*. The agency also seems to have begun introducing more physical series into its estimates as a proxy for hidden inflation. See CIA, *Measures of Soviet Gross National Product in 1982 Prices*, 34–5; Michael Boretsky, "The Tenability of the CIA Estimates of Soviet Economic Growth," *Journal of Comparative Economics* 11, no. 4 (1987): 517–42; John Pitzer, "The Tenability of the CIA Estimates of Soviet Economic Growth: A Comment," *Journal of Comparative Economics* 14, no. 2 (1990): 301–19.

8. Steven Rosefielde, "The Riddle of Postwar Russian Economic Growth: Statistics Lied and Were Misconstrued," *Europe-Asia Studies* 55, no. 3 (2003): 469–81. Cf. Harrison, "Postwar Russian Economic Growth," and Rosefielde, "Post-war Russian Economic Growth: Not a Riddle – A Reply."

9. *Narkhoz Narodnoe khoziaistvo SSSR za Let* (Moscow: Finansy i Statistika, 1987), 34.

10. Bergson, *The Real National Income of Soviet Russia since 1928*, 210. Cf. Rosefielde, "Knowledge and Socalism."

11. Bergson, *The Real National Income of Soviet Russia since 1928*, 34.

12. Abram Bergson, "Reliability and Usability of Soviet Statistics: A Summary Appraisal" *American Statistician* 7, no. 5 (1953): 13–16.

13. In "Reliability and Usability of Soviet Statistics," Bergson stated,

> Contrary to a common supposition, the Russians seem generally not to resort to falsification in the sense of free invention and double book-keeping. I have explained that there is falsification of a local sort. . . . I am now concerned primarily with falsification of a comprehensive character at the center. This distinction, I fear, is a fine one. Almost all the deficiencies that have been discovered lead to unduly favorable impressions of the Soviet economy. If the Russians do not wilfully introduce such deficiencies to create such impressions, they are at least notably tolerant of them. (p. 15)

The judgment that "the Russians seem generally not to resort to falsification in the sense of free invention" is restated more broadly:

> While it has seemed in order to distinguish in this essay between falsification by lower echelons and falsification at the center, it will be evident that in a number of the grounds for thinking that the latter is not a general practice must also apply to the former. As a result, there is some upper limit to the margin of error introduced by falsification by lower echelons. (p. 16)

Bergson engages in a clever balancing act, acknowledging the suspiciousness of subaggregate data while suggesting that it is manageably limited. But there are sound grounds for skepticism beyond the obvious illogic of assuming that the subaggregates are sound, for Bergson's own reestimates showed that the aggregates were overstated more than could be explained by NMP accounting and indexing. He attributed this gap to abusive new goods pricing in the early 1930s, but Stanley Cohn's subaggregate estimates indicated that there was more to it. A brief quote from Alec Nove may suffice to bring home the point that Soviet statisticians were not shielded from political pressure to "objectively" compute "accurate" statistical series: "In the general atmosphere of terror, it could well be that statisticians concealed (or were ordered to conceal) the truth about deaths in the early Thirties and when it did emerge in a 1937 census, the reaction was to shoot the statisticians and suppress the census" ("Robert Conquest, The Great Terror," *Soviet Studies* 20 [April 1969]: 538). The statisticians were literally shot. See Abram Bergson, "Soviet National Income Statistics," in Vladimir Treml and John Hardt, eds., *Soviet Economic Statistics* (Durham, NC: Duke University Press, 1942), 148–52. Cf. Stanley Cohn, "National Income Statistics," in Treml and Hardt, *Soviet Economic Statistics*, 120–47, esp. p. 123, table 5.1; Richard Moorsteen, "On Measuring Productive Potential and Relative Efficiency," *Quarterly Journal of Economics* 75 no. 6 (1961): 451–67; Bergson, *The Real National Income of Soviet Russia since 1928*; Alexander Gerschenkron, "The Soviet Indices of Industrial Production," *Review of Economics and Statistics* 29, no. 4, (1947): 217–26; Jasny, *Soviet Industrialization, 1928–1952*; Nutter, *The Growth of Industrial Production in the Soviet Union*.

14. Adjusted ruble factor costing entailed subtracting retail turnover taxes and accounting profits from ruble prices and replacing them with imputed interest charges. The neoclassical supply-side criterion requires ruble output prices to be

proportional to enterprise marginal rates of product transformation. Bergson's attitude toward planners' preferences was ambivalent. Sometimes he stressed their theoretical and practical significance, other times he was notably skeptical. See Bergson, *Essays in Normative Economics*, 233–41. But he always insisted adjusted factor costing measured "production potential."

15. Growth theory strongly suggests that indexes computed with base-year prices should display more rapid increases than those valued in final-year prices during the initial phase of development. Indexes of Soviet growth during 1928–37 were consistent with this expectation. See Bergson, *Real National Income of the Soviet Union since 1928*, where he writes, "Where valuation is in 1950 ruble factor cost, growth generally is less than where valuation is at 1937 ruble factor cost. In the light of Professor Gerschenkron's principle, these results must also be reassuring regarding the reliability of the calculations. Moreover as he implies, prices are likely to behave in the required manner only if to begin with they correspond in some degree to scarcity relations" (pp. 210–11). The last point is incorrect, because Bergson is thinking about scarcity from the misleading "planners' preferences," "production potential" standpoint (see note 14, this chapter). Gerschenkron doubted that Soviet prices could be given any economic meaning ("The Soviet Indices of Industrial Production").

16. This conversion of Soviet data from NMP to GNP had a negligible impact on growth estimates. See CIA, *Measures of Gross National Product in 1982 Prices*, 3.

17. Rosefielde, "The Riddle of Postwar Soviet Economic Growth"; Rosefielde and Kuboniwa, "Russian Growth Retardation Then and Now."

18. CIA, *Measures of Soviet Gross National Product in 1982 Prices*, vii–ix. Although, the agency correctly inferred that properly constructed physical indexes preclude hidden inflation, nothing stopped Goskomstat from making "adjustments" for the improved "quality" of the physical input mix.

19. Abel Aganbegyan, in *The Economic Challenge of Perestroika* (Bloomington: Indiana University Press, 1988), writes,

In the Second World War, 20 million lives and one third of the nation's capital stock were lost. Simultaneously, the expensive problems of unraveling the secrets of the atomic bomb, and the creation of a rocket defense shield had to be undertaken to guarantee the peaceful labour of the Soviet people from the growing threat, above all from the USA. In these conditions energies and resources were concentrated on the development of heavy industry and armaments, and what was allocated to the development of welfare services and to raising the standard of living of the people was insufficient. (p. 15)

20. U.S. House Permanent Select Committee on Intelligence Review, Daniel Berkowitz et al., "Survey Articles: An Evaluation of the CIA's Analysis of Soviet Economic Performance, 1970–90," *Comparative Economic Studies*, Summer 1993, pp. 33–48. Cf. John Wilhelm, "The Failure of the American Sovietological Economics Profession," *Europe-Asia Studies* 55, no. 1 (2003): 59–74.

21. Mark Harrison, "Soviet Industrial Production, 1928 to 1955: Real Growth and Hidden Inflation," *Journal of Comparative Economics* 28, no. 1 (2000): 134–55. Harrison views the overstatement of the official Soviet growth indexes as the consequence of a "failed attempt to move toward a chain index number" (p. 144). He writes,

Comparison of the Soviet concept with a chain–Laspeyres index with frequent links shows how hidden inflation arose. When core inflation was combined with negatively correlated changes in relative prices and quantities, two factors conspired to bring it about. First, plan prices of old products lagged increasingly behind those of new products introduced at the absolutely higher price level prevailing after the base period; this rise in p_t resulted in a growing over-weighting of those products that were growing most rapidly. Second, plan prices were never adjusted downward for the relative deflation of new product costs, i.e., the fall in π_i, after the pilot stage; this resulted in over-weighting of new products as soon as they had ceased to be new. (p. 143)

Cf. Mark Harrison, "Prices, Planners, and Producers: An Agency Problem in Soviet Industry 1928–1950," *Journal of Economic History* 58, no. 4 (1998): 1032–62, esp. 1043–4. Harrison says that there is no direct evidence for "simulated innovation" (unjustified price markups) during 1928–50 (p. 1044). Bergson advanced a similar hypothesis earlier (see Bergson, "Soviet National Income Statistics," 148–52).

22. Alec Nove, along with others, doubted the importance of overreporting for the measurement of growth by supposing that the "padding" rate was constant, but he later questioned his own assumption. See Alec Nove, *Glasnost' in Action: Cultural Renaissance in Russia* (Boston: Unwin Hyman, 1989), 213–20.

23. Morris Bornstein and Gregory Grossman not only acknowledged the temptation but considered price discipline lax. See Morris Bornstein, "The Administration of the Soviet Price System," *Soviet Studies* 30, no. 4 (1978): 466–90; Gregory Grossman, "Price Controls, Incentives and Innovation in the Soviet Economy," in Alan Abouchar, ed., *The Socialist Price Mechanism* (Durham, NC: Duke University Press, 1977), 129–69; Vladimir Kontorovich, "Economic System and the Valuation of National Income" (unpublished manuscript, 2001). Cf. Vladimir Kontorovich, "Economists, the Soviet Growth Slowdown and the Collapse," *Europe-Asia Studies* 53, no. 5 (2001): 675–95. See also Grigorii Khanin, "Ekonomicheskii Rost: Al'ternativnaia Otsenka," *Kommunist* 17 (1988): 83–90; idem, *Sovetskii Ekonomicheskii Rost: Analiz Zapadnykh Otsenok* (Novosibirsk: EKOR, 1993). Cf. Richard Ericson, "The Soviet Statistical Debate: Khanin vs. TsSU," in Henry Rowen and Charles Wolf, Jr., eds., *The Impoverished Superpower: Perestroika and the Soviet Military Burden* (San Francisco: ICS Press, 1990).

24. James Steiner, *Inflation in Soviet Industry and Machinebuilding (BMW) 1960–1975*, SRM 78-10142, CIA, July 1978; Robert Leggett, "Measuring Inflation in the Soviet Machinebuilding Sector, 1960–1973," *Journal of Comparative Economics* 5, no. 2 (1981): 169–84.

25. See note 1, this chapter.

26. Steven Rosefielde and R. W. Pfouts, "The Mis-specification of Soviet Production Potential: Adjusted Factor Costing and Bergson's Efficiency Standard," in Steven Rosefielde, ed., *Efficiency and Russia's Economic Recovery Potential to the Year 2000 and Beyond* (Aldershot, England: Ashgate, 1998), 11–32. Cf. Bergson, "Neoclassical Norms and the Valuation of National Product in the Soviet Union and Its Postcommunist Successor States: Comment"; 1995, Rosefielde, "Post-war Russian Economic Growth: Not a Riddle – A Reply,"

27. See note 1, this chapter. Joan Robinson wrote, that "what seems most lacking is some method to direct the use of resources now available to securing the maximum

satisfaction of the constantly rising material and cultural requirements of the whole society" ("Socialist Affluence," in C. H. Feinstein, ed., *Socialism, Capitalism and Economic Growth: Essays Presented to Maurice Dobb* [London: Cambridge University Press, 1967], 187). Bergson came to doubt the usefulness of his own concept of planners' preferences by 1966 but wouldn't give ground on "production potential" (see Bergson, "Social Calculation: A Further Word").

28. In the view of Kurt Rothchild,

> At some future date it may appear as a joke of history that socialist countries learned at the long last to overcome their prejudices and to dismantle clumsy planning mechanisms in favor of more effective market elements just at a time when the rise of computers and of cybernetics laid the foundations for greater opportunites in comprehensive planning.... If the rise of new dogmas can be avoided and a flexible approach is secured the road should be open to a promising evolution of socialist systems of economic regulation. ("Socialism, Planning and Economic Growth," in C. H. Feinstein, ed., *Socialism, Capitalism and Economic Growth* [Cambridge: Cambridge University Press, 1967], 175).

29. Chang has shown how economic growth can be immiserizing in controlled economies. This probably doesn't accurately characterize changes in Russian living standards during the period 1961–90, but missed opportunities for doing better abounded. See Gene Hsing Chang, "Immisering Growth in Centrally Planned Economies," *Journal of Comparative Economics* 15 (1991): 711–17.

   Elizabeth Brainard, "Reassessing the Standard of Living in the Soviet Union: An Analysis Using Archival and Anthropometric Data," paper presented to the Abram Bergson, Memorial Conference, Harvard University, Davis Center, Cambridge, MA, November 23–24, 2003. Irwin Collier, "The 'Welfare Standard' and Soviet Consumers," paper presented at the Abram Bergson Memorial Conference, Harvard University, Davis Center, Cambridge, MA, November 23–24, 2003.

30. Steven Rosefielde, *Russian Economics, Russian Economics: From Lenin to Putin* (London: Blackwell, 2005).

31. Wilhelm, "The Failure of the American Sovietological Economics Profession." 2003.

CHAPTER 3

1. Gertrude Schroeder, "Post-Soviet Economic Reforms in Perspective," in *The Former Soviet Union in Transition*, vol. 1 (Washington, DC: Joint Economic Committee of Congress, February 1993), 57–80; idem, "Soviet Economy on a Treadmill of Reforms," in *Soviet Economy in a Time of Change* (Washington, DC: Joint Economic Committee of Congress, 1979), 312–40; idem, "Soviet Economic Reform Decrees: More Steps on the Treadmill," in *Soviet Economy in the 1980s: Problems and Prospects* (Washington, DC: Joint Economic Committee of Congress, 1982), 68–88; idem, "Organizations and Hierachies: The Perennial Search for Solutions," *Comparative Economic Studies*, Winter 1987, 7–28.

2. The Office of the Secretary of Defense (OSD), which characterized the Soviet Union as an "impoverished superpower," grasped reality better than most, but its influence was muted because it refused to publically challenge the CIA's flawed weapons valuation techniques, deferring to bureaucratic etiquette and the public

cultural imperative of conflict avoidance. OSD also acquiesced in this regard because the Defense Intelligence Agency's arms balance data carried substantial weight with Congress, enabling the Defense Department to satisfy its procurement needs. OSD's assessment of Soviet structural militarization, however, was sometimes off the mark. It occasionally overemphasized the USSR's impoverishment, misimplying that the long-term Soviet threat was self-limiting. See Henry Rowen and Charles Wolf, Jr., *The Impoverished Superpower: Perestroika and the Soviet Military Burden* (San Francisco: Institute for Contemporary Studies, 1990).

3. Dmitri Steinberg was the only specialist who believed that a large portion of defense spending was excluded from official NMP and GNP statistics, arguing that they were financed by profits, which were kept as a secret category outside Goskomstat's published system of accounts. See Dmitri Steinberg, *Reconstructing the Soviet National Economic Balance, 1965–1984: An Alternative Approach to Estimating Soviet Military Expenditures*, vol. 1, *Technical Discussion*, DSA Report no. 692 (Decision-Sciences Applications, March 11, 1986); vol. 2, Washington, DC, *Compilation of Working Tables* (March 21, 1986); idem, "Estimating Total Soviet Military Expenditures: An Alternative Approach Based on Reconstructed Soviet National Accounts," in Carl Jacobsen, ed., *The Soviet Defense Enigma* (New York: SIPRI, 1987), 27–58. Also see Dmitri Steinberg, "Trends in Soviet Military Expenditures, *Soviet Studies* 42, no. 4 (1990): 675–99; Steven Rosefielde, "Soviet Defense Spending: The Contribution of the New Accountancy," *Soviet Studies* 42, no. 1 (1990): 59–80.

4. Intelligence information obtained from the books of the Soviet Ministry of Defense in 1975 seemed to contradict this because weapons outlays exceeded the entire defense spending figure, but it was later revealed that weapons were excluded from Goskomstat's definition of "defense" and were instead treated as "capital." This convention goes back to the time when Abram Bergson was chief of the Russian Economic Subdivision of the OSS during World War II. See Bergson, *The Real National Income of Soviet Russia since 1928*, 362–77, app. E, "'Real' Defense Outlays." When Gorbachev revealed that the official defense budget excluded weapons, Bergson denied that this could have been the case before 1969. Another article of faith was that defense expenditures weren't dispersed in civilian activities. If you find this convincing, try to find the CIA's activities in America's GDP accounts.

5. Abraham Becker believed that weapons were priced without profits as an element of *sebestoimost'* (personal communication). Cf. Noel Firth and James Noren, *Soviet Defense Spending: A History of CIA Estimates, 1950–1990* (College Station: Texas A&M University Press, 1998), 190.

6. Abraham Becker, *Soviet National Income 1958–64* (Berkeley: University of California, Berkeley, 1969); CIA, *USSR: Measures of Soviet Economic Growth and Development 1950–1980*; Abraham Becker, *Soviet Military Outlays since 1958*, RM-3886-PR (Santa Monica, CA, Rand Corporation, June 1964); Franklyn Holzman, *Financial Checks on Soviet Defense Expenditures* (Lexington, MA: Lexington Books, 1975); idem, "Are the Soviets Really Outspending the U.S. on Defense?" idem, "Soviet Military Spending: Assessing the Numbers Game"; idem, "Politics and Guesswork: CIA and DIA Estimates of Soviet Military

Spending"; idem, "Politics, Military Spending, and the National Welfare." Notice that Holzman never acknowledged his error, even though Gorbachev disclosed in 1987 that Soviet defense spending was far higher than Holzman had been contending. See Firth and Noren, *Soviet Defense Spending*, 189.

7. Derk Swain, "The Soviet Military Sector: How It Is Defined and Measured," in Rowen and Wolf, *The Impoverished Superpower*, 93–109. The CIA's ruble estimates of Soviet defense include MVD troops, MOD railway and construction troops, military personnel in civilian activities, and space programs run by the MOD (p. 94).

8. The CIA estimated Soviet defense spending using its direct costing method. Outside analysts in Rand cross-checked the agency's figures against the Goskomstat's defense budgetary expenditure entry and Rand's own budgetary estimate derived from various Goskomstat subseries. All three series tracked each other closely from 1970 to 1975, giving the false impression that Soviet defense activities were constant in absolute terms and declining rapidly as a share of GDP (Table 3.3). See Steven Rosefielde, *False Science: Underestimating the Soviet Arm Buildup* (New Brunswick, NJ: Transactions, 1987), 186–7, table 13.11, 253, table 19.2, 294, table A11; Firth and Noren, *Soviet Defense Spending*; Maddison, "Measuring the Performance of a Communist Command Economy.

9. Rosefielde, *False Science*. The CIA's direct costing definition of Soviet defense activities was broader than Goskomstat's. It covered the American Department of Defense categories, military pensions, space, KGB border guards, militarized USSR Ministry of Internal Affairs (MVD) troops, railroad and construction brigades, and civil defense. See Firth and Noren, *Soviet Defense Spending*, 146.

10. Rosefielde, *False Science*, 294, table A11; Firth and Noren, *Soviet Defense Spending*, 59–66.

11. David Epstein, "The Economic Cost of Soviet Security and Empire," in Rowen and Wolf, *The Impoverished Superpower*, 153. Epstein was deputy director of the Office of Net Assessment, OSD.

12. Rosefielde, *False Science*, 294, table A11; Firth and Noren, *Soviet Defense Spending*, 59–66.

13. Rosefielde, *False Science*, 33, fig. 1.1. The revised series for 1965–87 is reported in Swain, "The Soviet Military Sector," 105, table 3.2.

14. The agency's latest revised defense spending estimates provided in 1982 ruble prices display the same trend, with the average burden in the vicinity of 16 percent. See Firth and Noren, *Soviet Defense Spending*, 129, table 5.10.

15. Peter Wiles and Moshe Efrat, *The Economics of Soviet Arms* (London: Suntory-Toyota International Center for Economics and Related Disciplines, 1985); Peter Wiles, "How Soviet Defense Expenditures Fit into the National Accounts," in Carl Jacobson, ed., *The Soviet Defense Enigma*, 59–94; idem, "Soviet Military Finance" (paper presented at the Third World Congress on Soviet and East European Studies, Washington DC, October 1985), 1–62. Cf. Becker, *Soviet National Income, 1958–1964*, 161–2; Alec Nove, *The Soviet Economic System* (London: George Allen & Unwin, 1977), 230–40.

16. Abraham Becker, *Military Expenditure Limitations for Arms Control: Problems and Prospects* (Cambridge, MA: Ballinger, 1977): "At the Twenty-Eighth General

Assembly in September 1973, Foreign Minister Gromyko proposed that the five permanent members of the Security Council reduce their military budgets by 10 percent" (p. 6). Although the CIA and RAND were burned by their belief in the "reliability" of the published Soviet defense budget, the former was drawn again to using it as a basis for assessing Soviet defense intentions in the late eighties (see Firth and Noren, *Soviet Defense Spending*, 128). The assertion that Soviet procurement spending nose-dived after 1987 is also inconsistent with the CIA's procurement series in current prices (p. 82).

17. Firth and Noren, *Soviet Defense Spending*, 188–90.

18. Vitaly Shlykov believes that the removal of weapons from the official defense budgetary statistic in 1970 and the Soviet gambit of challenging America to reduce its defense burden to Russia's level were coincidental (meeting, September 19, 2002, Moscow); see note 15, this chapter. Observe also that Gorbachev's disclosure refuted Holzman's claims about the reliability of the official defense budgetary statistics in *Financial Checks on Soviet Defense Expenditures*.

19. The difference between Gorbachev's and the CIA's defense spending estimates could be partly explained by subsides and the provision of some military supplies and services on a nonpecuniary basis. Various organizations had obligations to supply services and materials gratis to the military. It has been conjectured that profits weren't charged on weapons, that natural resources were acquired at discount, and that other costs were allocated to civilian activities in dual-production facilities.

20. See Steven Rosefielde, "The Civilian Labor Force and Unemployment in the Russian Federation," *Europe-Asia Studies* 52, no. 8 (2000): 1435, table 1. Some intelligence analysts like William Lee estimate Soviet military personnel at upwards of 5 million, while Goskomstat reports a figure of 4 million (see *Narodnoe Khozyaistyo SSSR 1990* [Moscow, 1991], 97). The actual number of Russian active-duty military personnel is uncertain and disputed by Russian officials and Western analysts. Estimates range from 1.2 million to as high as 1.8 million. The official authorized strength is 1.7 million, although Russian officials often say 1.8 million. Most analysts place actual troop strength at 1.2–1.5 million. The figure 1.27 million from *The Military Balance* is near the low end of the range. But the practice of padding unit rosters with "ghost" contract soldiers is believed to be widely used as a way to get larger payroll disbursements. Authoritative data on military manpower published in *Izvestiya*, July 18, 1997, indicate a total of 1.32 million. The Ministry of Defense is currently conducting a unit-by-unit census in order to determine actual troop strength. A further complication is that Russia has another 1 million armed men in uniform in 15–23 paramilitary agencies classified as part of the civilian labor force. Forty to 50 percent of these are Interior Ministry troops or in the Federal Border Guard Service, Federal Security Service, Ministry of Emergency Situations, or Federal Road Construction Department. But since only the regular armed forces are supposed to be equipped, trained, and dedicated to the war-fighting mission, most analysts do not include paramilitary personnel in military manpower. Vitaly Shlykov, former co-chairman of the Russian Defense Committee, contests this view, however. He asserts that paramilitary troops are equipped with advanced war-fighting weaponry and contends that

the current number of military and paramilitary personnel could be as high as 4.0 million. He gets this figure by adding 1.3 million MVD and KGB troops paid out of non-MOD budgets to Baturin's estimate of 2.7 million paid MOD soldiers. See Steven Rosefielde, "Russian Military Power and Defense Industrial Potential" (unpublished manuscript, December 1997), table 7. Cf. Stuart Goldman, *Russian Conventional Armed Forces: On the Verge of Collapse?* (Washington, DC: Library of Congress, Congressional Research Service, September 1997); International Institute of Strategic Studies, *The Military Balance, 1996–1997* (London: International Institute of Strategic Studies, 1997). As of 2002, Putin had provided a figure of 3 million troops. Cf. Firth and Noren, *Soviet Defense Spending*, 211, table A.1. They report that there were 5–6.1 million troops, including KGB, MVD, and railroad troops in mid-1988. The armed forces component was 4.4–5.2 million (see footnote 15, "Russian Army More Than Halved since 1992 – Defense Ministry," interfax, reprinted in *Johnson's Russia List*, no. 7139, art. 3, April 9, 2003). General Vasily Smirnov, a senior official from the Russian General Staff stated on Echo Moskvy radio that in the past eleven years the general number of Russian armed forces has been reduced by more than 50 percent: "At the moment, the Russian army numbers 1.162 million people. In 1992, this index was 2.88 million people."

21. For more comparable figures, see CIA, *USSR: Measures of Economic Growth and Development 1950–1980*; Rosefielde, *False Science*; William Lee, *The Estimation of Soviet Defense Expenditures for 1955–1945*; idem, *CIA Estimates of Soviet Military Expenditures: Errors and Waste* (Washington, DC: American Enterprise Institute, 1995); Firth and Noren, *Soviet Defense Spending*, 179–85. Hidden inflation, as the CIA perceived it, was value that was falsely claimed and therefore never really added. Unlike the rest of CIA's Soviet GNP statistics, the figures for Soviet weapons didn't reflect ruble factor cost and should not have been treated as if they did. The agency's practice of classifying current ruble priced estimates as legitimate factor cost estimates violates this principle and reflects a deep confusion about the determinants of value in the Soviet economic system.

22. The CIA collected sample prices of weakly comparable ruble prices for 1970 and 1982. It found that the change in the cost of various defense bundles including procurement, manpower, construction and O&M were greater than seemed justified, and it attributed the excess to hidden inflation because the increases weren't confirmed in official price indexes. The concept of "hidden inflation" is broader than the concept of "spurious innovation" discussed in chapter 2, which suggests that the entire problem is attributable to sampling error. Indeed, Firth and Noren write, "The new analysis, however, found no difference between inflation in old products versus new products." See Firth and Noren, *Soviet Defense Spending*, tables 6.1 and 6.2, associated text on pp. 150–62, and p. 82, fig. 4.2.

23. Rosefielde, *False Science*, 158, table 13.1. Compare columns 1 and 3, the agency's pre- and postrevision weapons estimates. If the difference between these two series, priced in 1970 rubles, constitutes hidden inflation, then the former, not the later, should have been combined with other defense expenditures in uninflated 1970 prices in the postrevision estimates.

24. Swain, "The Soviet Military Sector."

25. According to Vitaly Shlykov, KGB and other paramilitary troops had standard-issue weapons, including long-range bombers with nuclear ordnance. The Soviet Union maintained a reserve system comprising 20 million conscripts, and factories and public institutions were designed to military specs so that they could be quickly converted from civilian to military use in time of war. Vitaly Shlykov estimated in 2000 that Russia had 1.3 million MVD, KGB, and border guard troops.
26. Epstein, "The Economic Cost of Soviet Security and Empire," 153, table 5.4.
27. Vitaly Shlykov and Academician Yuri Yaremenko (private discussions, 1998). Yaremenko, who was responsible for reviewing the numbers for the politburo, estimated the figure at 30 percent but said no exact calculation was possible because of price anomalies. Cf. Vitaly Shylkov, *Chto Pogubilo Sovetskii Soiuz?* Also see Lev Dudkin and Anatol Vasilevsky, "The Soviet Military Burden: A Critical Analysis of Current Research," *Hitotsubashi Journal of Economics* 28, no. 1 (1987): 41–62.
28. The CIA preferred to interpret dollar estimates as measures of input cost rather than output value and added other innocuous caveats. See Firth and Noren, *Soviet Defense Spending*, 142–6.
29. Swain, "The Soviet Military Sector," 105, fig. 3.2. The same basic picture is confirmed in rubles. See Firth and Noren, *Soviet Defense Spending*, 149, fig. 6.1.
30. Rosefielde, *False Science*, 31–90.
31. Rosefielde, *Comparative Economic Systems*, 26; Steven Rosefielde, "The Underestimation of Soviet Weapons Prices: Learning Curve Bias," *Osteuropa Wirtschaft* 31 (March 1986): 53–63. Cf. Armen Alchain, "Reliability of Progress Curves in Aiframe Production," *Econometrica*, vol. 32, 1963, pp. 679–93.
32. Firth and Noren, *Soviet Defense Spending*, 160–1. This point is supposedly refuted by Donald Burton's study of thirty-two models of U.S. tactical aircraft in 1950–80 with the estimated dollar cost of growth of Soviet tactical aircraft in 1950–82, but the evidence cited in figure 6.2 refers to ruble data, making it impossible to evaluate the rebuttal. Note that the claim is inconsistent with the CIA's use of the SPIOER index. Burton asserts that Soviet weapons were qualitatively improved; SPIOER assumes they weren't! Holland Hunter, Haverford College, was the first MEAP (Military-Economic Analysis Panel) chairman (Firth and Noren, *Soviet Defense Spending*, 47).
33. Firth and Noren, *Soviet Defense Spending*, 155. The CIA's use of learning curves was questioned in the early 1980s. Norbert Michaud, an analyst at the Economic Affairs Branch of the Defense Intelligence Agency, told the Becker panel about an "interesting problem" that he wanted to bring up. He said that if the goal was to measure things in constant prices, learning shouldn't be taken into account; a given item should have the same price no matter when it was manufactured. Rosefielde also criticized the use of learning curves in his appearance before the Becker panel, saying that it violated the standard meaning of output and biased the constant-price dollar and ruble values downward. Derk Swain, replying to Rosefielde's charge, agreed that the agency was violating Rosefielde's definition of constant cost but maintained that the CIA was measuring the constant cost of producing a tank in terms of inputs. In its report, the working group labeled groundless the charge that the CIA had used learning curves incorrectly, arguing

that learning is a real phenomenon that does reduce military costs and that the CIA was applying learning curves in a conceptually correct and careful way. See Bergson, *The Real National Income of Soviet Russia since 1928*, 362–77, app. E.

34. The "input cost" growth trend was computed with the learning adjustment, and the 1970 value was extrapolated backward with this growth trend at the 1982 "price level." The alternative "output" growth trend apparently used the same trend modified in some minor way.

35. Firth and Noren, *Soviet Defense Spending*, 181. The agency's 1970 prices are postrevision, not prerevision. See William Lee, *Trends in Soviet Military Outlays and Economic Priorities 1970–1988*, U.S. Senate Committee on Foreign Relations, Republican Staff Memorandum, July 30, 1990, 8, table A-7. Weapons grew 7 percent per annum despite the CIA's claim of a pronounced slowdown in MBMW production during 1984–8.

36. Firth and Noren, *Soviet Defense Spending*. Cf. Abraham Becker, *Postwar Soviet Economic Growth: A Second Look* (Santa Monica, CA: Rand Corporation, February 2002).

37. Firth and Noren, *Soviet Defense Spending*, 62. They claim that their "new prices" only raised their defense estimate from 40.6 billion rubles to 49.6 billion rubles, although the table on p. 63 shows clearly their original number was 20 billion rubles. The disparity is due to some "undisclosed" revision. Likewise, the new prices had been discussed with Rosefielde at various conferences in the 1980s and were few in number and unpersuasive, a point on which Franklyn Holzman and William Lee agreed.

38. *Ibid.*, 155.

39. *Ibid.*, 129, table 5.10, 185–91. Also see ("Intracommunity Disputes over Economic Constraints on Soviet Military Programs"), and Lee, *Trends in Soviet Military Outlays and Economic Priorities 1970–1988*, pp. 93–7.

40. Aleksei Ponomarenko, "Gross Regional Product for Russian Regions: Compilation Methods and Preliminary Results," paper presented at Regions: A Prism to View the Slavic-Eurasian World, Slavic Research Center, Hokkaido University, Sapporo, Japan, July 22–4, 1998. Also see Rosefielde, *Efficiency and Russia's Economic Recovery Potential to the Year 2000 and Beyond*, xxii–xxiii, table S1; idem, *Comparative Economic Systems*, 172–73, n. 9.

41. Rapaway reports that there were 16 million workers in the machine-building and metalworking sectors in 1985, which should have been enough to encompass the 10 million military machine-building employees estimated by western intelligence. See Stephen Rapaway, "Labor Force and Employment in the U.S.S.R.," in *Gorbachev's Economic Plans*, vol. 1, Joint Economic Committee of Congress, Washington, DC, 23 November 1987, 200. The precedents for inclusion and exclusion are contradictory. The Soviet defense budget, as we now know, excluded weapons, but military hardware, based on William T. Lee's calculations, was included in the ruble statistics on MBMW. A full discussion of this complicated issue is beyond the scope of this book. See Rosefielde, *False Science*; Rosefielde, "Soviet Defense Spending"; pp. 59–80. Lee, *The Estimation of Soviet Defense Expenditures for 1955–1975*. Igor Birman ("Velichina Sovetskikh voennykh raskhodov: Metodicheskii aspekt," unpublished manuscript, 1990) reports that

4 million workers in the Soviet nuclear weapons sector, plus space-based mirrors for laser warfare, were excluded from Goskomstat's MBMW statistics. The figure was confirmed by Emil Ershov when he was a statistical chief at Goskomstat. See Lee, *CIA Estimates of Soviet Military Expenditures*, 151 n. 25. Cf. note 18.

42. Lennart Samuelson, *Plans for Stalin's War Machine: Tukhachevskii and Military-Economic Planning 1925–1941* (London: Macmillan, 2001); idem, *Rod Koloss pa Larvfotter*. In Dale Walton, "Book Review of Albert L. Weeks, *Stalin's Other War: Soviet Grand Strategy, 1939–41*, Rowman and Littlefield, Lanham, MD," *Johnson's Russia List*, no. 7292, art. 14, August 17, 2003,

   In mid-June 1941 Soviet Russia had "on paper" 303 infantry, tank, motorized, and cavalry divisions, of which one-quarter, however, was still in the process of being formed. Nor was the Red Navy unimpressive with, for example, 212 submarines and many surface ships. Equipped forces deployed along the western frontier numbered 163 infantry, tank, and motorized divisions consisting of 2,743,000 men with 57,000 guns and mortars, 12, 762 tanks, 8,696 military aircraft in good condition, and 545 naval ships. All these composed the first strategic echelon of the Soviet military forces in the west. To cover them the Red Army had deployed along the frontier thirteen general forces armies.

43. Donald Rumsfeld, "Transforming the Military," *Foreign Affairs* 81, no. 3 (2002): 20–32.

44. Vitaly Shlykov, *Chto Pogubilo Sovetskii Soeuz? Genshtab i Ekonomika*, Voennyi Vestnik, no. 9 (Moscow, September 2002); idem, *Chto Pogubilo Sovetskii Soiuz*? Shlykov's April 2001 article was a swift response to the proceeding of The CIA's Analysis of the Soviet Union 1947–1991, a conference held at Princeton University, March 9–10, 2001.

45. Cf. Clifford Gaddy, *The Price of the Past: Russia's Struggle with the Legacy of a Militarized Economy* (Washington, DC: Brookings Institution Press, 1996).

46. Shlykov, *Chto Pogubilio Sovetskii Soiuz*? 32–8. The *pushek i masla* strategy, which has deep historical antecedents, is also suggested by Vassily Klychevsky's observation that the "the state swelled up, the people grew lean." For discussions of the correlation between Russian poverty and excessive military expenditures, see Geoffrey Hosking, *Russia and the Russians* (Cambridge, MA: Harvard University Press, 2001), and Dominic Lieven, *Empire: The Russian Empire and Its Rivals* (New Haven, CT: Yale University Press, 2001).

47. Shlykov, *Chto Pogubilio Sovetskii Soiuz*? 28. The translation is Rosefielde's.

48. *Ibid.*, 33–8.

49. Gur Ofer, "The Service Sector in Soviet Economic Reforms: Does Convergence Finally Arrive?" paper presented at the Fourth World Congress for Soviet and East European Studies, Harrogate, England, July 21–26, 1990; idem, *The Service Sector in Soviet Economic Growth: A Comparative Study* (Cambridge, MA: Harvard University Press, 1972).

50. Steven Rosefielde, "The Distorted World of Soviet-Type Economies" (review article), *Atlantic Economic Journal* 17, no. 4 (1989): 83–6.

51. The production potential concept was elaborated as a device for interpreting ruble values in neoclassical terms but can be applied to the prices of any economy. Dollars cost for Russian assortments approximate American production potential.

52. Rosefielde, *Russian Economics, Russian Economics*; Rosefielde, *Efficiency and Russia's Economic Recovery Potential to the Year 2000 and Beyond*, xviii–xxiv. Not all specialists appreciated that the CIA's dollar purchasing power parities showed the Soviet Union to such advantage because they mistook its published geometric mean of 50 percent as the dollar estimate. The CIA inadvertently abetted the confusion by referring to its geometric mean figures as dollar values. See Clifford Gaddy and Barry Ickes, "Russia's Virtual Economy," *Foreign Affairs*, vol. 77, no. 5 (1998): 52–67.

53. CIA, *Handbook of International Economic Statistics*, CPAS92–1005, Washington, DC, September 1992. The value issue was also addressed in other ways. Dollar estimates were said to represent the cost of the assortment Russians preferred. Or geometric mean estimates (Fisher ideal) were treated as some sort of cost–value compromise. The Fisher ideal did indeed provide a better measure of comparative size, but those who produced the estimates failed to address the conceptual issue of undesirable characteristics. Cf. *Narodnoe Khozraistvo SSSR za to Let* (Moscow: Finansy i Statistika, 1987), 13. Goskomstat reported Soviet GNP to be 66 percent of America's in 1986 computed in dollars.

54. Holzman, for example, often expressed the opinion that Soviet trade in industrial manufactures with the West could be easily expanded if European and American tariff and quantitative barriers were abolished ("Foreign Trade Behavior of Centrally Planned Economies," in *Foreign Trade under Central Planning* [Cambridge, MA: Harvard University Press, 1974], 139–63).

55. See Steven Rosefielde, Aleksei Ponomarenko, and Roland Goetz, "Evidence of Transition: A Note on the Divergence of Russian and West European GDP Expenditure Patterns" (unpublished manuscript, October 2000).

56. Goskomstat, *Natsionalnie scheta Rossii*, 1997, 82.

57. Cf. Anders Aslund, "How Small Is Soviet National Income?" in Henry Rowen and Charles Wolf, Jr., eds., *The Impoverished Superpower: Perestroika and the Soviet Military Burden* (San Francisco: ICS Press, 1988), 13–62; Bergson, "The USSR Before the Fall: How Poor and Why?"

CHAPTER 4

1. Gregory Grossman, "Notes for a Theory of the Command Economy," *Soviet Studies* 15, no. 2 (1963): 103–23.

2. George Kleiner, *Mesoekonomika perekhodnovo perioda: Rynki, otrasli, predpriiatiia* (Moscow: Nauka, 2002).

3. Steven Rosefielde and R. W. Pfouts, "Economic Optimization and Technical Efficiency in Soviet Enterprises Jointly Regulated by Plans and Incentives," *European Economic Review* 32, no. 6 (1988): 1285–99.

4. Abram Bergson, *The Structure of Soviet Wages: A Study of Socialist Economics* (Cambridge, MA: Harvard University Press, 1944).

5. David Granick, "Soviet Use of Fixed Prices: Hypothesis of a Job-Right Constraint," in Rosefielde, *Economic Welfare and the Economics of Soviet Socialism*, 85–104.

6. Steven Rosefielde, "Gorbachev's Transition Plan: Strategy for Disaster," *Global Affairs* 6, no. 2 (1991): 1–21; idem, "The Grand Bargain: Underwriting Catastroika," *Global Affairs* 7, no. 1 (1991): 15–35.

7. Josef Brada and Arthur King, "Is There a J-Curve for Economic Transition from Socialism to Capitalism?" *Economics of Planning*, 25, no. 1 (1992): 37–53.

8. Stanislav Shatalin exemplified this attitude in a lecture presented in November 1991 at Duke University, where he declared, "It didn't matter whether transition took five hundred days or five hundred years, as long as it rid Russia of Communism!" Cf. Anders Aslund, "Heritage of the Gorbachev Era," in *The Former Soviet Union in Transition* (Washington, DC: Joint Economic Committee of Congress, February 1993), 184–95, where he argues that radical reform was essential but that Gorbachev stuck with a more conservative, inconsistent, and in the end destructive strategy of trying to build markets while retaining central control:

   In hindsight, it appears remarkable that Mikhail Gorbachev could receive so much acclaim for the economic policies that he pursued from 1985. From our perspective, it appears all too evident that his rule was characterized by an unprecedented confusion in economic policies. Virtually every mistake that could be made was made. The Gorbachev administration carried out a massive destruction of the old Soviet system. In history, Gorbachev will go down as one of the greatest destructors of evil, while he failed in all his many attempts at construction. Gorbachev's great achievement was that he swiftly and relatively peacefully broke down one of the most centralized and ruthless systems the world has seen to date. (p. 184)

9. Deng's "The Regulations on Transforming the Management Mechanism of State-Owned Industrial Enterprises," issued July 1992, authorized fourteen managerial control rights over (1) production, (2) pricing, (3) sales, (4) procurement, (5) foreign trade, (6) investment, (7) use of retained funds, (8) disposal of assets, (9) mergers and acquisitions, (10) labor, (11) personnel management, (12) bonuses, (13) internal organization, and (14) the refusal to pay unauthorized charges by the government.

10. Rosefielde, "Gorbachev's Transition Plan."

11. Ronald McKinnon, *The Order of Economic Liberalization: Financial Control in the Transition to a Market Economy* (Baltimore: Johns Hopkins University Press, 1991).

12. Bulat Stolyarov, "The Kremlin Wants the Natural Resources," Vedomosti, July 16, 2002, reprinted in *Johnson's Russia List*, no. 6272, July 2002. Mikhail Kochin, "The Lubyanka Strikes Back: Apostles of Controlled Democracy," *Russian and Eurasia Review* 1, no. 8 (2002): http://www.jamestown.org/publications_details. php?volume_id=15+issue_id=606+article_id=4461 September, 24, 2002. Putin has been systematically appointing FSB generals as ministers, board members of monopolies, and "elected" regional governors. Kochin envisions, "The restoration of a Soviet-style authoritarian command system." Cf. *RFE/RL (Un) Civil Societies*, Vol. 3, No. 39, September 25, 2002, reprinted in *Johnson's Russia List*, no. 6458, September 26, 2002, art. 3. But see chapter 9, note 7.

13. Stefan Hedlund, *Russian Path Dependence*, 2005. Hedlund argues that cultural-historical "mental frames" would have thwarted transition, even if structural

militarization had been properly understood. He believes that the Russian government and people are drawn to a strong central state (autocracy), where the autocrat (samoderzhava) rules with traditional devices like "patrimonialism" (fusion of sovereignty and property), pomestie (tenure land grants, or in the contemporary context oligarchic fiefs), kormlenie (tax collecting and rent-seeking agency), krugovaya poruka(informal networking and mutual support), duvan (plunder) and various types of ideological and psychological manipulation (slavophilism, cult of personality, domination, etc). These factors were clearly dominant in the event (see chapter 5), suggesting that Hedlund is right, but it is still important to grasp that culturally appropriate countermeasures like those described above could have worked if Yeltsin had been a virtuous autocrat.

14. Rosefielde, "The Civilian Labor Force and Unemployment in the Russian Federation"; Steven Rosefielde, "Premature Deaths: Russia's Radical Transition," *Europe-Asia Studies* 53, no. 8 (2001): 1159–76.

CHAPTER 5

1. Hedlund, *Russian Path Dependence*. Richard Pipes, *Property and Freedom*, New York: Alfred A. Knoph, 1999. Rent granting is the converse of rent seeking. The behavior is commonly exhibited in personal and state relations. It epitomizes the distinction between economic systems that stress dependency rather than individual self reliance founded on inalienable private property. Sovereigns in rent-granting societies secure power by fostering servility over efficiency, with a host of negative productive and human consequences. This makes rent granting the antithesis of democratic free enterprise, even though it may be carried out through the market. Rent granting has been a continuous feature of the Muscovite model since Czar Ivan the Great, but its character varies from epoch to epoch influenced by co-factors like autonomous markets and physical systems management. It works best from the ruler's perspective when coupled with conquest because rent seeking seldom augments national wealth and plunder provides a convenient surrogate. Another subtlety that merits comment is the status of the autocrat. When he or she is weak, economic outcomes may reflect survival tactics more than personal ideals, and result in co-sovereignty as was the case under Boris Yeltsin. Stronger leaders, like Vladimir Putin, by contrast have greater authority. They aren't totalitarian but are very powerful. See Robert Service, "Models of Soviet Historical Reality: Totalitarians and Revisionists," *Johnson's Russia List*, no. 8049, art. 15, February 5, 2004, where he agrues that not only was Soviet misreporting pandemic, but the system couldn't have functioned without winking at deceit. For a thorough discussion of the modalities of Muscovite rule during the Yeltsin period see Stephen Blank, "The 18th Brumaire of Vladimir Putin," *Succession Crises in Russia*, Boston University, Institute for the Study of Conflict, Ideology, and Policy, Boston, MA, April 20, 2004. Cf. Steven Rosefielde, "Rent Granting and National Security: The Economics of Russia's Re-emerging Superpower," paper presented at the Finnish Defence College, Helsinki, Finland, April 27, 2004. For a seminal paper on rent seeking see Anne Krueger, "The Political Economy of Rent-Seeking Society," *American Economic Review*, vol. 64,

no. 3, 1974, pp. 291–303. Cf. Leonid Polischuk and Alexei Savvatev, "Spontaneous (non) Emergence of Property Rights," *Economics of Transition*, vol. 12, no. 1, pp. 103–27. Donald Jensen, "Patrimonialism in One Country," *Johnson's Russia List*, no. 8137, art. 7, March 26, 2004.

2. See chapter 4 of this text, note 13. See also Yana Amelina, "Russia: Splendor and Miseries of the Social Split," *Pravda*, August 11, 2003, reprinted in *Johnson's Russia List*, no. 7285, art. 3, August 12, 2003. Amelina writes,

> The Director of the Institute for Social and Economic Problems of the Russian Population in the Russian Academy of Sciences, Natalya Rimashevskaya, reports that about 36 million of Russians are living below the poverty line now; one quarter of the Russian population and half of the group is children. About 35–40 per cent of Russia's population belongs to a group of indigent people. Incomes of the new poor are lower than the living wage officially fixed by the government for the year 1991. The 30 per cent increase of the population's incomes often mentioned by the official statistics is in fact lies. This increase characterizes the living standard of the high-paid group of the population which comprises about 7 million people or 5 per cent of the Russian population. These are the people who build gorgeous villas, buy expensive cars and do shopping at luxurious boutiques where ordinary people never appear. The polarization of the society is especially serious because the bulk of the population has been pauperized in the post-Soviet era. The Director of the Institute for Complex Social Research in the Russian Academy of Sciences Mikhail Gorshkov added new details to the portrait of the Russian poor. Their average age is 47 years. Contrary to the traditional stereotypes, these people are not pensioners (pensioners make up only one quarter of the poor), they are workers, even highly qualified ones (37 percent) and Russians with higher education (one fifth approximately). The Editor-in-Chief of the Sotsiologicheskiye Issledovaniya (Sociology Researches) magazine Zhan Toshchenko says that the characteristic feature of the category is that these people honestly work but are paid wages insufficient for normal living. Doctor of Psychological Sciences Mikhail Reshetnikov calls this category of people "the working poor". The poverty is particularly evident in small cities and in villages: only 17–19 per cent of the population belongs to the category in large cities while this group includes about one third of the rural population.

For the Khodorkovsky story see Chapter 9, note 6, and Chapter 8, note 18.

3. Economics is a subcase of production. Production regimes, including factor supply, factor allocation and use, product design and creation, finance, investment, and distribution, need not be "economic" in two fundamental senses. They may be unresponsive to demand and may disregard cost minimizing. Production begins to take on an economic aspect when supply responds to demand and when suppliers become cost conscious. These behaviors can occur in a single individual like Robinson Crusoe, without any possibility of negotiated exchange with others and hence markets. They can involve binary unstructured two-party exchange relations that are premarket, or they can be extended to include structured multilateral exchanges called markets, which may be productive in varying degrees depending on their design. A fully economic regime achieved through perfect planning, perfect markets, or some linear combination of these mechanisms will maximize utility for some individual or group or the community of individuals. Perfect authoritarian economies will benefit a narrow constituency; perfect democratic economies will be Pareto optimal. With these principles in mind, one can view Russia as moving from an authoritarian production regime

of a narrowly circumscribed economic character (i.e., a physically managed engineering control system) to a mixed regime comprising self-regulating physically managed subnetworks (the residue of the command economy after the dissolution of its higher level coordinating mechanism), subsistence markets, exclusionary markets, managed markets, motivationally disordered transactionary processes, and limited entrepreneurship – a rent-granting regime that lies much closer to the perfect authoritarian than the perfect Paretian end of the systems spectrum.

4. Hedlund, "Russian Path Dependence"; Stefan Hedlund, "Can They Go Back and Fix It? Reflections on Some Historical Roots of Russia's Economic Troubles," *Acta Slavica Iaponica* 20 (2003): 50–84; Mikkail Tugan-Baranovsky, *The Russian Factory in the 19th Century* (Homewood, IL: Irwin, 1970). Paul Gregory, *Behind the Facade of Stalin's Command Economy*, Princeton Univ. Press, Princeton, New Jersey, 2002.

5. *Russian Economic Trends* 2, no. 4 (2002): 97, 99, tables D10, D11, D13; Rosefielde, "The Civilian Labor Force and Unemployment in the Russian Federation." Current Statistical Survey, Goskomstat, no. 4, 2003.

6. The term "motivational dysfunction" suggests that Russian economic pathology is to be attributed more to deceitful games and fraud than to customs and institutions.

7. Some like former labor minister Vladimir Kosmarski argue that Yeltsin and Anatoli Chubais merely formalized the spontaneous seizure of assets under Gorbachev (RECEP, Moscow, May 23, 2002).

8. Kleiner, *Mesoekonomika perekhodnovo perioda*.

9. Anna Bedkhen, "Kremlin Can't Control Secretive Nuke Agency: Stalin's Creation Making Reactor for Iran," *San Francisco Chronicle*, September 1, 2002, reproduced in *Johnson's Russia List*, no. 6417, September 1, 2002. Minatom employs more than 600,000 people. It views the Bushehr reactor deal with Iran as a $800 million business venture even though everybody knows "Iran will get their weapons-grade plutonium to build a bomb."

10. Andrei Nesterenko, "Markets between Soviet Legacy and Globalization: Neoinstitutionalist Perspectives on Transformation," in Klaus Segbers, ed., *Explaining Post-Soviet Patchworks: Pathways from the Past to the Global*, vol. 2 (Aldershot, England: Ashgate, 2001), 78–103. According to Nesterenko, by the mid-1990s, more than half of public property was privatized, but many of these companies aren't truly private because their formal owners cannot exercise management and earn profit (p. 97). Unlike industry, finance, and services, where large-scale denationalization has been accomplished, agriculture remains under the control of collective farms. Cf. Aslund, *Building Capitalism*; Maxim Boyko, Andrei Shleifer, and R. Vishny, *Privatizing Russia* (Cambridge, MA: MIT Press, 1995); Joseph Blasi, *Ownership, Governance and Restructuring* (New Brunswick, NJ: Rutgers University School of Management and Labor Relations, 1994); Raj Desai and Itzhak Goldberg, "Stakeholders, Governance, and the Russian Enterprise Dilemma," *Finance and Development* 37, no. 2 (2000): 14–18; Aleksander Radygin, "Spontaneous Privatization: Motivations, Forms and Stages," *Studies on Soviet Economic Development* 3, no. 5 (1992): 341–7; Pekka Sutela, "Insider

Privatization in Russia: Speculations on Systemic Change," *Europe-Asia Studies* 46, no. 3 (1996): 417–35. Cf. Alexandr Radygin, "The Corporate Securities Market: Bridgehead or Barrier to Globalization?" in Segbers, *Explaining Post-Soviet Patchworks*, 193–226; John Earle, "After Voucher Privatization: The Structure of Corporate Ownership in the Russian Manufacturing Industry," Center for Economic Policy Research Discussion Paper no. 1736, John Earle and Saul Estrin, "Worker Ownership in Transition," in Roman Frydman, Cheryl Gray, and Andrezej Rapaczynski, eds., *Corporate Governance in Central Europe and Russia*, vol. 2, 1994 (Budapest: Central European University Press), 1–61.

11. Georgii Kleiner, "Person, Position, Power and Property: The General Director in the 'Economy of Individuals'," in Segbers, *Explaining Post-Soviet Patchworks*, 108–39. The term "economy of individuals" refers to a situation that is the antithesis of Pareto-optimal consumer sovereignty, for in this situation individuals like managers arrogate the rights of other shareholders, operating in their personal interest at the expense of other legitimate claimants. Cf. Andrei Shastitko and Vitalii Tambovtsev, "Institutionalization and Property Rights: The Reincarnation of Managerial 'Economic Authority' over State Property," in Segbers, *Explaining Post-Soviet Patchworks*, 281–302.

12. These ploys and others have been popularized in the West as Russia's "virtual economy." See Gaddy, *The Price of the Past*; Clifford Gaddy and Barry Ickes, "Russia's Virtual Economy," *Foreign Affairs*, vol. 77, no. 5 (1998): 53–67; idem, "Beyond a Bailout: Time to Face Reality about Russia's 'Virtual Economy'," (unpublished manuscript; available at
http://www.brook.edu/fp/articles/gaddy/gaddick1.htm).
The term "virtual economy" is used to make the point that Russian productive activities, as in the Soviet past simulate rather than replicate competitive market behavior, suffer from underproduction, and often lead to surreal results. Nesterenko traces the rise of the contemporary variant of the Russian virtual economy to mid-1992, when most government-owned enterprises built up bad debts as a consequence of hyperinflation, but he attributes the deeper problem to government complicitly in macropolicymaking and tolerance of soft budget constraints ("Markets between Soviet Legacy and Globalization," 90–1). These "assets" (debts) then infected the banking, public finance, and social sectors. The virtual economy peaked in 1998, when the total volume of mutual indebtedness was more than twice the GDP. Over half the mutual settlements were done through barter trade. Gaddy and Ickes claimed that the "virtual economy is fundamentally not market-based" and will ensure continued economic decline and crises "Russia's Virtual Economy," 54). Some of the distinguishing features of the virtual economy, according to them, are bad enterprise debts, business tax arrears, barter trade, quasi-money, multiple pricing keyed to the form of payment, a shadow economy, wage arrears, and dollarization. However, a better way to grasp the phenomenon is to recognize that it is simply a predictable adaptation to the underlying Soviet-type physically managed subnetwork system in the absence of Soviet-type administrative command planning. See Clifford Gaddy and Barry Ickes, *Russia's Virtual Economy* (Washington, DC: Brookings Institution Press, 2002); idem, "An Accounting Model of the Virtual Economy in Russia," *Post-Soviet Geography and Economics* 40, no. 3 (1999): 79–97; Dalia Marin, "Trust

versus Illusion: What Is Driving Demonetization in the Former Soviet Union?" *Economics of Transition* 10, no. 1 (2002): 173–200; Barry Ickes, "Illusion and Trust: Comment on Marin's Paper," (unpublished working paper, August 2002).

13. Valerii Makarov and Georgii Kleiner, "Barter v ekonomike perekhodnovo perioda: Osobennosti i tendentsii," *Ekonomika i matematicheskie metody*, vol. 33, no. 2 (1997): 25–41. Up to 90 percent of intercompany settlements involved barter and money surrogates. See Nesterenko, "Markets between Soviet Legacy and Globalization," 90.

14. Alena Ledeneva, "Networks in Russia: Global and Local Implications," in Segbers, *Explaining Post-Soviet Patchworks*, 59–77. Ledeneva captures an aspect of the phenomenon with the phrase "economy of favors." The concept includes *blat* (reciprocal favors of *tolkachi*), *vynos* (petty theft of state property), and personal contacts in the private sector. Also see Alena Ledeneva, *Russia's Economy of Favors: Blat, Networking, and Informal Exchange* (Cambridge: Cambridge University Press, 1998); Alena Ledeneva and Paul Seabright, "Barter in Post-Soviet Societies: What Does It Look Like and Why Does It Matter?" in Paul Seabright, ed., *The Vanishing Rouble: Barter Networks and Non-Monetary Transactions in Post-Soviet Societies* (Cambridge: Cambridge University Press, 2000). Cf. Nina Oding, "Profit or Production? Enterprise Behavior after Privatization," in Segbers, *Explaining Post-Soviet Patchworks*, 140–69. Oding cites Aukutsionek's study, which shows that only 24 percent of Russian manufacturing enterprises sought to maximize, increase, preserve, or improve profits, compared with 80 percent of Dutch firms (table 6.1). See S. P. Aukutsionek, "Rossiiskii motiv – bez pribyli!" *EKO*, no. 11 (1997) 2–14; Rostislav Kapeliushnikov, "Chto skryvaetsa za 'skrytoi' bezrabotsei?" in Tat'iana Maleva, ed., *Gosudarstvennaia i korporativnaia politika zaniatnosti* (Moscow: Moskovskii Tsentr Karnegi, 1998), 75–111. Klaus Segbers correctly traces those influences on productivity. See Klaus Segbers, "Institutional Change in Russia: A Research Design," in Segbers, *Explaining Post-Soviet Patchworks*, 10.

15. The Soviet division of labor was both over- and underspecialized judged from the Pareto norm. Post-Soviet despecialization therefore isn't entirely bad. It enhances the efficiency of those who are still gainfully employed but were previously overspecialized.

16. Russia's technology is higher than that of a "rude" natural economy, but this fact must be discounted because demand guides supply more effectively in cohesive, integrated primitive societies than in Russia.

17. Individual suboptimization in subsistence subnetwork markets is further constrained by custom, ritual, and reciprocal obligation, widening the gulf between Russian practice and Pareto efficiency.

18. Vitaly Golovachyov, "Splender and Poverty of the Regions," available at www.trud.ru/01.Today/07/2002070230601-htm.
Goskomstat reports a lower figure but reaches this figure by disregarding the unemployed and discouraged workers.

19. Russians also strongly prefer foreign goods. This may reflect a well-justified belief that Russian products are more likely to be adulterated. For example, ordinary fish roe is sometimes painted black and sold as caviar.
Nesterenko, "Markets between Soviet Legacy and Globalization," 100.

20. Andrew Jack, "Russia's Oligarchs Not Efficient Says World Bank, *Financial Times* (reprinted in *Johnson's Russia List*, no. 8154, art. 12, April 7, 2004). Gerald Easter, "Networks, Bureaucracies, and the Russian State," in Segbers, *Explaining Post-Soviet Patchworks*, 54–8; Radygin, "The Corporate Securities Market"; David Hoffman, *The Oligarchs: Wealth and Power in the New Russia* (New York: Public Affairs Press, 2002); Martha Brill Olcott, "Reforming Russia's Tycoons," *Foreign Policy*, May–June 2002, pp. 66–75. Peter Stavrakis writes,

    Neither the president nor the country's richest men could manage without one another. A magnate or two can be knocked off the field without much harm to the economy, but Russia's economy has shrunk so dramatically from the Cold War days that a handful of men working in concert could wreak havoc. Of course, they have no economic incentive to do so, and thus most generally promote Russian government interests abroad – including giving priority to investment in countries where Moscow has strong strategic political interests in the hope that this will speed up the creation of the domestic political and legal environment necessary for them to retain and expand their assets. But for all their voice, Russian billionaires – and their economic and political opportunities – are still largely shaped by the powers inherent in the Russian presidency. Putin is making the most of his strong hand, carving out his own policy in critical areas of natural-resource development ("Russia's Evolution as a Predatory State," in *Russia's Uncertain Economic Future* [Washington, DC: Joint Economic Committee of Congress, December 2001]).

21. Aslund, *Building Capitalism*; Shlykov, *Chto Pogubilo Sovetskii Soiuz?*

22. A neurosis is a mental and emotional disorder caused by repression or another structural anomaly that affects only part of the personality; is accompanied by a less distorted perception of reality than in a psychosis; does not result in disturbance of the use of language; and is accompanied by various physical, physiological, and mental disturbances (e.g., visceral symptoms, anxieties, or phobias). Neurotic behavior is persistent and often acontextual. It can be traced to repressed unconscious mental desires (as distinct from physical addiction or character flaws) that cannot be openly confronted and rationally resolved. A psychosis is a fundamental mental derangement (e.g., paranoia) characterized by defective or lost contact with reality.

23. Nonneurotic personality disorders may merely be moral failings. If so, reeducation may solve the problem. See Daniel Rancour-Laferriere, *Russian Nationalism from an Interdisciplinary Perspective: Imagining Russia* (Lewiston, NY: Edwin Melien Press, 2000). Rancour-Laferriere provides some insight into Russian productive behavior using the psychoanalytic theories of the British scholar Melanie Klein.

24. Aslund, *Building Capitalism*, 453–6; Segbers, "Institutional Changes in Russia" Nesterenko, "Markets between Soviet Legacy and Globalization," 104–6. Aslund believes that a new breed of postoligarchic big businessmen who have moved away from their dependence on state handouts will save the day (lecture, University of North Carolina, Chapel Hill, November 14, 2002).

25. The G8 institutions reversed field in the spring of 2004 and decided that the oligarchs weren't efficient after all. See note 20. Small is once again beautiful. Cf. Anders Aslund and Simon Johnson, "Small Enterprises and Economic Policy," *Russian and Eurasian Progress*, Carnegie Endowment for International Peace,

no. 43, March 2004. Nesterenko, "Markets between Soviet Legacy and Globalization," 97–100; Mancur Olson, *Power and Prosperity: Outgrowing Communist and Capitalist Dictatorships* (New York: Basic Books, 2000).

26. Dmitri Glinski and Peter Reddaway, "The Ravages of 'Market Bolshevism,'" *Journal of Democracy* 10, no. 2 (1999): 19–34; Peter Reddaway and Dmitri Glinski, *The Tragedy of Russia's Reforms: Market Bolshevism against Democracy* (Washington, DC: United States Institute of Peace, 2001); Joseph Blasi, M. Kroumova, and D. Kruse, *Kremlin Capitalism* (Ithaca, NY: Cornell University Press, 1997); Gerald Easter, *Reconstructing the State: Personal Networks and Elite Identity in Soviet Russia* (New York: Cambridge University Press, 2000); Thane Gustafson, *Capitalism Russian-Style* (Cambridge: Cambrdige University Press, 2000); Steven Solnick, *Stealing the State: Control and Collapse in Soviet Institutions* (Cambridge, MA: Harvard University Press, 1999).

27. Nesterenko, "Markets between Soviet Legacy and Globalization," 99; S. A. Pashin, "Chelovek v rossiiskom pravovom prostranstve," Moskovskaia vysshaia shkola sotsial'nkykh i ekonomicheskikh nauk, Interstsentr, 2001, 156–66; M. A. Shabanova, "Institutsional'nye izmeneniia i nepravovye praktiki," Moskovskaia vysshaia shkola sotsial'nykh i ekonomischeskikh, Intertsentr, 2001, 319–27. Pashin, a jurist and retired federal judge, asserts that "if you don't know what to do, then act in accordance with the law." Cf. Satoshi Mizobata, "Financial Moral Hazard and Restructuring in Russia after the Financial Crisis," Kyoto Institute of Economic Research, Discussion Paper no. 524, March 2001; idem, "Lessons from the Russian Transformation in the Yeltson Era," Kyoto Institute of Economic Research, Discussion Paper no. 523, March 2001.

28. Steven Rosefielde and Natalia Vennikova, "Fiscal Federalism in Russia: A Critique of the OECD's Proposals," *Cambridge Journal of Economics*, vol. 28, 2004, pp. 307–18.

29. Anders Aslund, "Rentoorientirovannoe povedenie v rossiiskoi perekhodnoi ekonomike," *Voprosy Ekonomiki*, no. 8 (1996): 99–108. Russian export trade margins provide telltale evidence of profiteering. Figures for the United States, Japan, and Russia are 7, 6.4, and 30.8 percent respectively. Most of this disparity is attributable to the oil and gas industry. Similar distortions characterized domestic trade margins. See Masaaki Kuboniwa, "The Hollowing out of Industry and Expansion of Trade Service Sector in Russia: Domestic Factors Determining Russia's Presence in the International Markets under Globalization," paper presented at the American Association for the Advancement of Slavic Studies, Pittsburgh, November 24, 2002. Cf. Shinichiro Tabata, "Flow of Oil and Gas Exports Revenues and Their Taxation in Russia," paper presented at the American Association for the Advancement of Slavic Studies, Pittsburgh, November 24, 2002, table 10, which shows that 13.3 percent of oil exports go to tax haven countries.

30. Putin's assault on Khodorkovsky and others has set limits, but hasn't slowed the relentless pursuit of rents and the state's assets. Vladimir Tikhomirov, "Capital Flight from Post-Soviet Russia," *Europe Asia Studies* 49, no. 4 (1997); 591–615; idem, "State Finances and the Effectiveness of the Russian Reform," in Vladimir Tikhomirov, ed., *Anatomy of the 1998 Russian Crisis* (Melbourne: Contemporary

Europe Research Centre, 1999), 164–203; idem, *The Political Economy of Post-Soviet Russia* (London: Macmillan, 2000), idem, "Capital Flight: Causes, Consequences and Counter-Measures," in Segbers, *Explaining Post-Soviet Patchworks*, 251–80. The battle between Chukotka governor Roman Abramovich's Sibneft Company and rival oligarch Sergey Pugachev of St. Petersburg's International Industrial Bank (MPB) for control of Slavneft shows that little has changed. See Wayne Allensworth, "Fiddling While Rome Burns: The Battle over Slavneft," *Johnson's Russia List*, no. 6309, June 15, 2002. On the Yukos affair, see chapter 9 of this text, note 6. Putin's attack on Khodorkovsky is intended to remind oligarchs that what they think are property rights are merely revokable user privileges.

31. Most of Russia's exports are natural resources. See *Russian Economic Trends* 11, no. 3 (2002): 107, table D6. Also see Paul Webster, "Suicide Rates in Russia on the Increase," *The Lancet* 363, no. 9379, reprinted In *Johnson's Russia List*, no. 7257, July 20, 2003. "Figures confirming that Russian suicide levels are among the world's highest were reported last week, putting a tragically human face on Russian economic decline since the Soviet collapse in 1990. Russia registered 39.7 suicides per 100,000 people in 2001, for a total of 57,000, according to a report released in collaboration with WHO by the Russian Ministry of Health's Research Institute of Psychiatry. The 2001 figure represents a slight decline from a peak in 1994 of 42.1 suicides per 100,000, when the Russian economy was rapidly shrinking, and a slight increase over the 1998 figure of 35.4, when the economy was rapidly growing. Russian men are now six times more likely to commit suicide than women, and the highest risk group among men consists of 45- to 54-year-olds, with 106.7 suicides per 100,000, according to study author Dmitry Veltischev. Russian women are most likely to kill themselves after the age of seventy-five, with 27.4 cases per 100,000 reported. The new figures represent a dramatic increase in Russian suicide rates since 1990, the last year of Soviet government in Russia, when the suicide rate was reported to be 26.4 per 100,000. While Russia's rate is well below Lithuania's – which, at 51 per 100,000, is the world's highest – it is greater than Western Europe's average of 5 suicides per 100,000 and North America's average of 4.1. Alexander Butchart, WHO coordinator for violence prevention, says that 'there was a dramatic increase in Russian suicide rates starting in the mid-1980s through to the mid-1990s, then a brief decline before it began growing again after 2000. The reasons are complex but the suicide rate is obviously linked to social and economic disintegration.'"

32. Rosefielde, "Premature Deaths." The stagnation deprecated by Gorbachev suggests that the problem may have begun earlier as massive corruption within the administrative command planning apparatus.

33. The IMF is slowly coming to the same conclusion. See Oleh Havrylyshyn, "Uncharted Waters, Pirate Raids, and Safe Havens: A Parsimonious Model of Transition Progress," paper presented at the BOFIT/CEFIR Workshop on Transition Economics, April 2–3, 2004, Helsinki, Finland.

34. Those who don't grasp this try to blame the Soviet system for Russia's economic debacle. See Strobe Talbott, *A Memoir of Presidential Diplomacy* (New York: Random House, 2002); Stephen Kotkin, *Armageddon Averted: The Soviet*

Collapse 1970–2000 (London: Oxford University Press, 2002); Martin Malia, "Brinksmanship," *Washington Post Book World*, June 9, 2002. Kotkin blames Gorbachev's erratic style for the USSR's demise and attributes its continuing illiberalism to an administrative class absorbed with plundering. Cf. Michael McFaul, *Russia's Unfinished Revolution: Political Change from Grobachev to Putin* (Ithaca, NY: Cornell University Press, 2001). McFaul blames Gorbachev only for failing to overhaul the system. Also see Jerry Hough, *The Logic of Economic Reform in Russia* (Washington, DC: Brookings Institution Press, 2001). Hough blames Russia's economic woes on perverse incentives created by Western liberal reformers and the failure to heed Yeltsin "conservatives."

35. Stanislav Shatalin et al., *Transition to the Market: 500 Days*, pt. 1 (Moscow: Arkhangelskoe, August, 1990).

36. Rose Brady, *Kapitalizm: Russia's Struggle to Free Its Economy* (New Haven, CT: Yale University Press, 1999), 135–43; David Satter, *Darkness at Dawn: The Rise of the Russian Criminal State* (New Haven, CT: Yale University Press, 2003). Marshall Goldman, *The Piratization of Russia: Russian Reform Goes Awry* (London: Routledge, 2003).

37. Anders Aslund, "Russia's Collapse," in *Foreign Affairs* 78, no. 5 (1999); 64–77. Cf. Bulat Stolyarov, "The Kremlin Wants the Natural Resources," *Vedomosti*, July 16, 2002, reprinted in *Johnson's Russia List*, no. 6272, July 2002.

38. Oding, "Profit or Production."

39. Simon Kordonskii, "Everyday Life as Flight from the State: 'Housing Portfolios' and the 'Diversified Way of Life,'" in Segbers, *Explaining Post-Soviet Patchworks*, 326–32.

40. See chapter 9 of this text.

41. For a discussion of Walrasian and Marshallian adjustment processes, see Rosefielde, *Comparative Economic Systems*, chap. 2.

42. Easter, "Networks, Bureaucracies and the Soviet State," 38. Easter refers to the phenomenon as "neo-appanage" (patrimonial) Russia.

43. Steven Rosefielde, "Keynes and Peter I: Managing Russia's Economic and Military Vulnerabilities," in Pentti Forsstrom, ed., *Russia's Potential in the 21st Century*, National Defense College, series 2, no. 14 (Helsinki, 2001), 75–91.

44. Lilia Shevtsova, "President Putin: Arbiter or Traffic Controller?" *Rossiskaya Gazeta*, no. 41, March 2003, reprinted in *Johnson's Russia List*, no. 7110, item 16, March 20, 2003. According to Shevtsova,

> Deep down, a process has begun in Russia that could come to upset lots of things. This involves the realisation that the Russian system, based on diffuse authority, bureaucratic control, imitation of legality, and parasitic business, is not working. Putin's attempts to rationalise it have failed. What is more, the system inescapably makes any president hostage to it.

45. Andrei Shliefer and Daniel Treisman, "A Normal Country," *Foreign Affairs*, vol. 84, no. 2, 2004, pp. 20–38. Anders Aslund, *How Russia Became a Market Economy* (Washington, DC: Brookings Institution, 1995); Michael Stedman, "Market Economy: Russia Is There, 'Irreversible Progress'?" strana.ru, April 27, 2002. Cf. Tatyana Zaslavskaya, "Kto i kuda stremitsia vesti Rossiiu?" Moskovskaia vysshaia shkola sotsial'nykh i ekonomicheskikh nauk, Intertsentr,

2001, 9–10. Zaslavskaya contends that authoritarian-coercive (favored by the Putin's KGB *siloviki*), conservative-statist (favored by legalist bureaucrats), and semi-criminal oligarchical alternatives are more likely than liberal-democratic or social-democratic futures.

46. Segbers, "Institutional Change in Russia."

47. Olcott, "Reforming Russia's Tycoons." The first wave of businessmen were former Soviet managers like Vagit Alekperov of Lukoil, Vladimir Bogdanov of Surgut, Vladimir Kadannikov of Avtovaz, and Vladimir Lisin of Novolipetsk. These "spontaneous privatizers," now in their fifties, were superseded by well-known oligarchs like Mikhail Khodorkovsky of Yukos, Mikhail Fridman and Peter Aven of Alfa, Vladimir Potanin of Norilsk Nickel/Interros, and Kakha Bendukidze. Olcott reports that the oligarchs have stacked the Federal Council with their representatives, tightening their collusion with the state (Carnegie Endowment for International Peace meeting report, "Russia's Big Conglomerates and the Country's Modernization," April 17, 2002, www.ceip.org). Alexander Dynkin, first deputy director of the Institute of the World Economy and International Relations (IMEMO) reported that Russia's integrated business groups (IBGs) have begun to shift the focus of their activities from simple resource extraction to higher value added sectors of the economy. Both Interros and Sistema have moved aggressively into communications and electronics, while Sibirski Aluminy-Sibneft and Severstal have started to develop enterprises in the engineering industries. Dynkin advocates state subsidization of interest rates on merger and acquisition financing, transferring state-owned stock to trust managements, and converting enterprises' tax debt into stock for sale to strategic owners to help the IBGs as part of a joint state–private sector systems development strategy. Clem Cecil, "Russian Oligarchs Fear Putin Inquiry into Their Wealth," *The Times*, July 18, 2003, reprinted in *Johnson's Russia List*, no. 7256, art. 2, July 18, 2003, provides this list of "Russia's richest":

1. Mikhail Khodorkovsky, 39. Menatep; Yukos Oil. Worth: $8 billion (26th richest in world)
2. Roman Abramovich, 36. Sibneft (oil); Russian Aluminium. Worth: $5.7 billion (49th)
3. Mikhail Fridman, 38. Tyumen Oil. Worth: $4.3 billion (68th)
4. Viktor Vekselberg, 45. Tyumen Oil. Worth: $2.5 billion (147th)
5. Vladimir Potanin, 42. Norilsk Nickel. Worth: $1.8 billion (222nd)
6. Mikhail Prokhorov, 37. Norilsk Nickel. Worth: $1.6 billion (256th)
7. Vladimir Yevtushenkov, 54. AFK Sistema. Worth: $1.5 billion (278th)
8. Oleg Deripaska, 34. Russian Aluminium. Worth: $1.5 billion (278th)
9. Vagit Alekperov, 52. LUK Oil. Worth: $1.3 billion (329th)
10. Alexei Mordashov, 37. Severstal (steel). Worth: $1.2 billion (348th)

48. David Yakubashvili has leased 200,000 hectares in Volgograd oblast, Potanin's Interros 250,000 hectares in Stavropol krai.

49. James Millar, "The Normalization of the Russian Economy: Obstacles and Opportunities for Reform and Sustainable Growth," *NBR Analysis* 13, no. 2 (2002): 5–44; Marshall Goldman, "The Coming Russian Boom–Again," in Michael Crutcher,

ed., *Russian National Security: Perceptions, Policies and Prospects* (U.S. Army War College, November 2001), Cerlisle Barracks, PA, 315–30; Eric Brunet, "Is Russian Economic Growth Sustainable?" in Arnaud Blin and Francois Gere, eds., *Puissance et Influences*, geopolitical and geostrategic (yearbook March 2002). Charles Léopold Mayer, *Descartes & Cu*, Paris, June 2002, pp. 55–74. Martin Hutchinson, in "Russia Takes Control of Gazprom," *Johnson's Russia List*, no. 7099, March 11, 2003, reported the following:

The Russian gas company Gazprom announced Tuesday that its corporate restructuring had been completed, and that the Russian state now owned 51 percent of its shares, up from 38 percent previously.

Gazprom is the largest gas company in the world and one of the leading joint stock companies in Russia. It accounts for 8 percent of Russia's total industrial output and provides 25 percent of total tax proceeds to the state budget.

Gazprom produces 20 percent of the world's gas and 90 percent of Russian gas. It controls about 65 percent of all gas reserves in Russia and 20 percent of all gas reserves worldwide, with estimated reserves of 26 trillion cubic meters.

In May 2001, following Putin's election, Gazprom Chairman Rem Vyakhirev was replaced by the little known Alexei Miller, then a 39-year-old deputy energy minister, who had been a Putin protégé since they had worked together in St. Petersburg in the mid-1990s.

A fierce power struggle has followed, during which old guard management has been replaced, core assets reclaimed and non-core businesses accumulated over the years have been prepared for sale

For example, Gazprom exercised a "call" option to regain a stake in Pourgaz, a gas field operator with significant reserves that it had sold to Itera for a nominal sum. It also attempted to negotiate the return of $800 million in loans and reconsolidate its control over Sibur, an alliance of petrochemical companies.

When this proved impossible, Gazprom provided information to the general prosecutor's office in January 2002, and three top Sibur officials were arrested.

During Miller's tenure there has been considerable discussion of the possibility of breaking Gazprom into several companies, but this now appears unlikely.

50. Many have an abiding belief in the power of saviors and argue the Putin is on their side. This should give particular encouragement to the Washington consensus, because in the aftermath of 9/11 Putin has wagered economically and politically on the West instead of forging a coherent exceptionalist economic strategy or coalition building with Iran, India, and China. Rhetoric and reality in Russia, however, seldom coincide, and actions in support of the rule of law, as distinct from the rule of men, remain thin. Anders Aslund more recently blames the EU for Russia's sluggish redevelopment and foresees a wave of vitalizing investment. See Anders Aslund and Andrew Warner, "The EU Enlargement: Consequences for the CIS Countries," Carnegie Endowment for International Peace, Working Paper no. 36 (Washington, DC, April 2003). Also Pekka Sutela, *The Russian Market Economy*, Kikimora Publications, Helsinki, Finland, 2003. But cf. Andrew Jack, "Russia's Oligarchs are not Efficient Says World Bank," *Johnson's Russia List*, no. 8154, art. 12, April 7, 2004.

51. *Reformirovanie i razvitie oboronno-promyshlennovo kompleksa, 2002–2006*, Pravitel'stva Rossiskoi Federatsii, no. 713, October 2001.

CHAPTER 6

1. Stephen Blank, "The General Crisis of the Russian Military," paper presented at Putin's Russia: Two Years On, Wilton Park, England, March 11–15, 2002, p. 4. According to Alexander Golts, "By preserving the conscription system, the Defense Ministry is preserving the Soviet-era military organization of society. The main aim of this system is to have millions of reserve soldiers available for mobilization if necessary" ("Conscription Syndrome: Military Reforms Stall Because the Top Brass Is Addicted to Conscription," *Yezhnedelnyi Zhurnal*, no. 48, December 10, 2002, reprinted in *Johnson's Russia List*, no. 6602, December 16, 2002).
2. Aslund and Warner, "The EU Enlargement." Aslund believes that, while Russian accession to the EU is desirable, important constituencies in the EU and Russia are adamantly opposed (lecture, University of North Carolina, Chapel Hill, November 15, 2002).
3. Wilhelm Unge, *Den Ruska Militartekniska Resursbasen* (Russian Military-Technological Capacity), FOR-4-0618-SE (Swedish Defense Agency, October 2002); idem, *The Russian Military-Industrial Complex in the 1990s: Conversion and Privatisation in a Structurally Militarised Economy*, FOA-R5-00-01702-170-SE (Stockholm Swedish Defense Establishment, December 2000).
4. Rosefielde, "The Civilian Labor Force and Unemployment in the Russian Federation." According to Vladimir Isachenkov, in "Putin Approves Military's Hiring Plans" (*Johnson's Russia List*, no. 7110, art. 13, March 19, 2003), Putin approved the defense ministry's plan to switch the core of Russia's armed forces to volunteers over the next four years. The plan calls for hiring 167,000 volunteers. Sergei Ivanov, defense minister, said, "Conscription will remain forever." According to Maria Golovina, in "Russia Speeds Up Military Reform, Analysts Skeptical," *Johnson's Russia List*, no. 7145, art. 1, April 15, 2003, nonconscript forces are scheduled to be instituted in 2004.
5. Lyuba Pronina, "Soaring Arms Sales Pass $5 Bln Mark," *Johnson's Russia List*, no. 8035, art. 8, January 27, 2004. Rosoboroneksport received 5.1 billion dollars of a total 5.4 billion dollars in arms sales during 2003. Sales included Su-30MKs, and Su275Ks. International Institute for Strategic Studies, *The Military Balance 2001–2002* (London: Oxford University Press, 2003, 111. Russia exported $3.4 billion worth of arms in 2000 computed at the official exchange rate. The purchasing power parity figure is roughly quadruple this figure, but most of these sales were probably transacted in dollars, so the lower estimate is closer to the mark. See *World Development Indicators 2001* (Washington, DC, World Bank, 2001). Stephen Blank notes that arms sales are surrogates for reform ("The Material Technical Foundations of Russian Military Power," draft, August 2002, 6).
6. Blank, "Material Technical Foundations," 28 n. 2. Blank points out that these receipts allow the government to circumvent civilian control (p. 5). See *Russian Economic Trends* 11, no. 3 (2002): 107, table 06.
7. Blank, "Material Technical Foundations," 3. Of course, in the case of EU national missile defense, the Russians hope to obtain valuable technical information from the West, in addition to any cost savings produced from the cooperative effort. For the petroleum story, see *Johnson's Russia List*, no. 6552, art. 16, November

14, 2002. Cf. "Russian to Run Out of Oil in Six Years," *Johnson's Russia List*, no. 8165, art. 9, April 13, 2004.

8. Anders Aslund reports that the top twenty Russian companies are awash in cash that they don't know how to invest (lecture, University of North Carolina, Chapel Hill, November 14, 2002). Transferring funds to the OPK shouldn't retard civilian growth if he is right.

9. Vladimir Mukhin, "Oil, Fish, and Defense," *Nezavisimaya Gazeta*, November 23, 2002.

10. Blank, "Material Technical Foundations," 4. Blank contends that information warfare (IW) can have strategic outcomes (p. 8) and that the Russians are so concerned that they have threatened to respond to an IW attack with nuclear weapons (p. 11), and he observes that IW can be combined with biological warfare (p. 12). The Kremlin has also warned that it would be justified in employing a nuclear first strike if menaced by advanced conventional weapons warfare (p. 13).

11. *Ibid.*, 25

12. *Ibid.*, 13, 35.

13. *Ibid.*, 14

14. *Ibid.*, 15. Cf. "Russia Possesses Secret Weapon," *Johnson's Russia List*, no. 8140, art. 4, March 28, 2004. Putin announced a new ICBM that can change course and thereby defeat America's NMD defenses.

15. *Ibid.*, 34.

16. *Ibid.*, 34–5. Blank believes that Kuroyedov is speaking for the entire defense establishment.

17. Rumsfeld, "Transforming the Military."

18. Rosefielde, "Premature Deaths"; Nicholas Eberstadt, "The Future of AIDS," *Foreign Affairs* 81, no. 6 (2002): 22–45. An article in *Johnson's Russia List* presented this picture: Nicholas Eberstadt, "The Demographic Factor as a Constraint on Russian Development. Prospects at the Dawn of the Twenty First Century," in Eugene Rumer and Celeste Wallender, *Sources and Limits of Russian Power*, National Defense University Press, Washington, DC, forthcoming.

According to the statistics committee, around 145,390,000 people live in Russia now. The number of the male population is: 67,790,000, female – over 77,600,000. The average expectation of life of Russian men is 58.5 years. Women live, on average, 72 years. All in all, Russian population dwindled down by 1,840,000 since 1989 or by 1.3 percent. The statistics committee explained that this decrease was caused mostly by natural decrease of population (excess of mortality incidence over birth rate) and emigration. The natural loss of population totaled 7.4 million people over the past 13 years, while immigration inflow topped 5.5 million. Russia has 13 cities with a population of over one million. Big cities include Moscow (10.4 million people), St. Petersburg (4.7 million) as well as Novosibirsk, Yekaterinburg, Nizhnyi Novgorod and others. While the number of Muscovites rose by 17 percent since 1989 when the previous census was conducted, the number of Petersburg residents declined by 6.4 percent. State committee materials show that 73.3 percent of the population lives in cities. According to the 2002 census, nearly a third of all villages in Russia are deserted. ("Census Shows Russia Ranks Seventh in World Population," *Johnson's Russia List*, no. 7155, art. 2, April 26, 2003.)

19. Murray Feshbach, *Russia's Health and Demographic Crises: Policy Implications and Consequences* (Washington, DC: Chemical and Biological Arms Control Institute, 2003); idem, "The Demographic, Health and Environmental Situation in Russia," draft report presented at The Future of the Russian State, Liechtenstein Institute on Self-Determination conference, Triesenberg, Liechtenstein, March 14–17, 2002; idem, "Russia's Demographic and Health Meltdown," testimony to the U.S. Congress, Joint Economic Committee, in *Russia's Uncertain Economic Future* (Washington, DC: Joint Economic Committee of Congress, 2002), 283–306. Preliminary census results indicate that Russia's population is more than 145 million, 1.6 million more than the State Statistical Committee's prior estimate (*Johnson's Russia List*, no. 6554, item 2, November 15, 2002). According to the article "Russia's Population Decreased by 760,000 People in 2002," *Johnson's Russia List*, no. 6618, art. 4, December 127, 2002, Vladimir Sokolin, chairman of the Russian State Statistical Committee, besides reporting a decrease in Russia's population, surmised that the census population was higher than expected because of Ukrainian and Belarussian immigration but held that this doesn't alter the negative long-range population trajectory.

20. Blank, "Material Technical Foundations," 29–30. Blank reports that 4,000 scientific research organizations are funded at only about 17 percent of the Soviet level. The average age of researchers is approaching 60 because low pay discourages new entrants. The number of researchers has fallen 67 percent to 910,000, 11 percent of whom are young scientists. Seventy-five percent of Russia's world-class mathematicians and 50 percent of its physicists have emigrated. Indeed, 85 percent of all Russian Ph.D. scientists are working abroad, which sheds some light on why Russia's share of the global high-tech market is 0.3 percent.

21. Vitaly Shlykov, "Russian Defense Industrial Complex after 9–11," paper presented at Russian Security Policy and the War on Terrorism, U.S. Naval Postgraduate School, Monterey, CA, June 4–5, 2002. For a discussion of earlier reforms, see Alexei Izyumov, Leonid Kosals, and Rosalina Ryvkina, "Privatisation of the Russian Defence Industry: Ownership and Control Issues," *Post-Communist Economies* 12, no. 4 (2001): 485–96; idem, "Defense Industrial Transformation in Russia: Evidence from a Longitudinal Survey," *Post-Communist Economies* 12, no. 2 (2001): 215–27.

22. Shlykov, "Russian Defense Industrial Complex after 9–11." The employment figure is too low, and the machinery data probably too high, but for the purposes at hand the official numbers provide an adequate impression of scale. Alexander Roubtsov put the OPK labor force at 3.5 million (Blank, "Material Technical Foundations," 36). Military manpower today is between 2.4 and 3 million according to Shlykov, citing Sergei Ivanov, Russia's defense minister, and Vladimir Putin, comparable to Soviet manpower on a territorially adjusted basis, but procurement is between 10 and 20 percent of the Soviet era level. If Shlykov is correct, the recent surge displayed by the OPK's weapons production statistics is bogus. OPK manpower, excluding MVD, FSB, and border troops but including those of the MOD, is in the vicinity of 6.5 million, or roughly 10 percent of the labor force. Felgenhauer estimates that there are 2 million soldiers.

23. *Reformirovanie i razvitie oboronno-promyshlennovo kompleksa 2002–2006 gody.* Cf. Shlykov, "Russian Defense Industrial Complex after 9–11."

24. Putin is commander-in-chief of the military under the control of the MOD, but due to a quirk in Yeltsin's constitution, he has no formal executive authority over the rest of the armed forces (Vitaly Shlykov, personal communication, September 19, 2002, Moscow). Also see Shlykov, *Chto Pogubilo Sovetskii Soiuz?*

25. Shlykov, *Chto Pogubilo Sovetskii Soiuz?* 6. Klebanov claims that Russia's defense needs are too pressing to wait for the OPK to successfully privatize according to the American pattern.

26. Even if Klebanov is right, the government need not effectively renationalize to capture part of weapons export rents. It can always tax. Following is a section of an interview of Nikolai Solortsov by Nikolai Proskov ("Satan Missiles to Remain in Use Until 2016: An Interview with Colonel General Nikolai Solovtsov, SMF Commander," *Vremya Novoati*, December 16, 2002, reprinted in *Johnson's Russia List*, no. 6602, art. 11, December 16, 2002):

Question: After the status of the SMF was lowered, there was talk that the SMF is fading away and has lost its previous significance. Have any changes occurred since then?

Nikolai Solovtsov: Everything has remained unchanged: four missile armies, training sites, arsenals, higher education institutions. As the Security Council's resolution approved by the president says, not a single launcher will be removed from combat duty until the prolonged service life elapses.

Question: In compliance with START II, the Satan MIRV heavy missiles (according to NATO classification) should be removed from combat duty and dismantled. Is this process underway?

Nikolai Solovtsov: It will remain in use until 2016–20. The state armaments program to 2006 includes some measures to prolong utilization of this missile. By the by, the combat railway missile systems have also been retained. In my opinion, the missile grouping will undergo no considerable changes within the next decade.

Question: How has the SMF responded to the US withdrawal from the ABM treaty? Supposedly, the single-warhead missiles have been replaced with MIRV on Topol-M missiles?

Nikolai Solovtsov: This opportunity is being considered, but not in connection to the ABM treaty. Some other decisions could be made as well. However, we haven't made any drastic steps and it is not our intention to make any.

Question: How is rearmament with Topol-M missiles progressing?

Nikolai Solovtsov: According to the rearmament program, some 6–10 missiles should be supplied to the SMF per year. In 2003, we will deploy a new regiment in the Tatishchevo Division.

27. Vitaly Shlykov, "Russian Security Policy and the War on Terrorism," paper presented at the U.S. Naval Postgraduate School, Montery, CA, June 2003. 15–17.

28. *Ibid.*, 18. Sukhoi was awarded the contract on April 26, 2002.

29. Shlykov, *Chto Pogubilo Sovetskii Soiuz?* Shlykov uses the term "guns and margarine" to underscore the point that high levels of weapons procurement were achieved during the Soviet era by compelling consumers to accept Spartan living standards.

30. *Ibid.*, 19. The following is from an article by Fyodor Virtsev, "Russian Government Determined to Deal with Defense Industry: The Privatization of 12 Defense Enterprises Will Be Announced until (*sic*) the End of the Year," *Pravda*, August 2, 2003, reprinted in *Johnson's Russia List*, no. 7274, art. 11, August 2, 2003:

> It has been recently announced, preliminary works to form the new State Rocket and Space Corporation have been completed in the Krasnoyarsk region. The new corporation will be the example of Russia's first inter-agency association of enterprises. The integrated organization will be formed on the base of the scientific and industrial applied mechanics association (the town of Zheleznogorsk, the Krasnoyarsk region). The project has been approved by a special committee, chaired by Ilya Klebanov, the Minister for Industry and Science. The following factories have expressed their wish to become members of the corporation: Polyus (Tomsk), Kvant (Moscow), Geofizika-Kosmos (Moscow), Kvant (Rostov-on-Don). At present moment, all these enterprise are subordinated to various agencies. This is an example of the targeted work of the Federal program about the reform and the development of the Russian defense industry in 2002–2006. The government is seriously intended (*sic*) to deal with industry's problems. In addition to it, the privatization of 12 defense enterprises will be announced until (*sic*) the end of the current year.

31. Shlykov, *Chto Pogubilo Sovetskii Soiuz?*
32. "Russia Pledges to Ratify US Nuclear Treaty Despite Delay in Vote March 19th, 2003," *Johnson's Russia List*, no. 7109, art. 22, March 19, 2003. The U.S. Senate ratified the treaty, which provides for a two-thirds reduction of each country's 6,000 warheads to under 2,200 by 2012. But see Andrei Zlobin, "Washington's Nuclear Barn: the United States Will Not Honor the Strategic Offensive Reductions," *Vremya Novesti*, March 26, 2004 (reprinted in *Johnson's Russia List*, no. 8138, article 4, March 26, 2004.
33. Blank, "The General Crisis of the Russian Military," 4.
34. Cf. William Wohlforth, "Russia," in Richard Ellings and Aaron Friedberg, eds. *Asian Aftershock* (NBR, Seattle September 2002), 17–18.
35. "Russia: Defense Economics," Center for Strategic and International Affairs, Russian and Eurasian Program, highlights of a briefing given by Christopher Hill, British Ministry of Defense, London, January 31, 2001; Christopher Hill, "Russia's Defense Spending," in *Russia's Uncertain Future* (Washington, DC: Joint Economic Committee of Congress, 2002). Cf. International Institute for Strategic Studies, *The Military Balance 2000–2001*, 115–17, 161–82. Hill puts the dollar "burden" in 2000 at 5 percent, accepting the World Bank's GDP figure of $1 trillion, with a defense expenditure estimate of $50 billion. If these figures are deflated back to a 1978 base, they are $450 billion and $22.8 billion respectively. The latter figure is between a third and a half of the extrapolated CIA number (depending on the territorial adjustment estimate). The bulk of the discrepancy appears attributable to troop size. In the old days, the CIA estimated 5 million men in arms (3 million adjusted for disunion), but Hill is only assuming 1.3 million, despite Putin's admission that Russian military manpower circa 2000 was 3 million. The official defense burden is 2.6 percent of GDP (the same as during the Soviet period). The Stockholm International Peace Research Institute estimates 4 percent (http://first.sipri.org). The International Institute for Strategic Studies puts the figure at 8 percent (*The Military Balance: 2001–2002*).

36. The CIA estimated Russia's 1989 GNP (computed in 1991 dollars) to be $2.3 trillion, but purchasing power parities developed only six years later by Goskomstat, using the 1993 System of National Accounts (SNA) methodology, reduced the figure to $1.4 trillion. Later computations by the deputy director of Goskomstat, Aleksei Ponomarenko, discounted purchasing power parities further to $1.1 trillion. This figure was revised upward in SNA 96 and SNA 99 (due to the jettisoning of adjustments for inferior services). SNA 99 is approximately 20 percent higher than the SNA 93 figure, which in turn is roughly treble the exchange rate figure. See Goskomstat, *Natsional'nie scheta Rossii*, 1997, p. 82, and Rosefielde, *Efficiency and Russia's Economic Recovery Potential to the Year 2000 and Beyond*, xxii, table S1. See also Rosefielde, Ponomarenko, and Goetz, "Evidence of Transition."

CHAPTER 7

1. Martin Crutsinger, "U.S. Calls Russia a Market Economy," *Johnson's Russia List*, no. 6293, June 7, 2002.

2. Ivan Samson and Xavier Greffe, *Common Economic Space: Prospects of Russia–EU Relations*, white paper, Russian-European Centre for Economic Policy, Moscow, October 2002; Alexis Belianin, "Protectionism, Restructuring, and the Optimum Strategy for Russia's Accession to the WTO," RECEP, August 2002.

3. Paul Marantz, "The Incomplete Realignment of Russian Foreign Policy," paper presented at the meetings of the American Association for the Advancement of Slavic Studies, Pittsburgh, November 22, 2002, p. 4. Peter Clement (CIA) reported Iran will have missiles with nuclear warheads in 2002 (statement made at the Russian Foreign Policy roundtable, meetings of the American Association for the Advancement of Slavic Studies, Pittsburg, November 22, 2002).

4. "American Diplomat, Russia–Nato Council Aims at Creating Collective Security System," *Johnson's Russia List*, no. 6591, item 5, December 6, 2002. As stated in this article, "American Ambassador to Russia Alexander Vershbow stresses the new spirit and possibilities of the Russia-America coalition." Yevgeny Primakov, in *The World after September 11* (Moscow: Mysl' 2002), maintains that the West and Russia must unite in a global war on terrorism. See *Johnson's Russia List*, no. 6594, art. 7, December 10, 2002. For other views on the nature of the new Russian-American relationship, see Marantz, "The Incomplete Realignment of Russian Foreign Policy"; Talbott, *The Russia Hand*, 410–11; James Goldgeier and Michael McFaul, "George W. Bush and Russia," *Current History* 101, no. 657 (2002): 317; Jessica Mathews, "September 11, One Year Later: A World of Change," policy brief (Washington, DC: Carnegie Endowment for International Peace, 2002), 3; Vladimir Shlapentokh, "Is the 'Greatness Syndrome' Eroding?" *Washington Quarterly* 25, no. 2 (2002): 133–6; Daniel Treisman, "How Different is Putin's Russia?" *Foreign Affairs* 81, no. 6 (2002): 58–72.

5. The term "*siloviki*" describes individuals who have been covertly active only for the last two or three years and try to exert pressure on Putin in his decisions on personnel appointments, control of financial flows, etc. Peter Reddaway, "Is Putin

Unable to Consolidate His Power?" *Post-Soviet Affairs* 17, no. 1 (2001): 23–44;
idem, "Is Putin's Power More Formal Than Real?" *Post-Soviet Affairs* 18, no. 1
(2002) 31–40; idem, email, November 30, 2002. Reddaway's usage is inconsistent
with the familiar idea that Russia's power ministries rule the nation.

6. *Johnson's Russia List*, no. 6577, item 3, November 28, 2002. Willem Buiter, chief
economist for the European Bank for Reconstruction and Development, states,
"What we have seen in Russia for the last several years by its nature cannot be
considered economic growth, but rather a catching up between available industrial
capacities and growth in productivity after the 1998 crisis." Cf. Vladimir Gurvich,
"Russia Economy: Analysis and Forecasts," *Johnson's Russia List*, no. 6577, item
4, November 28, 2002. Vladimir Mau, Rector of the Academy of the National
Economy, also sees Russia's future growth as being capacity constrained. Arina
Sharipova, "Private Capital Outflow from Russia Decreasing," *Johnson's Russia
List*, no. 6594, art. 5, December 10, 2002. Sharipova, citing Andrei Petrov, deputy
minister of finance, claims that capital flight in 2002 fell to $3 billion. However,
Stanislav Menshikov, in "Russian Economy at Year End" notes that new capital
formation (before depreciation) grew only 2 percent and that light industry didn't
grow at all in 2002. See Memshikov, *Johnson's Russia List*, "Russian Economy
at Year End," no. 6594, art. 12, December 10, 2002. Cf. "Industrial Output on
the Rise in Russia," *Johnson's Russia List*, no. 7250, art. 2, July 16, 2003. Russian
industrial output grew 6 percent per annum during the first half of 2003. Claims
of similar success, including the claim of a surge in capital inflows, were common
in the run up to Putin's election.

7. Vladimir Putin, *First Person: An Astonishingly Frank Self-Portrait by Russia's
President* (New York: Public Affairs Press, 2000), 211, 213.

8. World Bank Operations Evaluation Department, No. 225, Summer 2002. According to this document, "The CAE (Country Assistance Evaluation) found that an
assistance strategy oriented around analytical and advisory services (AAA) with
limited financial support for Russia would have been more appropriate than one
involving large volumes of adjustment lending, since such lending in 1996–97 may
have delayed rather than accelerated needed reforms." The document also states,
"The generic lesson of the Bank's experience in Russia is that country ownership
is crucial to the success of assistance. Thus, it is important for the Bank to pay
close attention to the political and institutional aspects of reforms and consult with
all relevant units of government and civil society, to improve the relevance and
design of its activities and avoid operations where commitment is weak." These
statement don't amount to a blanket rejection of applying standard macroeconomic solutions to transition economies, but they come close to acknowledging
the need for systems reengineering.

9. Evgeny Gavrilenkov, "Openness in the Russian Economy and the Quality of
Growth," paper presented at the American Association for the Advancement of
Slavic Studies, Pittsburgh, November 22, 2002. Ivan Sergeevitch Aksakov (1823–
86) was a Russian journalist, entrepreneur, and social activist. He was a founder
of the *slavyanofili* (Slavophil) movement, which advocated pre-Petrine traditions
and norms. But he wasn't reactionary. He favored the abolition of serfdom, supported political liberalism, and cofounded the Moscow merchant mutual credit

society. His farther was Sergei Aksakov, a well-known author of books and poetic fairy tales (information provided by Natalia Vennikova, November 30, 2002).

10. *Ibid.*
11. Alla Startsev, "Alarm Bells Ring over Slow Pace of Reform," *Moscow Times*, November 27, 2002, reprinted in *Johnson's Russia List*, no. 6575, art. 5, November 27, 2002.
12. Joseph Stiglitz, "Rewriting History," *Moscow Times*, November 27, 2002, reprinted in *Johnson's Russia List*, no. 6575, art. 6, November 27, 2002.
13. Anders Aslund, "How Russia Was Won," *Moscow Times*, November 21, 2002. Andrei Shleifer and Daniel Treisman, "A Normal Country," Foreign Affairs, vol. 84, no. 2, March/April 2004. Steven Rosefielde, "An Abnormal Country: Russian Authoritarianism Unique, Not Universal." BOFIT Discussion Papers 2004, no. 5, Bank of Finland, Institute for Economies in Transition, Helsinki, Finland, 2004.
14. Aslund, *How Russia Became a Market Economy*.
15. Aslund, "How Russia Was Won." Cf. Steven Rosefielde, "Anders Aslund's Perceptions of Post-Soviet Russia: Past, Present and Prospects," unpublished commentary on three lectures presented November 12–14, 2002, at the University of North Carolina, Chapel Hill. The topics of the lectures were (1) CIS, Eastern European, and Central European postcommunist transition and comparative performance, (2) Russia's business tycoons after the decline of oligarchy, and (3) EU protectionism as a barrier to CIS development.

The overarching thesis of the lectures was that predictions of rapid Russian transition and westernization advanced by "economic liberals" like Aslund (*How Russia Became a Market Economy*) were premature because of the federation's special structural characteristics and EU protectionism. Russia's industrial base, like Sweden's, is tied to natural resources, and it is also distinguished by economies of scale. Effective transition, therefore, doesn't just mean privatization but the concentration of ownership in skilled domestic hands. Foreigners can't do this because they don't understand how to operate in the culture and interact with the state. If direct foreign investment had captured Russia's mineral-industrial base, this sector would be paralyzed today, without any future prospects. For a while, it seemed that the process of concentration itself would depress productivity because key assets were seized by "oligarchs" beholden to the state and by the mafia, but twenty core companies have succeeded in transforming themselves into "big businesses" (Yukos Oil, Sibneft, Tumen Oil, Inteferros, etc.) and are now poised to carry out the capitalist transformation predicted a decade ago to occur in 500 days. Old-style "oligarchs" are passé, and the mafia has "vanished" (vanquished by the state). Among other things, the "new" big businesses have discovered that transparency, western management practices (good corporate governance), and "honesty" are best because they increase the market capitalization of their assets.

Many flies remain in the ointment. The state is too interventionist; corruption persists (especially in the state sector); democracy is impaired by big business's open purchase of Duma representatives; and the EU unreasonably restricts Russian steel, chemical, machinery, textile, and agricultural exports. But on the whole people are well off (because lost production was mostly "value subtracted" – weapons?), poverty is diminishing, and Russia is on the threshold of taking off and integrating into the global economy. Its success seems likely because it can hire foreign management (the coffers of the Big Twenty are bulging with cash, as are those of smaller entities), and EU Solons will soon confront their anti-CIS protectionism and repent. Presumably this means Russia doesn't need any more G-8 assistance and will swiftly repay its debts to the IMF and the World Bank. Moreover, even though aid is no longer essential, direct foreign investment will soon come pouring into the country to fund non-Big Twenty activities, and there could be some huge purchases of Russian oil companies by western majors. In this regard, past capital flight was transitionary.

Aslund also asserted that Russia's prospects are far brighter than those of Central Europe, despite the impending accession of the Central European countries to the EU, because they are social democratic (hamstrung by statism), whereas Russia combines Singaporean free enterprise and domination by huge natural resource firms (like Sweden in the recent past). The defense-industrial complex (OPK) and the systemic suppression of Paretian principles weren't addressed, perhaps because they seemed negligible in the big picture. Aslund understands that all market systems aren't alike but places the blame for Russia's past failures neither on its culture nor its institutions but on teething problems and external obstacles, which are now giving way to a model that can rival the EU's and America's.

It is possible to accept Aslund's liberal premises but deny that they apply to an economy governed by the rule of men, where authoritarianism and privilege have displaced consumer sovereignty and Pareto efficiency. The counterview stresses the fraudulence of Russian democracy, the limitations of its competition, corporate misgovernance, asset stripping, asset seizing, rent seeking, the warped character of property rights, moral hazard, the ineffectuality of the rule of contract law, the prevalence of barter, the persistence of the physical systems management, the repression of competition (except where it benefits the oligarchs), drastic underinvestment, capital flight, the preservation of structural militarization, mass involuntary unemployment, depression, rampant inflation, corruption, crime, and the pauperization of a large proportion of the population.

In addition, Aslund misconstrues the concept of "value subtracted." The existence of forgone gains from trade doesn't mean value was subtracted, only that utility wasn't maximized. Russia's depression is real and devastating, as attested by 3.4 million premature deaths and the fact that nearly 25 percent of the population live at or below the subsistence level. His lower poverty estimate exaggerates the contribution of the "second economy." It is probably true, as suggested, that EU practices have had some small detrimental impact on Russia's post-Soviet development, but less so than COCOM restrictions during the Cold War. Likewise, some firms may be on the verge of achieving effective corporate governance, but most of the Big Twenty are only profitable because the state sells them resources for processing at token prices. As during the Soviet period, when business was criminalized, Russia may achieve distorted growth and development with its market-assisted Muscovite authoritarian model, but it is difficult to understand why a professed economic liberal like Aslund takes all Russia's illiberal barriers to Pareto efficiency so lightly and is so buoyantly optimistic. See Aslund and Warner, *The Enlargement of the European Union.*

16. *Ibid.* But cf. Anders Aslund, "Amnesty the Oligarchs," *Moscow Times,* March 14, 2003, reprinted in *Johnson's Russia List,* no. 7102, art. 1, March 14, 2003. Cf. Andrew Jack, "Russia's Oligarchs Not Efficient Says World Bank," *Johnson's Russia List,* No. 8154, article 12, April 7, 2004.

17. Cf. Boris Fishman, "Investors Toast Putin in New York,"*Moscow Times,* March 17, 2003, reprinted in *Johnson's Russia List,* no. 7105, art. 12, March 17, 2003. There is a constant deluge of articles of this type, many funded by the oligarchs and the Putin administration to lure western investors back after the drubbing they took in 1998. British Petroleum has recently been enticed into investing an additional $6.74 billion. For a sobering analysis of the travails of investing in Russia, see Jeanne Whalen and Bhushan Barhee, "How BP Learned to Trust an Ally That Once Burned It," *Wall Street Journal,* February 27, 2003, reprinted in *Johnson's Russia List,* no. 7081, art. 11, February 27, 2003; Simon Targett, "Fighting Its Risky Reputation: A New Survey Shows That Russia Has a Long Ways to Go to Put Itself on the Investment Map,"*Financial Times,* March 24, 2003, reprinted in *Johnson's Russia List,* no. 7113, art. 16, March 24, 2003.

18. Stiglitz, "Rewriting History." Cf. Joseph Stiglitz, *Globalization and Its Discontents.* New York, W.W. Norton Company Allen June, 2002. On November 29, 2002, *Pravda* reported that the World Bank acknowledged having given faulty advice to Russia since 1992. See *Johnson's Russia List,* no. 6579, November 29, 2002. *Moscow Times,* November 15, 2002.

In a series of exchanges shedding more heat than light, commentators have lost sight of Aslund's central thesis. Has Russia been won? If yes, then the causes of success can be debated. Otherwise, Aslund is wrong, and Stiglitz's explanations of Russia's purported post-1998 turnaround are problematic.

Aslund has gotten the best of the discussion because his critics tacitly accept his contention that Yeltsin's failures have been surmounted by Putin – that Russia has become a western market economy with unbounded prospects for overtaking Portugal.

It is therefore important to recognize that Russia's transition to competitive free enterprise was stillborn. Neither Yeltsin nor Putin embraced the concept of consumer sovereignty under the rule of contract law, where markets serve as transactionary mechanisms permitting individual utility maximizing without moral hazard, adverse selection, rent seeking, asset grabbing, and other forms of predation. Russia's Muscovite productive system, by contrast, manages markets and the "virtual economy" (barter circles) for the benefit of a coterie, including the president and his entourage, the Yeltsin "family," oligarchs, governors, the security services, new Russians, and assorted scoundrels. This empowerment of privilege and moral hazard has substituted the rule of men for the rule of law and thwarted equal opportunity. It has transformed Russia from a resource mobilization to a resource demobilization regime characterized by idle capacity, mass employment (including discouraged workers), profiteering, corporate misgovernance, and misinvestment.

No one knows if these characteristics are immutable. The Muscovite model has undergone rapid albeit inconclusive institutional change, offering hope that Russia may yet adopt the idea of the West. Democratic free enterprise under the rule of contract law, where equilibrium is competitively determined, isn't an impossibility, but for the moment it remains only an elusive dream that neither Aslund's nor Stiglitz's policies have been able to realize.

19. Jacques Sapir, "Heated Economic Debate," *Moscow Times*, November 2, 2002. The term "hollowing out" means that domestic industrial production is going offshore and is being replaced by foreign imports. The Dutch disease and the "resource curse" are special cases of this phenomenon stressed by many commentators. See Samson and Greffe, *Common Economic Space*. Cf. Masaaki Kuboniwa, "The Hollowing out of Industry and Expansion of Trade Service Sector in Russia: Domestic Factors Determining Russia's Presence in the International Markets under Globalization," paper presented at the American Association for the Advancement of Slavic Studies, Pittsburgh, November 24, 2002, p. 7, Table 1. Kuboniwa, using input-output data at constant producer prices, demonstrates that the machine-building and metalworking GDP share during 1991–9 fell from 13.6 to 7.2 percent. In this same period, light industry's share declined from 9.3 to 1.1 percent, vivifying the severity of the "hollowing out." Cf. Iikka Korhonen, "Institutional Cure of Resource Curse?" Paper presented at the BOFIT/CEFIR Workshop on Transition Progress, Helsinki, Finland, April 2–3, 2004. Cf. Anders Aslund, "Russia's Curse," *Moscow Times*, January 16, 2004. http://www.themoscowtimes.com/stoues/2004/01/16/006.html

20. Cf. Daniel Treisman, "Russia Renewed?" *Foreign Affairs*, vol. 81, no. 6 (2002): 58–72. According to Treisman, "Most observers think Vladimir Putin is remaking Russia. In fact, although faces may have changed, Putin's Russia is more like Yeltsin's than is generally recognized." It isn't true that "the new president tamed both oligarchs and regional barons and began replacing corruption with a 'dictatorship of law.'" Also see "The World Bank Confesses Its Sins: The World Bank Acknowledged That Its Activity in Russia Was Useless for the Last Decade, *Pravda*, November 29, 2002. According to the article "Risks and Threats for Russia in 2003," *Johnson's Russia List*, no. 7105, art. 13, March 17, 2003, "Russian oligarchs expanded their power in 2002 by privatizing 75 percent of Slavneft (oil producer), illegally grabbing state forest reserves, struggling for control of Gazprom, preferentially acquiring shares of Russian Joint Energy System by Russian Aluminum, and by the state imposed transfer of control over NTS and TVS television into the hands of compliant oligarchs."

21. Eberstadt, "The Future of AIDS," Valery Stepanov, "Etnicheskaia identichnost' i uchet naseleniia: Kak gosudarstvo provodilo Vserossiiskuiu perepis' 2002 goda" (Ethnic Identity and the Counting of the Population: How the State Conducted the 2002 Russian Census), paper presented at The 2002 Russian Census as a Catalyst for Change, Watson Institute for International Studies, Brown University, Providence, RI, April 7, 2003, reprinted in *Johnson's Russia List*, no. 7136, art. 5, April 9, 2003. Stepanov argues that Russia's recent census overestimated the population, implying that excess deaths may have been as high as earlier estimated.

22. Harry Dent, Jr., *The Roaring 2000s Investor* (New York: Simon & Schuster, 1999).

23. Valeria Korchagina and Lyuba Pronina, "Illarionov Raises Fear of Civil War," *Moscow Times*, July 15, 2003, reprinted in *Johnson's Russia List*, no. 7247, art. 3, July 15, 2003. In this article, Illarionov is quoted as saying, in response to the Yukos affair, "If we start now to revisit privatization, it will not be easy to stop this process, and it is not inconceivable that such action will lead to a new civil war." Was the post-Soviet "transition" the "old civil war"? See chapter 9, note 6.

24. Robert Bartley, "Bush: Foreign Policy to Take Seriously," *Wall Street Journal*, December 9, 2002, A17. Bartley, to describe the "Bush Doctrine," quotes this statement: "To forestall or prevent such hostile acts by our adversaries, the United States will if necessary, act peremptorily." He also quotes the following as explanation: "Our forces will be strong enough to dissuade potential adversaries from pursuing a military buildup in hopes of surpassing or equaling the power of the United States." These quotations are from *The National Security Strategy of the United States*, White House, September 2002. According to John King ("Bush Rolls out Missile Defense System: First Interceptors to Be Deployed by 2004," CNN.com, December 18, 2002),

   President Bush announced plans to deploy within two years the first phase of a limited system designed to protect the United States against a ballistic missile attack. The initial deployment will serve as a "starting point" for an expanded system that still is being developed. The initial system will consist of ground-based interceptor missiles based at Fort Greeley, Alaska. The first battery of interceptors is to be deployed by 2004, with an additional battery scheduled to be in place within a year or two of that. In addition, a system designed to destroy short-range and medium-range missiles would be deployed aboard Navy ships equipped with the advanced Aegis radar system.

   Cf. Bryan Bender, "U.S.–Russia: Moscow Treaty Tops U.S. Senate Agenda, but Delays Expected," *Global Security News Wire*, December 16, 2002. Bender writes,

   The United States plans to implement the treaty by reducing its number of operationally deployed nuclear weapons to fewer than 2,200 warheads by the end of 2012 and to store many of the reduced warheads. Russia is expected to do the same, although the treaty does not explicitly say how both sides should shrink their nuclear arsenals, only that they must "reduce and limit" them. Because the new treaty lacks any verification measures, the two countries will use the existing arms control verification regimes to provide a basis for confidence and predictability in future arms reductions.

   But see Andrei Zlobin, "Washington's Nuclear Barn: The United States Will Not Honor the Strategic Offensive Reductions," *Vremya Novesti* (reprinted in *Johnson's Russia List*, no. 8138, article 4, March 26, 2004).

25. Samson and Greffe, *Common Economic Space*.

26. Shlykov, "*Chto Pogubilo Sovetskii Soiuz?*

27. International Institute for Strategic Studies, *Military Balance 2002*. Wohlforth, "Russia."

28. Following is a selection from the article "Can Russia Create Novel Strategic Armaments?" (*Arguenty i Fakty*, no. 21, May 2003, reprinted in *Johnson's Russia List*, no. 7195, art. 7, May 24, 2003):

   The Strategic Offensive Reductions Treaty (SORT treaty) stipulates the reduction of Russian and US nuclear warheads to 1,700–2,200. What should Russia do in this situation and what did Vladimir Putin mean when he spoke about novel types of strategic weapons? Radmir SMIRNOV, deputy director general of the Vityaz 21st

Century research and production company who had held leading posts in the space-related research institutes of the Defence Ministry for 20 years, in an interview with Sergei OSIPOV.

Question: Does the SORT treaty suit Russia?

Answer: Certainly. We should slash our nuclear missile capabilities, if only because they cost too much in their present form. Regrettably, our nuclear missile shield is the basic factor of global respect for Russia. But unless we do something now, it will cease to exist in the 2010s, above all because of the creation of the US NMD system.

Question: But the Americans say their NMD system is spearheaded against terrorists.

Answer: It is absolutely clear now that the NMD system will be strategic, which means that it will be not only spearheaded at repelling the missile strikes of rogue countries and international terrorists but will be also designed for defense against a large-scale nuclear strike. In US view, only two countries – Russia and China – can hypothetically deliver such a strike.

Question: What will be the structure of the new NMD system?

Answer: It will consist of three echelons. The task of the first echelon will be to hit ICBMs at the boost phase. With this purpose in view, a group of up to 30 Space Based Lasers (SLB) is to be orbited in 10–12 years in addition to a large group of space-based interceptors, meaning small satellites that will use anti-missiles to hit ICBMs at the launch phase. The anti-missiles were created during Reagan's Star Wars program. One such satellite weighs 75 kg and the USA will need 5,000–6,000 of them.

The USA has also created tiny 8–10 kg nano-interceptors, which have essentially similar combat ability. The Americans may produce 15,000–20,000 of them and orbit them very quickly, as one space shuttle can orbit up to 3,000 of these tiny killers. A considerable part of Russian ICBMs can thus be destroyed at the initial stage.

But the USA stipulated the second and third echelons for guaranteed defense against a nuclear strike. I mean the land-, sea- and air-launched missiles that can destroy nuclear warheads at the ballistic trajectory. The USA has held eight tests of such missiles, three of them successful.

Question: What will happen to the other components of the nuclear triad – submarines and strategic aircraft – after the deployment of the NMD system?

Answer: I think their effectiveness will decline. The Americans may soon create space-based laser weapons that would hit not only ICBMs but also aircraft. Worse still, in 10 to 15 years they may learn to track submerged submarines.

Question: President Putin said in his address to the Federal Assembly that Russia's program of novel strategic weapons had reached the stage of practical implementation. Is it connected with the effort to counterbalance the NMD system?

Answer: Russia will not be able to create a similar system, as it would cost 300–400 billion dollars. But it can give an asymmetrical reply, meaning the destruction of vital NMD elements. It will be most probably space-based weapons, which must be given priority attention. We may use ordinary shrapnel shells or more effective systems based on novel physical principles to hit American satellites.

On the other hand, the Americans may find out, after spending vast sums of money on their NMD system, that Russia has elaborated effective reply measures that would fully neutralise the military and political advantages of the US system. Moreover, these novel Russian weapons would cost no more than 3–4 billion dollars, or a hundred times less that the NMD system.

29. Marantz, "Incomplete Realignment of Russian Foreign Policy." Cf. Dmitri Trenin, "From Pragmatism to Strategic Choice: Is Russia's Security Policy Finally

Becoming Realistic?" in Andrew Kuchins, ed., *Russia after the Fall* (Washington, DC: Carnegie Endowment for International Peace, 2002).

30. Steven Rosefielde, "Economic Foundations of Russian Military Modernization: Putin's Dilemma," in Michael Crutcher, ed., *The Russian Armed Forces at the Dawn of the Millennium* (U.S. Army War College, Cerlisle Barracks, PA) December 2000, 99–114.

31. Andrei Lipsky and Viktor Myasnikov, "Why Was the FSB Enlarged?" *Johnson's Russia List*, no. 7101, art. 6, March 13, 2003. Following is a selection from Pavel Felgenhauer, "KGB: Big, Bad and Back?" *Moscow Times*, March 12, 2003:

After the collapse of communism, the KGB was broken up into five separate agencies, but it was not fully disbanded nor was the successor organizations' mode of operation seriously reformed. Now President Vladimir Putin, a former KGB operative, is reassembling the dreaded Soviet secret police.

The president announced that two former KGB agencies, the Federal Border Service and Federal Agency for Government Communications and Information, will be reintegrated with the main KGB successor agency, the FSB.

It was FAPSI's job not only to encode and secure government communications, but also to intercept e-mails, faxes and other private communications, as well as to record telephone and radio conversations in Russia and abroad. Now the enlarged FSB will be able to listen to anything any Russian (including government officials) says or sends – without the need to involve other government agencies or explain its actions.

Everything will be concentrated in one big secret police agency: the authority to investigate suspected "foreign spies" and other wrongdoers the state does not like; and the ability to intrude deeply into the private lives of citizens using the most modern electronic means.

It is typical that while announcing the recreation of a KGB-style super secret police, Putin did not propose the creation of any, even superficial, public system for controlling its activities. Of course, an authoritarian state does not envisage any such controls.

The old-time all-powerful KGB not only controlled the lives and souls of its subjects, it also controlled the external borders of the Soviet Union. It seemed logical to bundle all the jobs into one super agency, including the border guards.

Now the FSB will also have its own massive armed force, the border guards – with more than 100,000 soldiers, armor, an air force and a navy. Why would a truly democratic country need such a hybrid super agency? The rumors that President Vladimir Putin was planning to form a single super security agency, the Federal Investigations Service, have not come true, at least not yet. Instead, Putin abolished or broke up a number of security agencies on Tuesday: FAPSI, the Federal Border Service and the Tax Police. He also created one new agency, the State Committee for the Control of Narcotics. In the short term, the shake-up could be viewed as part of the struggle for power and influence in the crucial security and intelligence sectors – either as a reaction to the events of Sept. 11, 2001, or as a preemptive strike ahead of the upcoming national elections. The changes can also be viewed as part of Putin's long-term strategy for government reform, and in this context Tuesday's reshuffle is the third round of these reforms.

In the Soviet era, the state's security and intelligence services were concentrated in three agencies: the Defense Ministry, KGB and Interior Ministry. After the collapse of the Soviet Union, the big three quickly disintegrated, leading to a sharp increase in the number of agencies – a dozen or so in the early 1990s. By the end of the decade, 14 agencies possessed armed troops. This diffusion of responsibilities and functions led to confusion, the lack of a unified command and loss of manageability.

After the first war in Chechnya, the Russian leadership's concern about this disintegration hardened into a resolve to make some fundamental changes. Under a decree signed in July 1998, all agencies containing armed forces were ordered to redraw the borders of their territorial subdivisions to conform with Russia's military districts. However the reform, in which Putin was involved first as a member of the Security Council and later as its secretary, was not implemented in full at that time. Round One of Putin's reforms took place on May 13, 2000, with the decree creating seven federal administrative districts. One week later Viktor Cherkesov, deputy director of the FSB, was appointed a presidential envoy along with Deputy Interior Minister Pyotr Latyshev, Tax Police General Georgy Poltavchenko, two army generals and two civilians. Over the next three months the envoys assembled their staffs, assigning officials from the so-called power agencies a leading role. All federal security and law enforcement agencies created federal district subdivisions except for the FSB.

Round Two. In March, 2001, Sergei Ivanov, secretary of the Security Council, took over as defense minister, while his first deputy, Mikhail Fradkov, was installed as Russia's top tax cop. Boris Gryzlov moved into the interior minister's office, and the former minister, Vladimir Rushailo, became head of the Security Council. Far-reaching staff changes were soon carried out in all four agencies. Round One of the reform established federal district-level divisions as the structural center of the reorganized agencies. In Round Two the so-called chekists seized control of the main power agencies. And in Round Three, Putin has redistributed turf and resources among the power agencies.

So, who are the winners and losers in all this?

The last round of transformations has substantially strengthened the three traditional Soviet power agencies. Putin's St. Petersburg allies in the power agencies – Nikolai Patrushev at the FSB, Ivanov and Gryzlov – are joined by Cherkesov, whose anti-drug agency has been given the disbanded Tax Police's buildings, funding, equipment and personnel.

Putin's official explanation for the secret service reforms is that "government structures are not acting efficiently enough or duly coordinating their efforts in this very important sphere." Nikolai Petrov, "Putin Reform: Round 3," *Moscow Times*, March 13, 2003.

CHAPTER 8

1. Vladimir Isachenkov, "Russia's Putin Announces Government Shakeup," *Johnson's Russia List*, no. 7098, art. 1, March 11, 2003. Isachenkov writes,

Russian President Vladimir Putin on Tuesday dramatically bolstered the clout of the KGB's main successor agency by giving it control over the country's border guards and government communications. The move gives the Federal Security Service, known by its Russian acronym FSB, most of the authority enjoyed by its predecessor. Putin said that from now on, the FSB would oversee the border guards and, together with the Defense Ministry, inherit the functions of the Federal Agency for Government Communications and Information (FAPSI), which he disbanded. The border guards chief, Gen. Konstantin Totsky, was appointed Russia's envoy to NATO, and the head of FAPSI, Vladimir Matyukhin, was named a deputy defense minister in charge of weapons industries, Putin said in televised remarks to his Cabinet. Putin said the changes were intended to more effectively stem the spread of drugs and bolster the fight against terrorism. "We can't say that the government structures are acting efficiently enough and duly coordinating their efforts in this very important sphere," he said. The KGB was split into several separate agencies in the turbulent months that closely preceded and followed the December 1991 collapse of the Soviet Union. The reform was then presented as a way to break with the KGB's repressive traditions, limit its sweeping powers and make it more open for public control. As part of the reform, the KGB was split into the FSB, which was put in charge of domestic security, and the Foreign Intelligence Service, intended to oversee spying abroad. The KGB department in charge of border guards also became a separate agency as did the KGB's branch overseeing sensitive government communications, which became FAPSI. Following Putin's announcement Tuesday, the Foreign Intelligence Service will remain the only major branch of the former KGB outside FSB control. Putin, a 16-year KGB veteran, headed the FSB before becoming Russia's prime minister and then president. In addition to bestowing new powers on the FSB, Putin also disbanded the Federal Tax Police and split its functions between the Interior Ministry and the newly-created anti-drug service. He appointed tax police chief Mikhail Fradkov to be Russia's representative at the European Union. Putin also made his envoy to northwestern Russia, Viktor Cherkesov, the chief of the new government committee in charge of combating drugs.

Regarding the restoration of press censorship in Russia, see the U.S. State Department's *Human Rights Report*, 2002. Cf. Nabi Abdullaev, "Soldiers and Chechens Criticized in U.S. Report," *Johnson's Russia List*, no. 7128, art. 2, April 2, 2003.

2. Cf. Martin Indyk, "We Forgot the Russians," *Johnson's Russia List*, no. 7113, art. 4, March 24, 2003.

3. Martin Lee, "Russian Company Accused of Aiding Iraq against Allies," *Johnson's Russia List*, no. 7113, art. 7, March 24, 2003; Arshad Mohammed, "US Believes Russians in Bagdad Are Aiding Iraq," *Johnson's Russia List*, no. 7114, art. 1, March 25, 2003. According to another article published at the same time, "George Bush telephoned Vladimir Putin to complain about sale of night-vision goggle, anti-tank missiles, and GPS jamming systems which violate the Iraq sanctions regime. Former Deputy Defense Minister and current Chairman of the Duma Defense Committee Andrei Kokoshin denies these allegations" ("MP Denies Russia Delivers Weapons to Iraq," *Johnson's Russia List*, no. 7114, art. 2a, March 25, 2003). Cf. Stephen Blank, "Russian Weapons and Foreign Rogues," *Johnson's Russia List*, no. 7116, art. 16, March 25, 2003. Blank shows not only that Russian export of arms to Iraq has been big business since 1990 but that Russia's leaders have shielded Saddam and obstructed sanctions to protect its profits. Blank's assessment is confirmed by Pavel Felgenhauer, "Sanctions Busting Skeletons," *Johnson's Russia List*, no. 7118, art. 4, March 27, 2003. Felgenhauer reports that in 1997 he personally informed Kokoshin, who was in charge of arms exports for many years, of three major breaches of Russia's weapons export law and the UN's sanctions regime vis-à-vis. These included the sale of twenty MI-24 Hind helicopters, the sale of spare weapons parts, and the sale of antitank missiles. But the United States never imposed sanctions.

4. H. Joseph Hebert, "Russia's Nukes May Be Vulnerable," *Johnson's Russia List*, no. 7115, art. 10, March 25, 2003. Hebert writes, "Senator Richard Lugar said it would be absurd to abandon the program now, despite a lengthy list of cases where America has been barred from nuclear sites that should have been open." According to another article ("Russia Says Needs Cash to Maintain Space Station," *Johnson's Russia List*, no. 7125, art. 6, March 31, 2003), "Russia is trying to extract another 50 million from the US to cover expenses for shouldering extra launches in the wake of the Columbia shuttle disaster."

5. Armen Asrian and Pavel Sviatenkov, "The End of the World: Having Started to Strive for World Domination, American Will Be Unable to Stop," *Johnson's Russia List*, no. 7114, art. 14, March 25, 2003.

6. "Russian Refusal over Iraq, US Arms Sales Charges, Fuel Cold War Talk," *Johnson's Russia List*, no. 7116, art. 4, March 25, 2003; Bill Nichols, U.S.–Russian Relations Chilliest since Cold War," *Johnson's Russia List*, no. 7119, art. 1, March 27, 2003. Cf. Robert Kaplan, "Supremacy by Stealth, "*Atlantic Monthly*, July–August 2003, 67–83.

7. Mikhail Gorbachev, "America Needs a Perestroika, and UN Funeral Is Way Too Premature," *Johnson's Russia List*, no. 7115, March 25, 2003.

8. "Making a Russian World Order," *Johnson's Russia List*, no. 7114, art. 6, March 25, 2003; "Russia Seeks to Bring US Back into the International Fold, Wants Role in Postwar Iraq," *Johnson's Russia List*, no. 7116, art. 14, March 25, 2003.

9. "Russia's Defence Minister Questions Reality of Strategic Partnership with Nato," *Johnson's Russia List*, no. 8154, art. 1, April 7, 2004. Alex Keto, "Russian Def Min Warns of Return to Cold Peace with West," *Johnson's Russia List*, no. 8154, art. 4, April 7, 2004. For a positive interpretation of Russia's new course, see the article by Russia's Foreign Minister Sergei Lavrov, "What a Strong Russia Wants," *Wall Street Journal* (reprinted in *Johnson's Russia List*, no. 8146, art. 4, March 31, 2004). He contends that Russia can have it all: a pragmatic policy based on domestic development interest and strong relations with America and the EU. Cf. James Billington, Russia in Search of Itself, Woodrow Wilson Press, Washington, DC, 2004.

10. "EU Must Compensate Russia for its Expansion, Says Economist," *Johnson's Russia List*, no. 8033, art. 12, January 16, 2004. Alexander Livschits said that Russia suffers poor terms of trade with EU because it faces high tariffs.

11. "Estonia Might Face 'Caribbean Crisis': Estonia's Policy of Provocation Can Trigger A Serious Crisis Between Russia and the West," *Johnson's Russia List*, no. 8138, art. 3, March 26, 2004. Sergei Ivanov, "As Nato Grows, So Do Russia's Worries," *New York Times* (reprinted in Johnson's Russia List, no. 8154, art. 9, April 7, 2004). RIA Novosti, "Moscow Believes Nato May Deploy Nuclear Weapons in Baltic Republics," *Johnson's Russia List*, no. 8166, art. 10, April 14, 2004. Yuri Baluyevsky, First Deputy Chief of General Staff, said that the Genshtab doesn't rule out Nato nuclear deployment in Lithuania, Latvia and Estonia. David Holley, "Russia Sees U.S. Nato Actions as Reason to Watch its Back: New Nuclear Arms and Alliane Expansion May Lead to Tougher Policy by Moscow," *Los Angeles Times*, March 26, 2004 (reprinted in *Johnson's Russia List*, no. 8138, art. 1, March 26, 2004). Yevgeny Grigoriev, "Russia in the Tenacious Grip of Nato: The Treaty on Conventional Armed Forces in Europe Can Be Given up for Lost," *Nezavisimoe Voennoe Obozrenie*, March 26, 2004 (reprinted in *Johnson's Russia List*, no. 3128, art. 5, March 16, 2004). "Russian Defence Ministry to Launch 'Patriotic Channel,'" *Johnson's Russia List*, no. 8138, art. 16, March 2004.

12. "Russia Starts Military Exercise Involving Nuclear Forces," *Johnson's Russia List*, no. 8058, art. 2, February 10, 2004. For a discussion of the troubled history of the

RSM-54 missiles which misfired during the exercise and during a subsequent test, see Moskovskiy Komsomolets, "Another Failed Missile Launch Claimed reprinted in *Johnson's Russia List*, no. 8130, art. 20, March 22, 2004). Pavel Felgenhauer, "Old ICBMs, Old Thinking," *Johnson's Russia List*, no. 8070, art. 1, February 17, 2004. Felgenhauer contends that the main point of the exercise is to test aging ICBMs. The war-game scenario is antiquated. The military is caught in a time warp: its hardware is old, its strategic ideas outdated.

13. Vladimir Putin announced Russian strategic missile forces would be equipped with the newest intercontinental missile complexes able to hit their targets at hypersonic speed, altering their initial flight pattern to defeat America's NMD system. "Russia Possesses Secret Weapon," *Johnson's Russia List*, no. 8140, art. 4, March 28, 2004.

14. Dmitri Suslov, "The United States Will Get Bogged Down in the CIS: Uzbekistan, Tajikistan, and Kyrgyzstan Waiting for Rapid Response Forces US Military Infrastructure is Moving Closer to Russia's Borders," *Nezavisimaya Gazeta*, March 26, 2004 (reprinted in *Johnson's Russia List*, no. 8318, art. 6, March 26, 2004). "Ivanov Opposed to Permanent US Military Presence in CIS States," *Johnson's Russia List*, no. 8154, art. 8, April 7, 2004. Sergei Ivanov, "Russia's Armed Forces and Geopolitical Priorities," *Johnson's Russia List*, no. 8043, art. 17, February 1, 2004. http://www.globalaffairs.ru

15. "Government Approves Economic Development Scenarios for 2005–2007," *Johnson's Russia List*, no. 8136, art. 4, March 25, 2004. Minister of Economic Development and Trade German Gref announced that Russia's GDP growth was forecasted to reach 6.4 percent in 2004, and 6.2 percent in 2005. The inflation rate is expected to decline to 10 percent in 2004, and 2–4 percent by 2010. Talk of catching up with Portugal and extending the triumphs of liberalization have become the official party line. In a fit of pique after essentially being told at the fifth international conference on the Economy's Competitiveness and Modernization by Deputy Prime Minister Alexander Zhukov that all must agree that there are only blue skies ahead, German Gref Minister of Economic Development retorted that Putin's plans can only be realized if there is luck with oil prices. See "Economy Minister Voices Doubts over President's Economic Plans," *Johnson's Russia List*, no. 8158, art. 1, April 9, 2004. For the full text see "Remarks by Presidential Staff and Government Top Officials at a Conference of the Higher School of Economics," *Johnson's Russia List*, no. 8158, art. 1, April 9, 2004. Cf. "Yavlinsky: Growth Without Development" *Russkii Fokus*, no. 12, April 5–11, 2004 (reprinted in *Johnson's Russia List*, no. 8155, art. 16, April 8, 2004). Also see "Russian Finance Ministry Submits the Concept of Continued Tax Reform to the Government," *Johnson's Russia List*, no. 8129, art. 10, March 21, 2004. As before tax reform will be regressive to "spur" development. The maximum unified social tax rate will fall from 35.6 to 26 percent. The value added tax will be reduced from 18 to 16 percent beginning in 2006.

16. Valeria Korchagin, "Putin Launches War on Poverty," *Moscow Times* (reprinted in *Johnson's Russia List*, no. 8130, art. 5, March 22, 2004). After his re-election Putin announced a war on poverty: the number of people living below the poverty line will halve from 20.4 to 10 percent by 2007. The poverty line is 2,143 rubles,

or $75 per month. This will be accomplished by increasing taxation on oil and reducing it on other sectors to help the economy diversify and grow more rapidly. Andrei Denisov and Natalia Rozhkova, "Putin Calculates the Cost of the Yeltsin Era," *Johnson's Russia List*, no. 8065, art. 8, February 11, 2004. Putin criticized Yeltsin for toying with people's longing for democracy, serious economic and social policy errors causing one-third of the population to live below the poverty line, widespread wage arrears, loss of savings, strikes, tax hikes, dependency on international assistance, foreign exploitation, international weakness, disregard for law, and separatism. "Russia, World Bank Agree on Poverty Reduction Strategy," *Johnson's Russia List*, no. 8155, art. 3, April 13, 2004.

17. "No New Redistribution of Private Property – Stepashin," *Johnson's Russia List*, no. 8141, art. 4, March 29, 2004. Russia's Audit Chamber Chairman and former Prime Minister Sergei Stepashin reported that "the analysis of the 10-year-long privatization, which is currently conducted by the Russian Audit Chamber, may reveal only 2 or 3 cases of violations," and suggest that they can be settled by supplementary payments.

18. Vitaly Shlykov, "The Anti-Oligarchic Campaign and Its Implications for Russia's Security," presented at the conference on Russian Security and the Continuing War on Terrorism, United States Naval Postgraduate School, Monterey, California, September 16–17, 2003. On March 28, 2004, Mikhail Khodorkovsky reportedly wrote a letter defending liberalism and declaring his support for Vladimir Putin. After many days of speculation about its meaning and ramifications, Khodorkovsky disclaimed authorship. He continues to languish in prison, providing an object lesson to all rent seekers who desire to turn the tables on Muscovy, converting rent into inalienable private property and setting themselves free. Mikhail Khodorkovsky, "The Crisis of Russian Liberalism," *Vedomosti*, March 29, 2004, reprinted in *Johnson's Russia List*, no. 8142, art. 2, 2004. Ron Popeski, "Business Must Accept Putin, Share Wealth – Khodorkovsky," *Johnson's Russia List*, no. 8142, art. 1, March 29, 2004. "Yabloko Agrees with Khodorkovsky's View of Russian Liberalism in Crisis," *BBC Monitoring*, March 30, 2004 (reprinted in *Johnson's Russia List*, no. 8143, art. 1, March 30, 2004). Irina Nagornykh, Natalia Gevorkjan, Illya Bulavinov, "The True Author of Mikhail Khodorkovsky's Article?" *Kommersant*, March 30, 2004 (reprinted in *Johnson's Russia List*, no. 8144, art. 1, March 30, 2004). "Liberal Leader Nemtsov Doubts Authenticity of Khodorkovsky's Article," *Johnson's Russia List*, no. 8144, March 30, 2004. Khodorkovsky Denies Writing Liberalism Article," *Johnson's Russia List*, no. 8153, art. 1, April 6, 2004. Nikolai Gulko, "Oligarchic Folklore. Deputy Justice Minister Yuri Kalinin Says He Has Evidence that Mikhail Khodorkovsky Did Not Write the "Crisis of Russian Liberalism Article. However This Doesn't Mean That Khodorkovsky Had Nothing to Do with the Article at All: It Is Based on His Thoughts, as Written Up by His Lawyers," *Kommersant* (reprinted in *Johnson's Russia List*, no. 8154, art. 21, April 7, 2004). Justice Ministry Probes into Khodorkovsky Article Origin," *Johnson's Russia List*, no. 8155, art. 7, 2004. Peter Baker, "Targets Another Mogul: Oil Firm Ordered to Pay $1 Billion in Back Taxes," *Washington Post* (reprinted in *Johnson's Russia List*, no. 8100, art. 7, 2004). Roman Abramovich's Sibneft billed 1 billion for underpaid taxes 2000–01.

19. The new Prime Minister Mikhail Fradkov has been hailed as friend of economic liberalization. However, he is an old FSB buddy of Putin, and was Sergei Ivanov's deputy on the Security Council before Ivanov became Minister of Defense. The administrative reforms he is touting as revolutionary are Soviet era reruns. See Yevgenia Obukhova, "The New Prime Minister Breaks Down the System," *Nezavisimaya Gazeta* (reprinted in *Johnson's Russia List*, no. 8151, April 5, 2004). Obukhova writes "From now on – as in Soviet times – the key role will be played by ministers responsible for specific sectors: Viktor Khristenko (Industry and Energy Ministry), Igor Levitin (Ministry of Transport and Communications), Andrei Fursenko (Ministry of Education and Science). Henceforth, they will set objectives for their sectors independently. There will no longer be a single center for economic reforms. In the previous government, planning was handled by the Economic Development and Trade Ministry, responsible for developing the concepts of all reforms. But now German Gref risks losing the leading role in the Cabinet." Nikolai Petrov, "4 Years of Reforming the Federal System," *Johnson's Russia List*, no. 8070, art. 16, February 17, 2004. Federal districts are Putin's vision of a monolitic society organized along military lines. Olga Kryshtanovskaya, "Dangerous People in Civilian Clothing: The Rise of the Security and Law Enforcement People," *Yezhenedelnyi Zhurnal* (reprinted in *Johnson's Russia List*, no. 8130, art. 13, March 22, 2004). Albert Weeks, "Siloviki – Soviet and Post–Soviet," *Johnson's Russia List*, no. 8014, art. 8, January 14, 2004. Weeks argues that siloviki are no more dominant today than during the Soviet period.

20. Arkady Ostrovsky, "Is Russian Democracy Becoming an Illusion," *Financial Times* (reprinted in *Johnson's Russia List*, no. 8042, art. 13, February 2004). Caroline McGregor, "New Yavlinsky Book (Peripheral Capitalism, 2003) Says Russia Run by 'Gosklan'," *Johnson's Russia List*, no. 8067, art. 4, February 15, 2004. Yavlinsky asserts that less than 150 people (Gosklan) make all the decisions in Russia, and stresses the importance of contingent property rights. Donald Rayfield reminds us that Russia "is ruled by a man who is, by career and choice, a successor to Yagoda and Beria," and today's FSB "has taken, in alliance with bandits and extortioners, the commanding heights of the country's government and economic riches, and goes on lying to, and when expedient murdering its citizens." See Simon Montefiore, book review of *Stalin and His Hangmen: an Authorittive Portrait of a Tyrant and Those who Served Him*, Viking 2004 (reprinted in *Johnson's Russia List*, no. 8114, art. 6, March 13, 2004).

21. Anna Badkhen, "Democracy on the Brink: Russia Back on Track to Absolute Rule, Democracy Activists Again Out in the Cold," *Johnson's Russia List*, no. 8109, art. 1, March 10, 2004. Simon Montefiore, "Democratic Despot," *New York Times*, (Op–Ed), March 14, 2004: "Vladimir Putin, who will be handily re-elected president of Russia today, is never going to become a Western-Style, liberal-democratic politician, no matter how much we wish it. He is a quintessentially Russian leader, with very traditional aspirations and interests, and until the West gets used to it, he will continue to be a tanatalizing source of frustration and disappointment." A reforming liberal leader in Russia is the Holy Grail of Kremlinology, but the search for one is as misguided and hopeless as that for the relic of the Last Supper. Believe it or not, some Western anaylsts in the 1930s

insisted that Stalin was a 'moderate,' controlled by extremists like the secret police chief Nikolai Yezhov." Anders Aslund "President Putin's Imitation of a Tsar
Is Doomed to Failure," *Sunday Telegraph* (reprinted in *Johnson's Russia List*,
no. 8116, art. 10, March 14, 2004. Aslund's assessment of Russia's government
after Putin's re-election was "Putin's system appears to be modelled on Tsarism.
The Tsar follows any whim without bothering with consultation. The bureaucracy
is given a free hand, and the secret police is perceived as the jewel in the crown.
Corruption is not only accepted but favoured." "The big question is not whether
Putin's system can survive – it cannot – but whether the hard nationalist trend
will be continued as Yegor Gaidar, the former prime minister, thinks or whether
Putin's restoration of Tsarism is a brief nightmare which will be followed by a new
liberalization." Nikolai Petrov, Stalin's System Reduplicated," *Kommersant-
Vlast*, no. 14 (reprinted in Johnson's Russia List, no. 8165, art. 7, 2004).

22. Mikhail Yuriev, "Krepost' Rossiia: Kontseptsiia dlia presidenta" (Fortress
    Russia: Concept for President Putin), *Novayagazeta*, no. 17, March 15, 2004
    (http://2004.novayagazeta.ru/nomer/2004/17n7n17n-s44.shtml). On Yuriev's
    background see http//www.biograph.comstar.ru-bank/yuriev.htm For a debate
    on similar views see Filosofko-ekonomicheskoe uchyonoe sobranie, Akademiia
    gumanitarnykh nauk, Moskovskii Gosudarstvennyi Universitet im. M. V.
    Lomonosova, Moscow, 17-18, 2002, http://eurasia.com.ru/mgu.html. Yuriev's
    views echo themes associated with Vladimir Zhirinovsky's Liberal Democratic
    Party of Russia.

23. George Tenet, Director of Central Intelligence, "The Worldwide Threat 2004:
    Challenges in a Changing Global Context," testimony before the Senate Select
    Committee on Intelligence, 24 February 2004, excerpted in *Johnson's Russia List*,
    no. 8089, art. 10, February 27, 2004. Douglas Jehl, "C.I.A. Says Russia Could Try
    to Reassert Itself After a Putin Victory, *New York Times* (reprinted in *Johnson's
    Russia List*, no. 8116, art. 11, March 14, 2004). "The re-election of Mr. Putin to a
    second four-year term would be the culmination of a process that has recentralized
    power in the Kremlin, including a domination of Russia's news organizations."
    Russia is "attempting to reclaim great power status. On balance, Russia's relations
    with the United States were more cooperative than not."

24. Andrew Jack, "Russia's Oligarchs Not Efficient Says World Bank," *Financial
    Times* (reprinted in *Johnson's Russia List*, no. 8154, art. 12, April 7, 2004). Ac-
    cording to the World Bank report after sampling more than 1,300 companies, the
    study concludes Russia's 23 largest business groups control more than a third of its
    industry by sales and at least a sixth of its jobs. The report concludes that oligarchs
    are not more efficient than companies controlled by foreign investors and other
    private owners. Only companies owned by federal and regional governments per-
    form worse." Christof Ruhl, chief economist for the World Bank's Moscow office,
    who coordinated the research said, "Russia needs to do what the Americans did
    100 years ago by introducing tough antitrust rules and anti-monopoly regulation
    to create fair competition." Also see Christof Ruehl, "Structural Change and
    Economic Growth: Transition to Development," *Vedomosti* (reprinted in *John-
    son's Russia List*, no. 8164, April 13, 2004. Cf. Carl Mortished, "Growing Power of

the Oligarchs Defies Putin; New Signs of Tycoons' Political Influence in Russia," *Times* (reprinted in *Johnson's Russia List*, no. 8160, art. 7, April 11, 2004. The tycoons account for the majority of the powerbrokers named in the 2004 edition of the Russia Index.

25. According to James Goldgeier, "Except for the three Baltic nations, the former Soviet Union (Russia, Ukraine, Belarus, the Caucasus, Moldova and Central Asia) is not on a path to integration with the West." Goldgeier, "A New European Divide," *Washington Post* (reprinted in *Johnson's Russia List*, no. 8140, art. 9, March 28, 2004).

26. Robert Hunter, "The West Must Now Reassess its Gamble on Russia," *Johnson's Russia List*, 8146, art. 16, March 19, 2004. Hunter, who was a former US ambassador to NATO from 1993 to 1998, asserts that the West must be clearer and more precise in setting benchmarks for acceptable Russian political reform.

27. Andrei Zlobin, "Washington's Nuclear Barn: The United States Will Not Honor the Strategic Offensive Reductions," *Vremya Novesti*, March 26, 2004 (reprinted in *Johnson's Russia List*, no. 8138, art. 4, March 26, 2004). Ian Hoffman, "U.S. Keeps Guard up Against Russia: Pentagon May Aim More Missiles at Russia," *Johnson's Russia List*, no. 8130, art. 1, March 22, 2004. This could reflect "the Air Force's desire to reinforce targeting of Russia's most threatening multi-warhead missiles, SS-18s and SS-19s. They were to have been scrapped under an early 1990s arms-reduction treaty that also committed the United States to single-warhead missiles."

28. On March 31, 2004, the U.S. House of Representatives passed a resolution stating Russia's continued inclusion in the G-8 should be conditioned on its acceptance and adherence to the "norms and standards of democracy." Analytical Department of RIA RosBusinessConsulting, "USA Intimidating Russia: "Americans are Threatening to Oust Russia from the G8, if Moscow Conducts Independent Domestic and Foreign Policies," (reprinted in *Johnson's Russia List*, no. 8166, art. 1, April 14, 2004). Peter Lavelle, "Analysis: No VIP Pass for Russia?" *Untimely Thoughts*, vol. 2, no. 45 (94) G–8, April 5, 2004, http://www.untimely-thoughts.com

29. Oliver Bullough, "Nato Chief Tries to Sweet-Talk Russia on Expansion," *Johnson's Russia List*, no. 8155, art. 6, April 8, 2004. Stephen Cohen however sees the administration's "autocratic" attitude as the cause of a new cold war. See "U.S. Professor Sees New Cold War Starting, Blames US," *Johnson's Russia List*, no. 8146, art. 11, March 19, 2004.

30. "Russian Party Leaders' Iraq Positions Reviewed: Russia Seen Lacking Power to Influence," *Johnson's Russia List*, no. 7118, art. 9, March 27, 2003; "Russia Says to Defend Postwar Oil Interests," *Johnson's Russia List*, no. 7119, art. 6, March 27, 2003.

31. Andrei Lipsky, in "What Iraq Means to Russia" (*Johnson's Russia List*, no. 7117, art. 3, March 26, 2003), quotes Vladimir Ryzhkov, Duma representative, as saying, "We shouldn't expect to gain anything. The Moscow-Berlin-Paris alliance is a complete fiction.... Has the Iraqi crisis drawn Russia and Europe closer together? No, it has not."

CHAPTER 9

1. This caveat applies to the Korean and Japanese models, neither of which are viewed as appropriate models for Muscovite economic reform.
2. Conquest can be viewed as a surrogate for direct foreign investment. It boils down to direct foreign misappropriation.
3. Andrew Hurst, "Russian Tycoon Says Wealth Must Be Spread More Widely," *Johnson's Russia List*, no. 7124, art. 2, March 31, 2003.
4. Aslund, "Amnesty the Oligarch." Cf. Philby Burgess, "The Tigers of Wrath Are Wiser Than the Horses of Instruction," March 27, 2003.
5. Evgeny Arshiukhin, "Oligarchs Demand – A Second Free One," *Rossiiskaya Gazeta*, April 1, 2003, reprinted in *Johnson's Russia List*, no. 7138, art. 3, April 10, 2003. Arshiukhin reports that the lower house's committee on property, supported by the RSPP (Russian Union of Industrialists and Entrepreneurs), demanded that the land on which enterprises stand should be transferred without cost to factory owners. This requires a revision of the land law passed just last year and will cost the government an estimated $100 billion dollars. According to "Russia to Privatize All Federal Property?" (*Johnson's Russia List*, no. 7252, art. 3, July 17, 2003), the Ministry of Property Relations plans to sell all federal property by 2008, and privatization revenues are $1.3 billion annually.
6. Rosefielde, "Illusion of Transition. According to an article published in *Johnson's Russia List*,

   Platon Lebedev, Chairman of the Board of the financial group MFO Menatep, and a major shareholder in Yukos oil company headed by Russia's wealthiest oligarch Mikhail Khodorkovsky was arrested on July 2, 2003 charged with stealing a 20 percent stake in the company Apatit worth 283 million dollars in 1994. Lebedev was subsequently incarcerated in the FSB prison, Lefortovo with access to an attorney. The action has been widely interpreted as a warning shot to Khodorkovsky to rein in his political opposition to Vladimir Putin. ("Yukos Head Decides to Stay Longer in the U.S.," *Johnson's Russia List*, no. 7249, art. 3, July 15, 2003)

   The action triggered a firestorm of speculation about a power play by the *siloviki*, presaging a "junta," and presidential denial. Whatever the ultimate outcome, the flap reveals the unsettled foundations of Putin's Muscovite system. The rise of Russian economic oligarchy was haphazard, with little thought given to its evolutionary trajectory beyond the belief that the president could make or break whoever he chose and thereby establish ultimate authority. Oligarchs were supposed to advocate democratic free enterprise but grasp its limits. Khodorkovsky, like Berezovsky before him, has opted to test these boundaries, leaving Putin with the option of slapping him down or compromising. Either way, there is a lesson: FSB cadre are more reliable than uppity oligarchs. If Putin is the idealist many imagine, this won't matter. Otherwise, he will grow increasing wary of independent-minded, monied opposition. See "Chekists in the Corridors of Power," *Novaya Gazeta*, no. 50, July 2003, reprinted in *Johnson's Russia List*, no. 7255, art. 4, July 18, 2003; Igor Fedotkin, "Confiscate and Divide," *Vedomosti*, July 18, 2003, reprinted in *Johnson's Russia List*, no. 7255, art. 3, July 18, 2003.

   ROMIR Monitoring has done a poll and discovered that the people of Russia take an extremely negative view of the role of oligarchs while supporting the idea of revising the outcomes of privatization – even going as far as criminal prosecution for "capitalists." Pollsters hope that the attitude to entrepreneurs will gradually improve, but meanwhile they describe Russian society as "a dangerous swamp." Fifteen hundred Russian citizens were approached by ROMIR Monitoring between July 9 and July 14. Poll results indicate that negative views of capitalists are steadily exacerbating: 74 percent of respondents view the role of entrepreneurs in Russia's history over the last decade as negative or partially negative, and 77 percent blame entrepreneurs for the current state of affairs. Only 19 percent of respondents praise the oligarchs for the role they played in the 1990s, and 17 percent praise them for their current role. Seventy-seven percent of respondents believe that the outcomes of privatization should be revised, fully or partially; only 18 percent categorically object to the idea. The revisionists include business owners (77 percent), administrators (88 percent), and people with college degrees (87 percent). College students (53 percent) and young people (between 18 and 34) are the least revolutionary. Among the latter, only 63 percent of respondents advocate revising privatization results. Moreover, 57 percent of respondents would not object to seeing the state prosecute entrepreneurs, while 31 percent do not rule out the possibility in "special cases." This attitude is based on the firm belief that fortunes were made unlawfully in the first place: 88 percent of respondents are convinced that all the big fortunes in Russia were made "dishonestly," and only 6 percent are prepared to believe in their legitimate origins. Even 72 percent of business owners taking part in the poll are sure that Russia's big fortunes have unlawful origins. "The public views oligarchs rather as representatives of the regime who ended up with property and assets because of fraud, not as particularly successful businesspeople," said Alexander Muzafarov of ROMIR Monitoring.

According to Clem Cecil, writing in *The Times*,

The billionaire tycoons who control Russia's economy are alarmed by signs that President Putin may order an investigation into the burst of privatisations which handed them the country's most valuable natural assets. The Moscow stock market fell sharply this week, tumbling another 5 per cent yesterday, after police raided the offices of Yukos, Russia's largest oil company, to investigate allegations of embezzlement and tax fraud. Armed men in masks forced the company's security guards to the ground and searched the archive through the night. They left 17 hours later, carrying videos and documents. The judicial campaign against Yukos has prompted fears among Russia's richest men that they, too, might be investigated. They made their wealth almost overnight during the flawed privatizations of state-owned natural resources in the 1990s. A dozen "oligarchs", such as Mikhail Khodorkovsky, became billionaires after assets they acquired for relatively modest sums were revalued. Hoping to halt the fall in the stock market, which threatened to precipitate an economic crisis, Mikhail Kasyanov, the Russian Prime Minister, told investors that the privatisations were irreversible. He admitted that the process had been imperfect, but said it had provided advantages by introducing competition. Yet investors are alarmed by the prospect of a civil war between business and the Government. Yesterday a lobby group representing the oligarchs urged parliament to approve a law barring any review of privatizations that took place more than three years ago. Arkadi Volsky, the head of the Union of Industrialists and Entrepreneurs, said: "I believe it would be wrong to re-examine the results of the privatisations. I believe that the longest period a review of privatisations should stretch back is three years." The criminal investigation into Yukos appears to violate a secret truce between the oligarchs and Mr Putin, who agreed not to examine the privatisation deals if the oligarchs did not stray into politics. But Mr Khodorkovsky has ventured into the political arena, even hinting that he might run for president in 2008. The country's richest man, he is thought to be worth Pounds 5 billion. He has outgrown Russia's stock market and the "rules of play" that exist between the state and business in a country where the rule of law is hazy. This week he suggested that the investigation against Yukos was politically motivated. "Law enforcement agencies are using the law for personal interests," he said. "It will be clear by the end of the year what damage the country has suffered from this." Mr Khodorkovsky has taken steps to protect Yukos in case it is seized and he is forced into self-imposed exile to avoid prison, as the oligarchs Boris Berezovsky and Vladimir Gusinsky have been. He has drawn up an emergency plan which includes the appointment of Lord Rothschild as a potential chief executive of Yukos. A fellow oligarch, Roman Abramovich, has also been in the line of fire, accused by Sergei Stepashin, head of the Russian Parliament's Accounting Chamber and a close ally of Mr Putin, of evading Pounds 175 million in taxes. Mr Stepashin implied that Mr Abramovich had used the money to buy Chelsea Football Club. ("Russian Oligarchs Fear Putin Inquiry into Their Wealth," *The Times*, July 18, 2003, reprinted in *Johnson's Russia List*, no. 7256, art. 2, July 18, 2003.)

On July 17 the results of the privatisation were brought up by TV station TVTs which asked its viewers to answer the question: "if the results of privatisation were revised would people live better or worse?" 9.5 thousand of the 10 thousand respondents said they would live "better." (Dissatisfaction with Privatisation in Russia Rings Out," *Johnson's Russia List*, no. 7257, art. 5, July 20, 2003.)

7.   "Chekists in the Corridors of Power," *Novaya Gazeta*, no. 50, July 2003, reprinted in *Johnson's Russia List*, no. 7255, art. 4, July 18, 2003:

THE CLAN OF "SECURITY PEOPLE FROM ST. PETERSBURG", TO ALL APPEARANCES A BONA FIDE JUNTA, NUMBERS UP TO 6,000 PEOPLE. PERSONNEL WITH A BACKGROUND IN THE FEDERAL SECURITY SERVICE – THE FSB, SUCCESSOR TO THE KGB – PROVIDE A FOUNDATION FOR THE INCUMBENT REGIME.

Vladimir Putin – President of the Russian Federation. Lieutenant Colonel of the Federal Security Service (FSB).

Administration, Security Council

Viktor Ivanov – Deputy Director of the Presidential Administration (personnel). In 1999 and 2000 he was deputy director of the FSB. Igor Sechin – Deputy Director of the Presidential Administration. In the Soviet era he worked in Mozambique under cover as a Tekhnoeksport official (officially a translator from Portuguese).

Vladimir Osipov – head of the Presidential Personnel Directorate. Ex-officer of the central apparatus of the KGB.

Igor Porshnev – head of the Presidential Information Directorate. Worked at the foreign broadcasting service of the Soviet Gosteleradio (State Television and Radio) and in India (officially a journalist).

Vyacheslav Soltaganov – Deputy Secretary of the Security Council. Served in the Border Troops of the Soviet KGB.

Regional Leaders

Murat Zyazikov – President of Ingushetia. Deputy chief of the Astrakhan Regional Directorate of the FSB between January 1996 and January 2002.

Vladimir Kulakov – Voronezh governor. Chief of the Voronezh Regional Directorate of the FSB.

Viktor Maslov – Smolensk governor. Chief of the Smolensk Regional Directorate of the FSB.

Government, Ministries, Departments

Sergei Ivanov – Defense Minister. Officer of the KGB in the Soviet era. Andrei Chernenko – Deputy Interior Minister and Chief of the Immigration Service. Ex-chief of the PR Department of the Interior Ministry. Vyacheslav Trubnikov – Deputy Foreign Minister. Former head of the South Asia Department in the Soviet KGB. Anatoly Safonov – Deputy Foreign Minister. Former head of the Krasnoyarsk Territorial Directorate of the KGB. Yuri Demin – Senior Deputy Justice Minister. Former senior investigator of the Oktyabrsky District Department of the Moscow Regional Directorate of the KGB. Alexander Yelizarov – Deputy Justice Minister. Former KGB officer. Yevgeny Sidorenko – Deputy Justice Minister (registration of parties and organizations). Former KGB officer. Anatoly Kotelnikov – Deputy Nuclear Energy Minister. Former head of the Yaroslavl Regional Directorate of the FSB. Vladimir Kozlov – Deputy Media Minister. Former KGB officer. Gennadi Moshkov – Deputy Transport Minister. Former head of the Kaliningrad Regional Directorate of the FSB (1999). Nikolai Negodov – Deputy Transport Minister. Former senior deputy chief of the St. Petersburg and Leningrad Regional Directorate of the FSB. Vladimir Strzhalkovsky – Deputy Minister for Economic Development. Former KGB officer. Vladimir Makarov – Senior Deputy Chairman of the State Customs Committee. Former deputy head of the Personnel Directorate of the Soviet KGB. Leonid Lobzenko – Senior Deputy Chairman of the State Customs Committee. Former KGB officer. Igor Mezhakov – Deputy Chairman of the State Customs Committee. Former deputy director of the FSB.

Sergei Verevkin-Rokhalsky – Senior Deputy Taxes and Duties Minister. Former head of the Sakhalin Regional Directorate of the FSB. Anatoly Tsybulevsky – Deputy Director of the Federal Tax Police Service. Former head of a directorate of the FSB.

Vladimir Lazovsky – Deputy Director of the Federal Tax Police Service. Former deputy head of the Rostov Municipal Department of the Rostov Regional Directorate of the KGB. Alexei Sedov – Deputy Director of the Federal Tax Police Service. Ex-senior investigator of the St. Petersburg and Leningrad Regional Directorate of the FSB.

Vladimir Senin – Deputy Director of the Federal Tax Police Service. Former KGB officer. Alexander Grigoriev – General Director of the Russian Agency for State Reserves. Former senior deputy chief of the St. Petersburg and Leningrad Regional Directorate of the FSB. Alexander Spiridonov – Deputy Chairman of the Financial Monitoring Committee. Former KGB officer.

Federation Council

Valery Bykov – representative of the Kamchatka regional administration. Former investigator of the special department of the KGB of the Black Sea Fleet. Yuri Volkov – representative of the administration of the Nenetsk Autonomous

District. Former KGB officer. Valery Golubev – representative of the Leningrad regional legislature. Since 1980 he has worked in foreign intelligence, resigning at the rank of lieutenant colonel. Nikolai Kosarev – representative of the Tambov regional legislature. Former KGB officer. Mikhail Margelov – representative of the Pskov regional administration. Former instructor of Arabic at the Supreme School of the Soviet KGB.

Vladimir Melnikov – representative of the Chita regional administration. Former officer of the Chita Regional Directorate of the KGB. Chandyr Udumbara – representative of the Supreme Khural of the Republic of Tyva. Chief of the Tyva Republican Directorate of the FSB between 1993 and 2001.

Igor Morozov – representative of the Ryazan regional legislature. Former officer of the 1st Main Directorate of the Soviet KGB and Russian Foreign Intelligence Service. Oleg Panteleev – representative of the Kurgan regional administration. Graduated from the Andropov Red Banner Institute of the KGB.

CHAPTER 10

1. James Schlesinger, CIA conference, Princeton, NJ, March 9, 2000.
2. The code still applies. The United States knew Russia was helping Saddam Hussein with senior military advisors, espionage, and prohibited weapons but said, and continues to say, little publically to protect the larger relationship. According to David Harrison,

> Top secret documents obtained by The Telegraph in Baghdad show that Russia provided Saddam Hussein's regime with wide-ranging assistance in the months leading up to the war, including intelligence on private conversations between Tony Blair and other Western leaders. Moscow also provided Saddam with lists of assassins available for "hits" in the West and details of arms deals to neighboring countries. The documents detailing the extent of the links between Russia and Saddam were obtained from the heavily bombed headquarters of the Iraqi intelligence service in Baghdad yesterday. Tony Blair is referred to in a report dated March 5, 2002, and marked: "Subject – SECRET." In the letter, an Iraqi intelligence official explains that a Russian colleague had passed him details of a private conversation between Mr Blair and Silvio Berlusconi, the Italian prime minister, at a meeting in Rome. The two had met for an annual summit on February 15, 2002, in Rome. The document says that Mr Blair "referred to the negative things decided by the United States over Baghdad". Another document, dated March 12, 2002, appears to confirm that Saddam had developed, or was developing nuclear weapons. The Russians warned Baghdad that if it refused to comply with the United Nations then that would give the United States "a cause to destroy any nuclear weapons". ("Revealed: Russia Spied on Blair for Saddam," *Johnson's Russia List*, no. 7143, art. 1, April 13, 2003.)

> Cf. Robert Collier, Bill Wallace, and Chronicle staff writers, "Iraq–Russia Spy Link Uncovered," *San Francisco Chronicle*, April 13, 2003, reprinted in *Johnson's Russia List*, no. 7143, art. 3, April 13, 2003. According to this article,

> A Moscow-based organization was training Iraqi intelligence agents as recently as last September – at the same time Russia was resisting the Bush administration's push for a tough stand against Saddam Hussein's regime, Iraqi documents discovered by The Chronicle show. The documents found Thursday and Friday in a Baghdad office of the Mukhabarat, the Iraqi secret police, indicate that at least five agents graduated Sept. 15 from a two-week course in surveillance and eavesdropping techniques, according to

certificates issued to the Iraqi agents by the "Special Training Center" in Moscow. The Russian government, which has expressed intense disagreement with the U.S.-led war on Iraq, has repeatedly denied giving any military or security assistance to the Hussein regime. Any such aid would violate U.N. sanctions that have severely limited trade, military and other relations with Iraq since 1991. The U.S. State Department reacted cautiously Friday to the information unearthed by The Chronicle, saying it could not comment on matters that are the subject of current intelligence operations. But Lou Fintor, a State Department spokesman, said the U.S. government has repeatedly criticized Russian officials for giving assistance to Iraq and has had recent contacts with the Russian government in which it complained about the problem. "We consider this a serious matter and have raised it with senior levels of the Russian government," Fintor said. "They have repeatedly denied that they are providing material assistance to Iraq, but we gave them sufficient information (during the last two contacts) to let them know that we expected them to take action." Experts in Iraqi and Russian intelligence operations were not surprised that Mukhabarat officials had received specialized training in Russia.

Nick Paton Walsh, in an article entitled "Russia Denies Helping to Train Iraqi Intelligence" (*The Guardian*, April 14, 2003, reprinted in *Johnson's Russia List*, no. 7144, art. 5, April 14, 2003), states that

Russia has dismissed reports of cooperation between its foreign intelligence service and the feared Iraqi mukhabarat, ranging from espionage training to passing on sensitive information about Tony Blair's meeting with the Italian prime minister, Silvio Berlusconi. An SVR spokesman said yesterday: "We do not comment on baseless and unproven assertions published in the tabloids". Yet the Guardian can reveal that two former generals in the Soviet military went to Baghdad in the weeks immediately before the war. Gen Vladislav Achalov, a former deputy defense minister and a former commander of airborne and rapid-reaction forces, and Gen Igor Maltsev, an expert in air defense systems, left Baghdad six days before the war began.

3. Joshua Kurlantzick, "Can Burma Reform?" *Foreign Affairs* 81, no. 6 (2002): 133–46.

4. See "Putin Russia May Forgive Soviet-Era Iraq Debt," *Johnson's Russia List*, no. 7142, art. 5, April 12, 2003, according to which Iraq owes Russia $8 billion for Soviet era weapons purchases. Also see "Russia May Seek Easier Conditions for Repaying Foreign Debts," *Johnson's Russia List*, no. 7142, art. 6, April 12, 2003. But cf. "Russia Ministers Say Moscow Won't Drop Iraq Debt," *Johnson's Russia List*, no. 7143, art. 7, April 13, 2003, according to which Finance Minister Alexei Kudrin flatly contradicted Vladimir Putin's statement that Russia will consider dropping some of its debt claims on Iraq. This is a typical example of Russia's evasive "glasnost." Finally, see Josef Hebert, "U.S. to Build Power Plants in Russia," *Johnson's Russia List*, no. 7198, art. 3, May 28, 2003.

5. The murder of the liberal parliamentarian Sergei Yushenkov on April 17, 2003 (the tenth Duma member and second Liberal Democratic Party leader to die since 1994), is particularly distressing. He was the principal advocate of Hayekian democratic free enterprise operating under the rule of law and had just won the right of his party to participate in the upcoming parliamentary elections. The assassination appears to have been motivated by a desire to take the liberal agenda off the table. Sergei Kovalyov, a leading liberal lawmaker, in an open letter to Putin accused his government or its "circle" of complicity. See "Russian Lawmaker's Slaying Marks Ominous Debut of Duma Vote," *Johnson's Russia*

List, no. 7147, art. 1, April 19, 2003. Cf. Mark Weir, "Sergei Yushenkov: Defender of Russian Democracy," *Johnson's Russia List*, no. 7147, art. 2, April 19, 2003; Amy Knight, "A Modern Crime and Punishment: Who Killed Russia's Leading Liberal?" *The Globe and Mail*, April 23, 2003, reprinted in *Johnson's Russia List*, no. 7153, art. 12, April 24, 2003. Knight, a specialist in Russian security affairs, is the author of several books, including, most recently, *Who Killed Kirov? The Kremlin's Greatest Mystery*. In "A Modern Crime and Punishment," she writes,

Don't even think about it – that last week's murder of Sergei Yushenkov, Russian Duma deputy and co-chairman of the pro-democracy Liberal Russia party, was politically inspired. Because when you start considering motives, it leads you straight to President Vladimir Putin's security police. Mr. Yushenkov, who was shot to death April 17 outside his Moscow apartment house, had long been a fierce critic of the Kremlin's war in Chechnya, orchestrated by the Russian security service, the FSB. Mr. Yushenkov also took a leading role in the Duma's ongoing investigation of the 1999 apartment bombings in Russia that killed more than 300 people. Vladimir Putin, who was prime minister at the time, blamed the Chechens for the bombings, and then used the tragedy as an excuse to invade Chechnya. But when FSB employees were caught red-handed planting a bomb in the basement of an apartment in the city of Ryazan, suspicions about the Moscow bombings were directed at their agency. Although FSB officials claimed that the whole thing was a hoax and that the explosive powder was just sugar, they never offered convincing proof. As if that were not enough to raise the ire of the FSB against him, Mr. Yushenkov had connections with business tycoon Boris Berezovsky, a fierce enemy of the Kremlin and Liberal Russia's chief financial backer when it was founded last year. The party later expelled Mr. Berezovsky, who lives in exile in London, for courting former Communists, and Mr. Yushenkov broke off relations with him. But the FSB probably never forgave Mr. Yushenkov for distributing Mr. Berezovsky's film alleging that the FSB was behind the 1999 bombings. Mr. Yushenkov was aware that his politics had made him enemies. After fellow Duma member and Liberal party co-founder, Vladimir Golovlev, was shot to death last August, Mr. Yushenkov, according to one source, was "clearly frightened" that he would be the next victim. But that did not deter him from furthering his democratic political goals. Just hours before he was killed, Mr. Yushenkov announced that Liberal Russia had managed to achieve the crucial registration necessary to run in the parliamentary elections next December. Imagine what a thorn in the FSB's side Liberal Russia could be during the election campaign, especially if its members continue to harp on the FSB's possible involvement in the 1999 bombings. What better way to intimidate Liberal Russia's supporters than to have one of their leaders knocked off? No, don't even go there. Because if you suggest that the FSB was behind the Yushenkov murder, then you can't ignore the question of where Vladimir Putin stands in all of this. President Putin is one of the FSB's staunchest advocates. Just last month, Mr. Putin announced that he was strengthening the FSB's already substantial powers. As of this July, the Federal Border Guard Service, which commands over 100,000 troops, will be placed under the FSB's authority. In addition, Russia's powerful Federal Agency for Government Communications and Information, known by its Russian acronym as FAPSI, is being disbanded. The FSB will inherit all its domestic electronic- intelligence functions. (As one observer noted, it is like the FBI taking over the operations of the U.S. National Security Agency.) In transferring the border guards and key FAPSI functions to the FSB, the Russian President is transforming this agency into a supra security body, much like the former KGB. Why does President Putin continue to give the FSB so much power, especially considering its reputation for corruption and organized-crime connections? Because this agency is a crucial base of support for him. When Mr. Putin himself headed the FSB in 1998–1999, he brought in many of his former KGB colleagues from St. Petersburg, including the current director, Nikolai Patrushev, to serve under him. These men can be counted on to help preserve Mr. Putin's authority in the face of political challenges, including those that could arise in the upcoming parliamentary and presidential elections. The fact that Mr. Yushenkov is the third liberal lawmaker to be killed in less than five years suggests that politics in Russia can be a dangerous business, particularly if you are a critic of the Kremlin. The FSB is supposed to help solve these killings, along with a host of other apparent contract murders of politicians and journalists. But no one expects this to happen. Ironically, Vladimir Putin was head of the FSB when Duma deputy and human-rights activist Galina Starovoitova – another harsh critic of the security services – was gunned down outside her St. Petersburg apartment in November, 1998. Although Mr. Putin vowed to find the killers, and the FSB detained hundreds of suspects in the immediate aftermath, Ms. Starovoitova's murder has never been solved. Unfortunately, the same scenario will probably be repeated with the investigation of Mr. Yushenkov's killing. Despite the FSB's awesome powers and the vast arsenal of forensic expertise at its disposal, this agency has a dismal record of protecting Russian citizens from the violence and lawlessness that pervade their country. On Friday, Sergei Kovalev, a former dissident who was imprisoned by the KGB for his political beliefs and who is now a prominent Russian parliamentarian, sent an open letter to the Russian President in which he dared to express the unthinkable: "The people who ordered and organized Yushenkov's death . . . could be people who are supporting the current vector of political development in Russia, secret or open co-authors of this course – in other words, your supporters, Mr. President." Although Mr. Kovalev was careful to say that he had no reason to suspect current FSB officials, this possibility cannot have been far from his mind.

6. Rosefielde, *Comparative Economic Systems*, chap. 9.
7. Charles Hanley, "U.S., Russia Sign Reactor Shutdown Deal," *Johnson's Russia List*, no. 7100, art. 6, March 12, 2003. According to Hanley,

The United States and Russia signed agreements on Wednesday reviving an on-again, off-again deal to shut down the last three Russian reactors producing nuclear weapons–grade plutonium. Under terms of the accords, the United States will spend an estimated $500 million on two new fossil-fuel power plants to replace the reactors, which provide heat and electricity to Seversk and Zheleznogorsk. The Siberian cities once were secret, "closed" locations of the Soviet military establishment. They signed the documents at Vienna's Hofburg Congress Hall, on the sidelines of a three-day global conference, co-sponsored by their governments, on another non-proliferation concern, the potential for development of terrorist "dirty bombs" – conventional, non-nuclear bombs packed with radioactive materials. A U.S.–Russian deal under which Washington was to help phase out the plutonium reactors was first signed in 1997, and was celebrated as a historic event in the costly U.S. campaign to ensure that Moscow safeguarded and reduced its vast nuclear stockpile. The Russians, who have shut down 10 other plutonium-producing plants, continued operating the two at Seversk and one at Zheleznogorsk because they were vital to the power supplies of the cities, formerly known as Tomsk-7 and Krasnoyarsk-26. They continued reprocessing the spent uranium fuel from the power plants into plutonium not to make bombs, but because indefinite storage of the spent fuel would have been prohibitively expensive. The 1997 deal foundered, however, because its original goal of modifying the reactors proved impractical, and because of Russian financing problems and disputes over American audits on use of U.S. funds. The original plan envisioned conversion by 2001. Now, under Wednesday's agreements, the Seversk shutdown is to take place by 2008, and the shutdown at Zheleznogorsk by 2011. The governments hope displaced staff will be re-employed under the "Nuclear Cities" program, a U.S.-financed effort to develop jobs elsewhere in Russia for workers from the former "closed cities." The three plants are the source of 3,300 pounds of plutonium a year, roughly enough to make one nuclear bomb per day.

8. Wayne Merry, "State Department Remains Non-Transparent on Russian Policy," *Johnson's Russia List*, no. 7153, art. 3, April 24, 2003. Merry writes,

> It is an irony of the post–Cold War world that our former adversaries are sometimes more forthcoming in releasing policy-related documents about East-West policy than is Washington (but, then, we won the Cold War, didn't we?). As a case in point, consider the following story of the State Department, its Dissent Channel, and the Freedom of Information Act. While serving in the Political Section of the US Embassy in Moscow in the early Nineties, I became disenchanted (to put it diplomatically) with the "Washington consensus" and US missionary efforts – led by the Treasury and IMF – to attempt to remake Russia in our image of what it should be. Many more astute commentators have written publicly about this subject in recent years, but I was among the few insiders who put doubts down on official paper at the time. The Moscow Embassy, to its credit, has a tradition of encouraging dissenting views (within limits). Ambassadors Strauss, Pickering and Collins allowed me to send in doubting analyses on a number of occasions, labeled as solely my views rather than as cleared Embassy product. In early 1994, my conviction that US "reform" policy in Russia was badly misconceived and likely both to fail and to damage US interests led to my "long dissent telegram", a fairly massive denunciation of official policy. While Ambassador Pickering was willing to send it as an expression of individual views, vehement objections from Embassy officers serving the Gore-Chernomyrdin Commission persuaded me the message was more appropriate for the State Department's Dissent Channel. Dissent Channel, a product of the Vietnam War era, is an established vehicle for the submission of dissenting views on important policy issues. Messages in this channel are not subject to clearance procedures and are distributed to the top policy officials of the State Department, but not to other parts of the government. Dissent Channel rarely changes policy, but is a venting mechanism (and a way of identifying troublemakers). It has been used more often than one might think. My long Dissent Channel message of 1994 was submitted and, predictably, had no influence on policy whatsoever. Then-Deputy Secretary of State Strobe Talbott did respond to the message in a thoughtful and respectful letter which showed he had given my arguments time and consideration. I appreciated the courtesy, which is a good deal more than most State dissenters ever receive. After retiring from the Foreign Service, it occurred to me that this text, ineffectual though it had been, would be a useful addition to the material under review by scholars examining the Clinton-Yeltsin years of US policy toward Russia. I therefore requested its release under the Freedom of Information Act on July 27, 1999. Hearing nothing for months, I made discrete inquiries and was told my request was viewed as politically "hot" in light of the upcoming 2000 presidential contest. This struck me as silly, as my views on Russia of five years before could not alter a single vote in an American election. Therefore, I renewed my request on March 29, 2000, and received only a "Dear Sir or Madam, Don't Call Us, We'll Call You" response. Imagine my surprise this week actually to receive a formal response to my FOIA request! Dated April 17, and thus almost four years after my initial request, the State Department denies release of the message on the grounds that "release and public circulation of Dissent Channel messages, even as in your case to the drafter of the message, would inhibit the willingness of Department personnel to avail themselves of the Dissent Channel to express their views freely." In addition, as "Dissent Channel messages are deliberative, pre-decisional and constitute intra-agency communications" they cannot be released. Doublethink lives! It strikes me that making Dissent Channel messages public at the request of the drafters would probably attract Department personnel to use the mechanism rather than the contrary. In addition, I should think scholars

would find "pre-decisional" documents of greater interest than post-decisional ones. That dissent is so threatening to the established order of the State Department that it cannot be revealed even years after the event reflects a mindset familiar to anyone who has had the opportunity to examine the materials made public from former Communist governments about their decision-making processes. Let me conclude by dissuading any reader from the notion that my 1994 Dissent Channel message could constitute any kind of "smoking gun" indictment against US policy or policymakers of the time. So far as I recall the message (and it was about seventy-five paragraphs long), it expressed doubts that Russia could or would respond to US-designed reform stimuli and argued that US intrusion into Russian decisions about how to restructure their own economy would both fail and produce resentment toward the United States. I am sure the analysis would, in retrospect, appear lacking in many keys points of criticism and add little to the detailed writings on the subject of respected scholars. Nonetheless, I see no reason why it should not become part of the public record, along with the vast number of pre-decisional documents declassified to accommodate the memoirs of senior officials from administrations of all political hues. The difference is that former policymakers cherrypick documents for declassification to demonstrate how they did everything right. Is it so terrible that less than the statutory thirty years must pass before some documentation to the contrary can become public? In any case, I intend to appeal, with every expectation the next denial will also consume years. E. WAYNE MERRY, Senior Associate, American Foreign Policy Council, 1521 16th Street, NW, Washington, DC 20036, 202-462-6055, Fax 202-462-6045, Email merry@afpc.org

9. Kaplan, "Supremacy by Stealth."
10. Andrei Kokoshin, "Seven Surprises from the War in Iraq: The Anglo-Saxons have Suffered a Moral and Political Defeat," *Nezavisimaya Gazeta*, April 7, 2003, reprinted in *Johnson's Russia List*, no. 7133, art. 5, April 7, 2003. Kokoshin, chairman of the Duma committee for affairs of the CIS and compatriots, former senior deputy defense minister and secretary of the Russian Security Council, and corresponding member of the Russian Academy of Science, argues as follows:

The course of the Iraqi war enables arriving at several conclusions regarding the constellation of surprising political-military, strategic and operational-tactical phenomena (surprises), which the U.S. and Britain have faced.

First surprise: the Anglo-Saxons don't possess the overwhelming supremacy in the media sphere. Availability of the Euro news has undermined the television news monopoly of CNN and the BBC, at least in the Euro-Atlantic area. The Al-Jazeera television channel has become a factor of political-psychological influence not in the Arab East alone, but also the world community on the whole, penetrating even the information space of CNN.

This is a radical distinction of the current situation from that of March–April 2003 and what was taking place during Operation Desert Storm in 1991 and during the war of the United States and its NATO allies in Yugoslavia in 1999.

The electronic media eventually determine the winner and the loser in the war, especially in the moral and political aspects.

Second surprise: behavior of Turkey, which has been considered America's most significant outpost in the Middle East along with Israel (and established specific relations with Israel). Turkey's refusal to be involved in the war against Iraq in the alliance with the coalition forces has proved to be unexpected for the White House especially since Turkey is coming through financial and economic hardships. The finance worth of approximately $30 billion (grants and loans), which the U.S. offered, is imperative for the Turkish economy.

For the first time over many decades, the leadership of the Turkish General Staff, which was trying to influence the government and the parliament to ensure Turkey's direct involvement in the coalition headed by the U.S. has failed.

The third surprise concerns absence of mass actions on the part of the Shiites in south Iraq against Saddam Hussein's regime in support of the United States and its allies. Moreover, as some sources say, the Shiite clergy have been active at speaking against the United States, especially because two (Najaf and Karbala in Iraq) of the main Muslim sacred places (the town of Kum in Iran being the third) are jeopardized.

The fourth surprise is that the methods of psychological influence on the armed forces of Iraq, which, contrary to expectations of Washington and London, are not hastening to surrender their weapons on the scale similar to the events of 1991, are working very bad. In the meantime, the Anglo-Saxons are said to be remarkable experts of the propaganda.

Fifth surprise: inability of the U.S. military machinery, having its powerful reconnaissance-intelligence and the striking components, to destroy the system of state and military control of Iraq.

Sixth surprise: relatively high efficiency of semi-armed formations.

Seventh surprise: in the eye of the Arab and the Muslim world on the whole, Saddam Hussein is changing the cloak of the tyrant into apparel of a hero, the leader, who didn't break under the pressure of the gigantic political, economic, military and propaganda might of the United States. (The fact that many groups of Iraqi emigrants previously opposed to Hussein have decided to stop criticizing him mirrors that phenomenon.) In particular, this has been a bad service to moderate regimes at many of the Arab states, which are becoming more vulnerable to the radicals.

All of these unforeseen events and phenomena, which by far exceed the common "war debate" (under Clausewitz) and some other circumstances have brought the U.S. government and military command to face the hardest dilemma: either to take Baghdad by storm, or start besieging it (using raids by the special forces, high-precision strikes, etc.).

If the coalition forces initiate a storm, they'd lose their main advantage – ability to have the enemy detected and hit at a larger distance than that at which the enemy may locate and kill them. The last time the U.S. troops were involved in the city fights during the Vietnam War, in the town of Hue, fighting almost an equal by its strength grouping of the ground forces (two Vietnamese divisions), but having the overwhelming supremacy in the firepower, as a renowned U.S. expert B. Posen says, [the U.S.] lost 600 soldiers killed and 3,600 wounded. At the same time, the major part of the city was razed to the ground. Over the past few years, among the U.S.'s allies Israel has alone worked out the tactics of city fights using heavy military hardware (from the experience of extensive studies of the Grozny fights during the first Chechen campaign), including the special armored personnel carrier vehicle produced on the basis of T-55 Soviet tank, an armored bulldozer and the Mercava tank. However, no evidence proving that the American and the British soldiers adopted this experience (judging at least by the fights in Basra) is available. However, even this kind of experience has a restricted significance for fights in any Iraqi city, since the Israelis use their tactics to destroy relatively small and isolated groups of Palestine radicals.

Siege of Baghdad, a city with the population of 5 million, is pregnant with tremendous losses among the civilians, a humanitarian catastrophe. Under the absence of the Anglo-Saxon media supremacy, this will echo in all spots of the world, including the United States, where the peak of the anti-war movement and its influence on the U.S. political elite might not [have] been passed yet.

It goes almost without [saying that] a military victory [for] America and the coalition partners will be obtained – even though with huge losses and not as soon as many have expected. It is, however, clear that in the political respect this victory will prove to be something else than the Washington "hawks" and their listeners in Washington, London and other capitals have been counting on.

The war may entail quite different economic aftermaths, at least the short- and medium-term consequences. They may increase the probability that the recession may be prolonged in the three "centers of force" of the global economy (the United States, European Union and Japan) for a few months, which will negatively affect the Russian economy as well.

The leaders and countries, which, because they belong to the "axis of evil," are expecting similar actions on the part of the U.S. will make most serious conclusions [from] these surprises (and some other which may emerge).

Cf. Pavel Felgenhauer, "The Elite's Feeling the Heat," *Moscow Times*, April 10, 2003, reprinted in *Johnson's Russia List*, no. 7139, art. 5, April 10, 2003. According to Felgenhauer,

As the war in Iraq winds to its inevitable end, uneasy reflections are taking over Russia's political and military elite. No one in Moscow ever seriously believed that Saddam Hussein might indeed "defeat" the allied forces. But the speed and decisiveness of the offensive has bewildered many.

Russian generals were expecting another prolonged so-called non-contact war, like the one against Yugoslavia in 1999, in Afghanistan in 2001 or the first gulf war in 1991, when a four-day ground offensive was preceded by a 39-day air bombardment. It was believed that the Americans were afraid of close hand-to-hand encounters, they would not tolerate the inevitable casualties, and that in the final analysis they were cowards who relied on technical superiority.

In the first week of the war, allied forces rapidly fanned out of Kuwait, occupied most of southern Iraq and moved deep into the central part of the country without prolonged preliminary air bombardment. This successful blitz caused shock in Moscow. Then came news of the first U.S. casualties and prisoners, of severe sandstorms hampering movement, of increased Iraqi attacks and an overall pause in the offensive.

As the allies' push into Iraq seemed to falter, many hearts in Moscow and in Europe rejoiced. In a poll taken in late March, 52 percent of Russians were of the opinion that the U.S.-led military action in Iraq was unsuccessful; 58 percent believed it would be a long war; 35 percent were convinced the United States would win in the end, while 33 percent assumed Iraq would prevail.

Last week it was disclosed that two retired three-star generals – Vladislav Achalov (a former paratrooper and specialist in urban warfare) and Igor Maltsev (a specialist in air defense) – visited Baghdad recently and were awarded medals by Hussein. The awards were handed out by Iraqi Defense Minister Sultan Khashim Akhmed.

It was reported that the retired generals helped Hussein prepare a war plan to defeat the Americans. Achalov confirmed he was in Baghdad just before the war and received medals from Hussein for services rendered. He also told journalists that the defense of Baghdad was well organized, U.S. tanks would be burned if they enter the city and U.S. infantry would be slaughtered. According to Achalov, the only way the allies could ever take Baghdad and other Iraqi cities was to raze them to the ground by carpet bombing.

Last week, Defense Minister Sergei Ivanov echoed Achalov's opinion: "If the Americans continue to fight accurately, avoiding high casualties, the outcome is uncertain. If the Americans begin carpet bombing, Iraq will be defeated." Ivanov also announced that the Defense Ministry was attentively studying the war in order to learn how to build a stronger Russian army.

It seems that up to now the result of the study has been negative. It would appear that Russian generals and Ivanov assume it's the Americans that should be learning from them how to flatten cities – the way our military destroyed the Chechen capital, Grozny.

Many Russian generals truly believe that a bombing campaign that leaves some buildings still standing is ineffective. Precision-guided munitions are widely considered to be costly pranks – not real weapons. In Chechnya, we tried to use some of these gadgets, but they did not work, as most Russian officers and men have not been trained in how to use the limited number of modern weapons our military inherited from the Soviet armed forces.

The worst possible outcome of the war in Iraq for the Russian military is a swift allied victory with relatively low casualties. Already many in Russia are beginning to ask why our forces are so ineffective compared to the Brits and Americans; and why the two battles to take Grozny in 1995 and 2000 each took more than a month to complete, with more that 5,000 Russian soldiers killed and tens of thousands wounded in both engagements, given that Grozny is one tenth the size of Baghdad.

The Russian media is generally avoiding the hard questions and serving up anti-American propaganda instead. It is alleged that the U.S. government is "concealing casualties" (like its Russian counterpart), and that hundreds if not thousands of U.S. soldiers have already been killed. Maybe this deceit will become the main semi-official excuse for disregarding the allied victory.

Or perhaps our generals who do not want to build a modern post-Soviet military will come up with some other propaganda ploy.

11. Nikolai Glushkov, "Russia: Demography Hits Economy," *Nezavisimaya Gazeta*, no. 61, March 28, 2003, reprinted in *Johnson's Russia List*, no. 7139, art. 4, April 9, 2003. Glushkov writes,

Between January 1 and December 1, 2001, according to official statistics, the population of the Russian Federation diminished by 781,800 people – 103,700 people more than in the same period of 2000. For a country that occupies a territory of 17.1 million square kilometers and is traditionally sparsely populated, a sharp population decrease means destruction of the territorial infrastructure, which in its turn threatens the country's economic security. Already today, masses of immigrants from neighboring countries are aiming at our vacant lands. Such immigration goes beyond simple replenishment of Russia's human resources potential. It is a cultural and global political expansion fraught with a loss of territories and influence as well as with heavy economic losses. Between 2001 and 2016, the population of Siberia and the Far East will drop by 7.6% and that of the northern territories or similar areas by 12.0%. The population density in the Asian part of the Federation and in border districts will be reduced, too, which means a threat to the national security and territorial integrity of Russia. Low birth rate also weakens the defensive potential since it might be difficult to keep up the strength of the army and the number of people engaged in the defense industry. No wonder the authorities consider the forming of a professional army one of their priorities. One of the reasons is that the number of potential conscripts keeps falling.

12. Evgeny Primakov, former prime minister under Boris Yeltsin and chairman of the Russian Chamber of Industry and Commerce, advised Russians "not to seek direct confrontation with the United States," even though it should foster "a multipolar world and an independent-minded Europe as a counterweight to American unilateralism." See "Anti-Americanism Not in Russia's Interest – Former PM," *Johnson's Russia List*, no. 7134, art. 1, April 7, 2003.

CONCLUSION

1. The CIA's tentative appraisal was different. The command system was conjectured to be disorganized by Gorbachev's "belated" curtailments of military procurement, which compounded problems of reform implementation. See James Noren and Laurie Kurtzwig, "The Soviet Union Unravels: 1985–91," in *The Former Soviet Union in Transition* (Washington, DC: Joint Economic Committee of Congress, February 1993), 12.

2. Contemporary Russian democracy differs from Soviet democracy in several ways. Under the old regime, there was a single party, the Communists, and a nonelected leader who effectively appointed representatives to the Supreme Soviet (equivalent to today's Duma). The general secretary of the Communist Party ruled both the party and the state. The Communist Party periodically held balloted elections for all positions, including "supreme leader." Ninety-eight percent usually voted for the appointees, not too dissimilar to balloting for judgeships in the United States. Legislative representatives were powerless, and the electorate was effectively disenfranchised.

   Under Gorbachev, the title for the head of state was changed to "president." Yeltsin reformed this system by appointing himself "president" without even the fiction of party endorsement. Putin did the same. The president appoints a large portion of the legislators and governors. The rest of the positions are usually bought by the oligarchs. As before, balloting occurs, but not only is it pro forma (and rigged), but the president ignores the Duma at his discretion. The people's preferences simply don't count.

   Yes, you can conclude that in the period of the early 1990s there was a major geopolitical change (the USSR broke up), but there was little or no change in Russia's economic and political systems. The required qualification is that economic and political control is less heavy handed than before. Individuals have far greater autonomy over economic and political matters the leadership deems inessential. The system is not unlike the result of China's liberalization. The main difference is the willingness of Putin to indulge oligarchs by tolerating wholesale asset stripping, asset grabbing, rent seeking, and protectionism, which lie at the core of Russia's resource demobilization. In both cases, the state has experimented with individual economic autonomy and interest group advocacy (the admission of "capitalism" into communism in order to realize the potential benefits), and both face inferior long-term prospects if they stick with their nonwestern systems.

3. Simon Saradzhyan, "Army's Plan for Reform Wins Out," *Moscow Times*, April 25, 2003. According to Saradzhyan,

   Prime Minister Mikhail Kasyanov approved Defense Minister Sergei Ivanov's military reform proposal – an incremental expansion of volunteer service – over a fast-track, cheaper plan put forward by liberal lawmakers. But he balked at providing sufficient funding, which threatens to stall if not derail the much-needed reform. The plan calls for replacing all conscripts with professional soldiers at so-called permanent readiness units in both the armed forces proper and other forces by 2008. Only after these 209 combat units, which range in size from border guard posts to airborne divisions, are manned with a total of 170,000 professional sergeants and soldiers, will the Defense Ministry and other so-called power agencies consider cutting compulsory military service from two years to one, according to the plan described by Ivanov. The four-year plan, which will be formally considered by Kasyanov and President Vladimir Putin in June, would cost 135 billion rubles ($4.34 billion) to implement over four years, Ivanov said. The bulk of this sum would be spent on reconstructing barracks and paying wages. Boris Nemtsov, the leader of the Union of Right Forces, or SPS, who attended the meeting, said the Cabinet is not prepared to spend more than 50 billion rubles and Kasyanov made that clear. Nemtsov said SPS will continue to "battle with military bureaucrats" in the hope of convincing the government and the Kremlin to opt for its own plan, which provides for conscripts to serve only six months. Under the SPS plan, the 1.1 million-member armed forces proper could be transformed into a professional army in just three years at a cost of 91 billion rubles, Nemtsov told reporters after the Cabinet meeting.

Cf. Olga Tropkina and Maksim Glinkin, "Ivanov Drains Military Reform," *Nezavisimaya Gazeta* April 25, 2003.

Aktual'nye Zadachi Razvitüs Vooruzhennylih Sil Rossiikoi Federatsii (Priority Tasks of the Development of the Armed Forces of the Russian Federation), October 2, 2003. http://www.mil.ru/print/articles/article5005.shtml

4. According to Robert Kaplan ("Euphorias of Hatred," *Atlantic Monthly*, May 2003), "The signal error of the American elite after the end of the cold war was its trust in rationalism, which, it was assured would continually propel the world's societies toward systems based on individual rights and united by American style capitalism and technology" (p. 44).

5. Carol Giacomo, "Experts Fear U.S.–Russia Nuclear 'Perfect Storm,'" *Johnson's Russia List*, no. 7192, May 22, 2003. Giacomo writes,

More than a decade after the Cold War, the world faces a possible "perfect storm" of security factors that has increased the risk of an accidental or unauthorized nuclear arms attack between the United States and Russia, experts said on Wednesday. A study by the RAND think tank, strongly endorsed by former Sen. Sam Nunn and his nonprofit group The Nuclear Threat Initiative, paints a devastating picture of Russia's strategic capabilities and challenges assumptions about the degree to which better U.S.–Russian relations have improved security.

SELECTED BIBLIOGRAPHY

Abramowitz, Moses. "Catching up, Forging ahead, and Falling Behind." *Journal of Economic History* 46 (1986): 385–406.

Aganbegyan, Abel. *The Economic Challenge of Perestroika.* Bloomington: Indiana University Press, 1988.

Aktual'nye Zadachi Razvitiia Vooruzhennykh Sil Rossiiskoi Federatsii (Priority Tasks of the Development of the Armed Forces of the Russian Federation), October 2, 2003.

http://www.mil.ru/print/articles/article5005.shtml

Alchian, Armen. "Reliability of Progress Curves in Airframe Production," *Econometrica* 32 (1963): 679–93.

Arrow, Kenneth. *Social Choice and Individual Values.* 2nd ed. New York: Wiley, 1963.

———. "Optimal and Voluntary Income Distribution." In Steven Rosefielde, ed., *Economic Welfare and the Economics of Soviet Socialism.* Cambidge: Cambridge University Press, 1981, 267–88.

Aslund, Anders. "How Small Is Soviet National Income?" In Henry Rowen and Charles Wolf, Jr., eds., *The Impoverished Superpower: Perestroika and the Soviet Military Burden.* San Francisco: ICS Press, 1988, 13–62.

———. "Heritage of the Gorbachev Era." In *The Former Soviet Union in Transition.* Washington, DC: Joint Economic Committee of Congress, February 1993, 184–95.

———. *How Russia Became a Market Economy.* Washington, DC: Brookings Institution, 1995.

———. "Rentoorientirovannoe povedenie v rossiiskoi perekhodnoi ekonomike." *Voprosy Ekonomiki,* no. 8 (1996): 99–108.

———. "Russia's Collapse." *Foreign Affairs* 78, no. 5 (1999): 64–77.

———. *Building Capitalism: The Transformation of the Former Soviet Bloc.* Cambridge: Cambridge University Press, 2002.

———. "How Russia Was Won." *Moscow Times,* November 21, 2002.

———. "Amnesty the Oligarch." *Moscow Times,* March 14, 2003.

———. "The Drama Is Putin, But So Are the Results," *Moscow Times,* July 25, 2003.

Aslund, Anders, and Andrew Warner. *The Enlargement of the European Union: Consequences for the CIS.* Russian and Eurasian Program, Carnegie Endowment of International Peace, no. 36, April 2003.

Aslund, Anders, and John Hewko. "Reality to Clash with Idealism When Communism Collapses." *Washington Times*, July 2, 2002.

Aukutsionek, S. P. "Rossiiskii motiv – bez pribyli!" *EKO*, no. 11 (1997): 2–14.

Avineri, Shlomo. "The End of the Soviet Union and the Return to History." In Michael Keren and Gur Ofer, eds., *Trials of Transition: Economic Reform in the Former Communist Bloc*. Boulder, CO: Westview Press, 1992, 11–18.

Becker, Abraham. *Soviet Military Outlays Since 1958*. RM-3886-PR. Santa Monica, CA, Rand, June 1964.

———. *Soviet National Income 1958–64*. Berkeley: University of California, Berkeley, 1969.

———. *Military Expenditure Limitations for Arms Control: Problems and Prospects*. Cambridge, MA: Ballinger, 1977.

———. "Intelligence Fiasco or Reasoned Accounting? CIA Estimates of Soviet GNP." *Post-Soviet Affairs* 10, no. 4 (1994): 291–329.

———. *Postwar Soviet Economic Growth: A Second Look*. Santa Monica, CA: Rand, February 2002.

Belianin, Alexis. "Protectionism, Restructuring, and the Optimum Strategy for Russia's Accession to the WTO." RECEP, Moscow, August 2002.

Bergson, Abram. *The Structure of Soviet Wages: A Study of Socialist Economics*. Cambridge, MA: Harvard University Press, 1944.

———. "Reliability and Usability of Soviet Statistics: A Summary Appraisal." *American Statistician* 7, no. 5 (1953): 13–16. 1953.

———. *Soviet National Income of and Product in 1937*. New York: Columbia University Press, 1953.

———. *The Real National Income of Soviet Russia since 1928*, Cambridge, MA: Harvard University Press, 1961.

———. "Socialist Economics." In Abram Bergson, *Essays in Normative Economics*. Cambridge, MA: Belknap Press, 1965, 234–6.

———. *Essays in Normative Economics*. Cambridge, MA: Harvard University Press, 1966.

———. "Soviet National Income Statistics." In Vladimir Treml and John Hardt, eds., *Soviet Economic Statistics*. Durham, NC: Duke University Press, 1972, 148–52.

———. "Social Choice and Welfare Economics under Representative Government." *Journal of Public Economics* 6 (1976): 171–90.

———. "Technological Progress." In Abram Bergson and Herbert Levine, eds., *The Soviet Economy: Toward the Year 2000*, London: Allen and Unwin, 1983, 34–78.

———. "The U.S.S.R. before the Fall: How Poor and Why?" *Journal of Economic Perspectives* 5, no. 4 (1991): 29–44.

———. "Neoclassical Norms and the Valuation of National Product in the Soviet Union and Its Postcommunist Successor States: Comment." *Journal of Comparative Economics* 21, no. 3 (1995): 390–3.

Bergson, Abram, and Herbert Levine. *The Soviet Economy Toward the Year 2000*, George Allen and Unwin, London, 1983.

Bergson, Abram, and Simon Kuznets. *Economic Trends in the Soviet Union*. Cambridge, MA: Harvard University Press, 1963.

Berkowitz, Daniel, Joseph Berliner, Susan Gregory, and James Millar. "An Evaluation of the CIA's Analysis of Soviet Economic Performance." *Comparative Economic Studies* 35, no. 2 (1993): 33–56.

Berliner, Joseph. *Factory and Manager in the USSR*. Cambridge, MA: Harvard University Press, 1957.

Birman, Igor. "Velichina Sovetskikh voennykh raskhodov: Metodicheskii aspekt." Unpublished manuscript, 1990.

Blank, Stephen. "The 18th Brumaire of Vladimir Putin," Paper Conference on Succession Crises in Russia, Boston, MA, April 20, 2004.

———. "The General Crisis of the Russian Military." Paper presented at Putin's Russia: Two Years On, Wilton Park, England, March 11–15, 2002.

———. "The Material Technical Foundations of Russian Military Power." Draft, August 2002.

Blasi, Joseph. *Ownership, Governance and Restructuring*. New Brunswick, NJ: Rutgers University School of Management and Labor Relations, 1994.

Blasi, Joseph, M. Kroumova, and D. Kruse. *Kremlin Capitalism*. Ithaca, NY: Cornell University Press, 1997.

Boretsky, Michael. "The Tenability of the CIA Estimates of Soviet Economic Growth." *Journal of Comparative Economics* 11, no. 4 (1987): 517–42.

Bornstein, Morris. "The Administration of the Soviet Price System." *Soviet Studies* 30, no. 4 (1978): 466–90.

Boyko, Maxim, Andrei Shleifer, and R. Vishny. *Privatizing Russia*. Cambridge, MA: MIT Press, 1995.

Brada, Josef, and Arthur King. "Is There a J-Curve for Economic Transition from Socialism to Capitalism?" *Economics of Planning* 25, no. 1 (1992): 37–53.

Brady, Rose. *Kapitalizm: Russia's Struggle to Free Its Economy*. New Haven, CT: Yale University Press, 1999.

Brainard, Elizabeth. "Reassessing the Standard of Living in the Soviet Union: An Analysis Using Archival and Anthropometric Data," paper presented to the Abram Bergson Memorial Conference, Harvard University, Davis Center, Cambridge, MA, November 23–24, 2003.

Broadman, Harry, ed. *Unleashing Russia's Business Potential: Lessons from the Regions for Building Market Institutions*. Washington, DC: World Bank, April 2002.

Brunet, Eric. "Is Russian Economic Growth Sustainable?" In Arnaud Blin and Francois Gere, eds., *Puissance et Influences*. Géopolitical and géostrátegic yearbook. Charles Léopold Mayer, Descartes & Cie, Paris, June 2002, 55–74.

Bukharin, Nikolai, and Evgeny Preobrazhensky. *The ABC's of Communism*. Baltimore: Penguin, 1969.

Chang, Gene Hsing. "Immisering Growth in Centrally Planned Economies." *Journal of Comparative Economics* 15 (1991): 711–17.

CIA, *USSR: Measures of Economic Growth and Development 1950–1980*. Washington, DC: Joint Economic Committee of Congress, December 8, 1982.

———. "The Soviet Economy Stumbles Badly in 1989," In *Allocation of Resources in the Soviet Union and China*. Washington, DC, April 20, 1990.

———. *Measures of Soviet Gross National Product in 1982 Prices*. Washington, DC: Joint Economic Committee of Congress, November 1990.

———. *Handbook of International Economic Statistics.* CIA, Washington, DC, CPAS92-1005. September 1992.

CIA and the Defense Intelligence Agency, "The Soviet Economy Stumbles Badly in 1989," in *Allocation of the Resources in the Soviet Union and China – Part 15*, U.S. Government Printing Office, Washington, DC, 1991, 18–103.

Clark, Colin. *The Conditions of Economic Progress.* London: Macmillan, 1957.

———. *A Critique of Soviet Statistics.* London: Macmillan, 1939.

Coase, Ronald. "The Problem of Social Cost." *Journal of Law and Economics* 3 (October 1960): 1–44.

Cohn, Stanley. "National Income Statistics." In Vladimir G. Treml and John P. Hardt eds., *Soviet Economic Statistics.* Durham, NC: Duke University Press, 1972, 120–47.

Collier, Irwin. "The 'Welfare Standard' and Soviet Consumers," paper presented at the Abram Bergson Memorial Conference, Harvard University, Davis Center, Cambridge, MA, November 23–24, 2003.

Davies, Robert. *Soviet Industrial Production 1928–1937: The Rival Estimates.* Soviet Industrialization Project Series no. 18. Birmingham, England: University of Birmingham, Center for Russian and East European Studies, 1978.

———. *The Industrialization of Soviet Russia.* Vol. 4, *Crisis and Progress in the Soviet Economy, 1931–33.* Basingstoke and London: Macmillan, 1996.

———. "Industry." In Robert Davies, Mark Harrison, and Stephen Wheatcroft, eds., *The Economic Transformation of the USSR, 1913–1945.* Cambridge: Cambridge, University Press, 1994, 131–57.

Davis, Christopher. *Defense Sector in the Economy of a Declining Superpower: Soviet Union and Russia, 1965–2001.* Defense and Peace Economics, London Overseas Publishers Association, 2001.

Dent, Harry, Jr. *The Roaring 2000s Investor.* New York: Simon & Schuster, 1999.

Desai, Padma. "The Production Function and Technical Change in Postwar Soviet Industry: A Reexamination." *American Economic Review* 66, no. 3 (1976): 372–81.

Desai, Raj, and Itzhak Goldberg. "Stakeholders, Governance, and the Russian Enterprise Dilemma." *Finance and Development* 37, no. 2 (2000): 14–18.

Dobb, Maurice. "Further Appraisals of Russian Economic Statistics." *Review of Economic Statistics* 29, no. 1 (1948): 34–8.

Dollar, David, and Aart Kraay. "Growth is Good for the Poor," *Foreign Affairs* 81, no. 1 (2002): 120–33.

Domar, Evsei. "A Soviet Model of Growth." In *Essays in the Theory of Economic Growth.* New York: Oxford University Press, 1957.

Dudkin, Lev, and Anatol Vasilevsky. "The Soviet Military Burden: A Critical Analysis of Current Research." *Hitotsubashi Journal of Economics* 28, no. 1 (1987): 41–62.

Earle, John. "After Voucher Privatization: The Structure of Corporate Ownership in Russian Manufacturing Industry." Center for Economic Policy Research discussion paper no. 1736.

Earle, John, and Saul Estrin. "Worker Ownership in Transition." In Roman Frydman, Cheryl Gray, and Andrezej Rapaczynski, eds., *Corporate Governance in Central Europe and Russia*, vol. 2. Budapest: Central European University Press, 1993, 1–61.

Easter, Gerald. *Reconstructing the State: Personal Networks and Elite Identity in Soviet Russia*. New York: Cambridge University Press, 2000.

———. "Networks, Bureaucracies, and the Russian State." In Klaus Segbers, ed., *Explaining Post-Soviet Patchworks*, vol. 2. Aldershot, England: Ashgate, 2001, 39–58.

Easterly, William, and Stanley Fischer. "The Soviet Economic Decline." *World Bank Economic Review* 9, no. 3 (1995): 341–71.

Eberstadt, Nicholas. "The Future of AIDS," *Foreign Affairs* 81, no. 6 (2002): 22–45.

———. "The Demographic Factor as a Constraint on Russian Development: Prospects at the Dawn of the Twenty First Century," in Eugene Rumer and Celeste Wallander, *Sources and Limits of Russian Power*, National Defense University Press, Washington, DC, 2004 forthcoming.

Epstein, David. "The Economic Cost of Soviet Security and Empire." In Henry Rowen and Charles Wolf, Jr., eds., *The Impoverished Superpower: Perestroika and the Soviet Military Burden*. San Francisco: ICS Press, 1990, 127–54.

Ericson, Richard. "The Soviet Statistical Debate: Khanin vs. TsSU." In Henry Rowen and Charles Wolf, Jr., eds., *The Impoverished Superpower: Perestroika and the Soviet Military Burden*. San Francisco: ICS Press, 1990, 63–92.

Feshbach, Murray. "Russia's Demographic and Health Meltdown." Testimony to U.S. Congress, Joint Economic Committee. In *Russia's Uncertain Economic Future*. Washington, DC: Joint Economic Committee of Congress, 2002, 283–306.

———. "The Demographic, Health and Environmental Situation in Russia." Draft report presented at The Future of the Russian State, Liechtenstein Institute on Self-Determination conference, Triesenberg, Liechtenstein, March 14–17, 2002.

———. *Russia's Health and Demographic Crises: Policy Implications and Consequences*. Washington, DC: Chemical and Biological Arms Control Institute, 2003.

Firth, Noel, and James Noren. *Soviet Defense Spending: A History of CIA Estimates 1950–1990*. College Station: Texas A&M University, 1998.

Fukuyama, Francis. *The End of History and the Last Man*. New York: The Free Press, 1992.

———. *Trust: The Social Virtues and the Creation of Prosperity*. New York: The Free Press, 1995.

———. *The Great Disruption: Human Nature and the Reconstitution of Social Order*. New York: The Free Press, 1999.

———. *Our Posthuman Future: Consequences of the Biotechnology Evolution*. New York: Farrar, Straus & Giroux, 2002.

Gaddy, Clifford. *The Price of the Past: Russia's Struggle with the Legacy of a Militarized Economy*. Washington, DC: Brookings Institution Press, 1996.

Gaddy, Clifford, and Barry Ickes. "Russia's Virtual Economy." *Foreign Affairs* 77, no. 5 (1998): 52–67.

———. "An Accounting Model of the Virtual Economy in Russia." *Post-Soviet Geography and Economics* 40, no. 3 (1999): 79–97.

———. *Russia's Virtual Economy*. Washington, DC: Brookings Institution Press, 2002.

Galbraith, James, Joe Pitts, and Andrew Wells-Dang. "Is Inequality Decreasing?" *Foreign Affairs* 81, no. 4 (2002): 178–83.

Gavrilenkov, Evgeny. "After Russia's Financial Crisis: Structural and Institutional Changes in an Era of Globalization," paper presented at the Allied Social Science Association meetings, Washington DC, January 5, 2003.

Gerschenkron, Alexander. "The Soviet Indices of Industrial Production." *Review of Economic Statistics* 29, no. 4 (1947): 217–26.

Glinski, Dmitri, and Peter Reddaway. "The Ravages of 'Market Bolshevism.'" *Journal of Democracy* 10, no. 2 (1999): 19–34.

Goldgeier, James, and Michael McFaul. "George W. Bush and Russia." *Current History* 101 (October 2002): 317.

Goldman, Marshall. "The Coming Russian Boom – Again." In Michael Crutcher, ed., *Russian National Security: Perceptions, Policies and Prospects*. U.S. Army War College, Carlisle Barracks, PA, November 2001, 315–30.

———. *The Piratization of Russia: Russian Reform Goes Awry*. London: Routledge, 2003.

Goldman, Stuart. *Russian Conventional Armed Forces: On the Verge of Collapse?* Washington, DC: Library of Congress, Congressional Research Service, September 1997.

Gorbachev, Mikhail. *Perestroika i Novoe Myshlenie*. Moscow: Politicheskie Literatury, 1987.

Granick, David. "Soviet Use of Fixed Prices: Hypothesis of a Job-Right Constraint." In Steven Rosefielde, ed., *Economic Welfare and the Economics of Soviet Socialism*. Cambridge: Cambridge University Press, 1981, pp. 85–104.

Gregory, Paul. *Behind the Facade of Stalin's Command Economy*, Princeton UP, Princeton, New Jersey, 2002.

Grossman, Gregory. "Notes for a Theory of the Command Economy." *Soviet Studies* 15, no. 2 (1963): 103–23.

———. "Price Controls, Incentives and Innovation in the Soviet Economy." In Alan Abouchar, ed., *The Socialist Price Mechanism*. Durham, NC: Duke University Press, 1977, 129–69.

Gustafson, Thane. *Capitalism Russian-Style*. Cambridge: Cambridge University Press, 2000.

Harrison, Lawrence, and Samuel Huntington, eds. *Culture Matters: How Values Shape Human Progress*. New York: Basic Books, 2000.

Harrison, Mark. "Prices, Planners, and Producers: An Agency Problem in Soviet Industry 1928–1950." *Journal of Economic History* 58, no. 4 (1998): 1032–62.

———. "Soviet Industrial Production, 1928 to 1955: Real Growth and Hidden Inflation." *Journal of Comparative Economics* 28, no. 1 (2000): 134–55.

———. Postwar Soviet Economic Growth: Not a Riddle." *Europe-Asia Studies* 55, no. 8 (December 2003): 1323–29.

Havrylyshyn, Oleh. "Uncharted Waters, Pirate Raids, and Safe Havens: A Parsimonious Model of Transition Progress, " paper presented at the BOFIT/CEFIR Workshop on Transition Economics, Helsinki, Finland, April 2–3, 2004.

Hayek, Fredrich. *Collectivist Economic Planning*. Critical Studies on the Possibilities of Socialism, London: George Routledge & Sons, 1935.

———. "Socialist Calculation: The Competitive Solution." *Economica*, 7 (May 1940): 125–49.

————. "The Use of Knowledge in Society." *American Economic Review*, September 1945.

Hedlund, Stefan. "Can They Go Back and Fix It?: Reflections on Some Historical Roots of Russia's Economic Troubles." *Acta Slavica Iaponica* 20 (2003): 50–84.

————. *Russian Path Dependency*. London, Routledge, 2005.

Hill, Christopher. *Russia: Defense Economics*. London: British Ministry of Defense, Center for Strategic and International Affairs, Russian and Eurasian Program, January 31, 2001.

————. "Russia's Defense Spending." In *Russia's Uncertain Future*. Washington, DC: Joint Economic Committee of Congress, 2002.

Hodgman, Donald. *Soviet Industrial Production, 1928–51*. Cambridge, MA: Harvard University Press, 1954.

Hoffman, David. *The Oligarchs: Wealth and Power in the New Russia*. New York: Public Affairs Press, 2002.

Hoffman, Stanley. "Clash of Globalizations." *Foreign Affairs* 81, no. 4 (2002): 104–15.

Holzman, Franklyn. "Foreign Trade Behavior of Centrally Planned Economies." In *Foreign Trade under Central Planning*. Cambridge, MA: Harvard University Press, 1974, 139–63.

————. *Financial Checks on Soviet Defense Expenditures*. Lexington, MA: Lexington Books, 1975.

————. "Are the Soviets Really Outspending the U.S. on Defense?" *International Security* 4, no. 4 (1980): 86–104.

————. "Soviet Military Spending: Assessing the Numbers Game." *International Security* 6, no. 4 (1982): 78–101.

————. "Politics and Guesswork: CIA and DIA Estimates of Soviet Military Spending." *International Security* 14, no. 2 (1989): 101–31.

————. "Politics, Military Spending, and the National Welfare." *Comparative Economic Studies* 36, no. 3 (1994): 1–4.

Hosking, Geoffrey. *Russia and the Russians*. Cambridge, MA: Harvard University Press, 2001.

Hough, Jerry. *The Logic of Economic Reform in Russia*. Washington, DC: Brookings Institution Press, 2001.

Huntington, Samuel. *The Clash of Civilizations and the Remaking of World Order*. New York: Simon & Schuster, 1996.

————. "The West: Unique, Not Universal." *Foreign Affairs* 75, no. 6 (1996): 28–46.

————. "The Lonely Superpower." *Foreign Affairs* 78, no. 2 (1999): 35–50.

International Institute of Strategic Studies. *The Military Balance, 1996–1997*. London: International Institute for Strategic Studies, 1997.

Izyumov, Alexei, Leonid Kosals, and Rosalina Ryvkina. "Defense Industrial Transformation in Russia: Evidence from a Longitudinal Survey." *Post-Communist Economies* 12, no. 2 (2001): 215–27.

————. "Privatisation of the Russian Defence Industry: Ownership and Control Issues." *Post-Communist Economies* 12, no. 4 (2001): 485–96.

Jasny, Naum. *The Soviet Economy during the Plan Era*. Stanford, CA: Stanford University, Food Research Institute, 1951.

————. *Soviet Industrialization, 1928–1952*. Chicago: University of Chicago Press, 1961.

Kapeliushnikov, Rostislav. "Chto skryvaetsa za 'skrytoi' bezrabotsei?" In Tat'iana Maleva, ed., *Gosudarstvennaia i korporativnaia politika zaniatnosti*. Moscow: Moskovskii Tsentr Karnegi, 1998, 75–111.

Kaplan, Norman, and Richard Moorsteen. "Indexes of Soviet Industrial Output," 2 vols. Research Memorandum RM-2495. Santa Monica, CA: Rand, 1960.

Kaplan, Robert. "Euphorias of Hatred." *Atlantic Monthly*, May 2003, 44–45.

————. "Supremacy by Stealth." *Atlantic Monthly* 292, no. 1 (July–August 2003): 66–83.

Karagonov, S. A., V. A Nikonov, and V. L Inozemtsev. "Russia and Globalization Trends: What Needs to Be Done?" Theses by the Council on Foreign and Defense Policy, November 2001.

Kaser, Michael. "Le Debat sur la Loi de la Valeur en URSS: Etude Retrospective 1941–1953." *Annuaire de l'URSS* (CNFS, Paris), 1965.

Khanin, Grigorii. "Ekonomicheskii Rost: Al'ternativnaia Otsenka." *Kommunist* 17 (1988): 83–90.

————. *Sovetskii Ekonomicheskii Rost: Analiz Zapadnykh Otsenok*. Novosibirsk: EKOR, 1993.

Kleiner, George. *Mesoekonomika perekhodnovo perioda: Rynki, otrasli, predpriiatia*. Moscow: Nauka, 2001.

Kleiner, Georgii. "Person, Position, Power and Property: The General Director in the 'Economy of Individuals.'" In Klaus Segbers, ed., *Explaining Post-Soviet Patchworks*, vol. 2. Aldershot, England: Ashgate, 2001, 108–39.

Kochin, Mikhail. "The Lubyanka Strikes Back: Apostles of Controlled Democracy," *Russian and Eurasia Review* 1, no. 8 (2002), http://www.jamestown.org/publications_details.php?volume_id=15+issue_id=606+article_id=4461.

Kontorovich, Vladimir. "Economists, the Soviet Growth Slowdown and the Collapse." *Europe-Asia Studies* 53, no. 5 (2001): 675–95.

Kordonskii, Simon. "Everyday Life as Flight from the State: 'Housing Portfolios' and the 'Diversified Way of Life.'" In Klaus Segbers, *Explaining Post-Soviet Patchworks*, vol. 2. Aldershot, England: Ashgate, 2001, 326–32.

Korhonen, Iikka. "Institutional Cure of Resource Curse?" paper presented at the BOFIT/CEFIR Workshop on Transition Progress, Helsinki, Finland, April 2–3, 2004.

Kotkin, Stephen. *Armageddon Averted: The Soviet Collapse 1970–2000*. London: Oxford University Press, 2002.

Krueger, Anne. "The Political Economy of Rent-Seeking Society," *American Economic Review* 64, no. 3 (1974): 291–303.

Krugman, Paul. "The Myth of Asia's Miracle," *Foreign Affairs* 73, no. 1 (1994): 62–78.

Kurlantzick, Joshua. "Can Burma Reform?" *Foreign Affairs* 81, no. 6 (2002): 133–46.

Landes, David. *The Wealth and Poverty of Nations: Why Some Are So Rich and Some So Poor*. New York: Norton, 1998.

Lange, Oskar and Fred M. Taylor. *On the Economic Theory of Socialism*, University of Minnesota Press, Minneapolis, 1938.

Ledeneva, Alena. *Russia's Economy of Favors: Blat, Networking, and Informal Exchange*. Cambridge: Cambridge University Press, 1998.

———. "Networks in Russia: Global and Local Implications." In Klaus Segbers, *Explaining Post-Soviet Patchworks*, vol. 2. Aldershot, England: Ashgate, 2001, 59–77.

Ledeneva, Alena, and Paul Seabright. "Barter in Post-Soviet Societies: What Does It Look Like and Why Does It Matter?" In Paul Seabright, ed., *The Vanishing Rouble: Barter Networks and Non-Monetary Transactions in Post-Soviet Societies*. Cambridge: Cambridge University Press, 2000.

Lee, William T. *The Estimation of Soviet Defense Expenditures for 1955–1975: An Unconventional Approach*. New York: Praeger, 1977.

———. *Trends in Soviet Military Outlays and Economic Priorities 1970–1988*. U.S. Senate Committee on Foreign Relations, Republican Staff Memorandum, July 30, 1990.

———. *CIA Estimates of Soviet Military Expenditures: Errors and Waste*. Washington, DC: American Enterprise Institute, 1995.

Leggett, Robert. "Measuring Inflation in the Soviet Machinebuilding Sector, 1960–1973." *Journal of Comparative Economics* 5, no. 2 (1981): 169–84.

Leontief, Wassily. "Domestic Production and Foreign Trade: The American Capital Position Re-examined." *Proceedings of the American Philosophical Society*, September 1953, 332–49.

———. "Factor Proportions and the Structure of American Trade: Further Theoretical and Empirical Analysis." *Review of Economics and Statistics*, November 1956, 386–407.

Lieven, Dominic. *Empire: The Russian Empire and Its Rivals*. New Haven, CT: Yale University Press, 2001.

Maddison, Angus. "Measuring the Performance of a Communist Command Economy: An Assessment of the CIA Estimates for the USSR." *Review of Income and Wealth* 44, no. 3 (1998): 307–23.

Makarov, Valerii, and Georgii Kleiner. "Barter v ekonomike perekhodnovo perioda: Osobennosti i tendentsii." *Ekonomika i Matematicheskie Metody* 33, no. 2 (1997): 25–41.

Marin, Dalia. "Trust versus Illusion: What Is Driving Demonetization in the Former Soviet Union?" *Economics of Transition* 10, no. 1 (2002): 173–200.

Marx, Karl. *The Economic and Philosophic Manuscripts of 1844*. New York: International Publishers, 1964.

McFaul, Michael. *Russia's Unfinished Revolution: Political Change from Gorbachev to Putin*. Ithaca, NY: Cornell University Press, 2001.

McKinnon, Ronald. *The Order of Economic Liberalization: Financial Control in the Transition to a Market Economy*. Baltimore: Johns Hopkins University Press, 1991.

Menshikov, Stanislav. "Putin as Seen by Talbott." *Moscow Tribune*, July 4, 2002.

Millar, James. "The Normalization of the Russian Economy: Obstacles and Opportunities for Reform and Sustainable Growth." *NBR Analysis* 13, no. 2 (2002): 5–44.

Mises, Ludwig von. *Socialism*. London: Jonathan Cape, 1936.

Moorsteen, Richard. "On Measuring Productive Potential and Relative Efficiency." *Quarterly Journal of Economics* 75, no. 6 (1961): 451–67.

———. *Prices and Production of Machinery in the Soviet Union, 1928–1958*. Cambridge, MA: Harvard University Press, 1962.

Moorsteen, Richard, and Raymond Powell. *The Soviet Capital Stock, 1928–1962*. Homewood, IL: Irwin, 1966.

Murrell, Peter, ed. *Assessing the Value of Law in Transition Economics*. Ann Arbor: University of Michigan Press, 2001.

Nesterenko, Andrei. "Markets between Soviet Legacy and Globalization: Neoinstitutionalist Perspectives on Transformation." In Klaus Segbers, ed., *Explaining Post-Soviet Patchworks: Pathways from the Past to the Global*, vol. 2. Aldershot, England: Ashgate, 2001, 78–103.

Noren, James, and Laurie Kurtzwig. "The Soviet Union Unravels.: 1985–91." In *The Former Soviet Union in Transition*. Washington, DC: Joint Economic Committee of Congress, February 1993, 12.

North, Douglass, and Robert Thomas. *The Rise of the Western World*. London: Cambridge University Press, 1972.

North, Gary. *The Coase Theorem: A Study in Economic Epistemology*. Tyler, TX: Institute for Christian Economics, 1992.

Nove, Alec. "'1926/7' and All That." *Soviet Studies* 9, no. 2 (1957): 117–30.

———. "Robert Conquest, The Great Terror." *Soviet Studies* 20 (April 1969): 538.

———. *An Economic History of the USSR*. Harmondsworth, England: Penguin, 1972.

———. *The Soviet Economic System*. London: George Allen & Unwin, 1977, 230–40.

———. *Glasnost' in Action: Cultural Renaissance in Russia*. Boston: Unwin Hyman, 1989, 213–20.

Nutter, Warren. *The Growth of Industrial Production in the Soviet Union*. National Bureau of Economic Research, Princeton, NJ, 1962.

Oding, Nina. "Profit or Production? Enterprise Behavior after Privatization." In Klaus Segbers, ed., *Explaining Post-Soviet Patchworks*, vol. 2. Aldershot, England: Ashgate, 2001, 140–69.

Ofer, Gur. *The Service Sector in Soviet Economic Growth: A Comparative Study*. Cambridge, MA: Harvard University Press, 1972.

———. "Soviet Economic Growth: 1928–85." *Journal of Economic Literature* 25, no. 4 (1987): 1767–83.

Olcott, Martha Brill. "Reforming Russia's Tycoons." *Foreign Policy*, May–June 2002, 66–75.

Olson, Mancur. *Power and Prosperity: Outgrowing Communist and Capitalist Dictatorships*. New York: Basic Books, 2000.

Pipes, Richard. *Property and Freedom*. New York: Alfred A. Knopf, 1999.

Pitzer, John. "The Tenability of the CIA Estimates of Soviet Economic Growth: A Comment." *Journal of Comparative Economics* 14, no. 2 (1990): 301–19.

Polischuk, Leonid, and Alexei Savvatev. "Spontaneous (Non) Emergence of Property Rights," *Economics of Transition* 12, no. 1, 103–27.

Ponomarenko, Aleksei. "Gross Regional Product for Russian Regions: Compilation Methods and Preliminary Results." Paper presented at Regions: A Prism to View the Slavic-Eurasian World, Slavic Research Center, Hokkaido University, Sapporo, Japan, July 22–24, 1998.

Primakov, Yevgeny. *The World after September 11.* Moscow: Mysl, 2002.

Putin, Vladimir. *First Person: An Astonishingly Frank Self-Portrait by Russia's President.* New York: Public Affairs Press, 2000.

Radygin, Aleksander. "Spontaneous Privatization: Motivations, Forms and Stages." *Studies on Soviet Economic Development* 3, no. 5 (1992): 341–7.

———. "The Corporate Securities Market: Bridgehead or Barrier to Globalization?" In Klaus Segbers, ed., *Explaining Post-Soviet Patchworks*, vol. 2. Aldershot, England: Ashgate, 2001, 193–226.

Rancour-Laferriere, Daniel. *Russian Nationalism from an Interdisciplinary Perspective: Imagining Russia.* Lewiston, NY: Edwin Melien Press, 2000.

Rapaway, Stephen. "Labor Force and Employment in the USSR," in *Gorbachev's Economic Plans*, vol. 1, Joint Economic Committee of Congress, Washington DC, 23 November 1987, 173–207.

Reddaway, Peter. "Is Putin's Power More Formal Than Real?" *Post-Soviet Affairs* 18, no. 1 (2002): 31–40.

Reddaway, Peter, and Dmitri Glinski. *The Tragedy of Russia's Reforms: Market Bolshevism against Democracy.* Washington, DC: United States Institute of Peace, 2001.

Reformirovanie i razvitie oboronno-promyshlennovo kompleksa 2002–2006 gody (The Reform and Development of the Defense-Industrial Complex 2002–2006). Pravitel'stva Rossiskoi Federatsei, no. 713, October 2001.

Robbins, Lionel. *An Essay on the Nature and Significance of Economic Science.* London: Macmillan, 1932.

Robinson, Joan. "Socialist Affluence," In C. H. Feinstein ed., *Socialism, Capitalism and Economic Growth: Essays Presented to Maurice Dobb.* London: Cambridge University Press, 1967.

Rosefielde, Steven. *Economic Welfare and the Economics of Soviet Socialism.* Cambridge: Cambridge University Press, 1981.

———. "Knowledge and Socialism: Deciphering the Soviet Experience." In Steven Rosefielde, ed., *Economic Welfare and the Economics of Soviet Socialism*, Cambridge: Cambridge University Press, 1981, 5–23.

———. "The Underestimation of Soviet Weapons Prices: Learning Curve Bias," *Osteuropa Wirtschaft* 31 (March 1986): 53–63.

———. *False Science: Underestimating the Soviet Arm Buildup.* New Brunswick, NJ: Transactions, 1987.

———. "The Distorted World of Soviet-Type Economies." Review article. *Atlantic Economic Journal* 17, no. 4 (1989): 83–6.

———. "Soviet Defense Spending: The Contribution of the New Accountancy." *Soviet Studies* 42, no. 1 (1990): 59–80.

———. "Gorbachev's Transition Plan: Strategy for Disaster." *Global Affairs* 6, no. 2 (1991): 1–21.

———. "The Grand Bargain: Underwriting Catastroika." *Global Affairs* 7, no. 1 (1991): 15–35.

———. "The Civilian Labor Force and Unemployment in the Russian Federation." *Europe-Asia Studies* 52, no. 8 (2000): 1433–47.

———. "Economic Foundations of Russian Military Modernization: Putin's Dilemma." In Michael Crutcher, ed., *The Russian Armed Forces at the Dawn of the Millennium.* The United States Army War College, Carlisle Barracks, December 2000, 99–114.

———. "Keynes and Peter I: Managing Russia's Economic and Military Vulnerabilities." In Pentti Forsstrom, ed., *Russia's Potential in the 21st Century.* National Defense College, series 2, no. 14. Helsinki: National Defense College, 2001, 75–91.

———. "Premature Deaths: Russia's Radical Transition." *Europe-Asia Studies* 53, no. 8 (2001): 1159–76.

———. "Back to the Future? Prospects for Russia's Military Industrial Revival," *Orbis* 46, no. 3 (Summer 2002): 499–509.

———. *Comparative Economic Systems: Culture, Wealth and Power in the 21st Century.* Oxford: Blackwell, 2002.

———. "The Riddle of Postwar Russian Economic Growth: Statistics Lied and Were Misconstrued." *Europe-Asia Studies* 55, no. 3 (2003): 469–81.

———. "'Tea Leaves' and Productivity: Bergsonian Norms for Gauging the Soviet Union." Paper presented at the Bergson Memorial Conference, Harvard University, Davis Center, November 23–24, 2003.

———. "An Abnormal Country: Russian Authoritarianism Unique, Not Universal," BOFIT Discussion Papers 2004, no. 5, Bank of Finland Institute for Economies in Transition, Helsinki, Finland, 2004.

———. "Illusion of Transition: Russia's Muscovite Future." *Eastern Economic Journal,* forthcoming.

———. *Russian Economics: From Lenin to Putin.* London: Blackwell, 2005.

Rosefielde, Steven, and Masaaki Kuboniwa. "Russian Growth Retardation Then and Now." *Eurasian Geography and Economics* 44, no. 2 (2003): 87–101.

Rosefielde, Steven, and Natalia Vennikova. "Fiscal Federalism in Russia: A Critique of the OECD's Proposals." *Cambridge Journal of Economics* 28, no. 2 (2004): 307–18.

Rosefielde, Steven, and R. W. Pfouts. "Economic Optimization and Technical Efficiency in Soviet Enterprises Jointly Regulated by Plans and Incentives." *European Economic Review* 32, no. 6 (1988): 1285–99.

———. "The Mis-specification of Soviet Production Potential: Adjusted Factor Costing and Bergson's Efficiency Standard." In Steven Rosefielde, ed., *Efficiency and Russia's Economic Recovery Potential to the Year 2000 and Beyond.* Aldershot, England: Ashgate, 1998, 11–32.

Rothschild, Kurt. "Socialism, Planning and Economic Growth," in C. H. Feinstein ed., *Socialism, Capitalism and Economic Growth.* Cambridge: Cambridge University Press, 1967.

Rowen, Henry, and Charles Wolf, Jr. *The Impoverished Superpower: Perestroika and the Soviet Military Burden.* San Francisco: Institute for Contemporary Studies, 1990.

Rumsfeld, Donald. "Transforming the Military." *Foreign Affairs* 81, no. 3 (2002): 20–32.

Russia's Uncertain Economic Future. Washington, DC: Joint Economic Committee of Congress, June 28, 2002.
http://www.access.gpo.gov/congress/joint/sjoint02.html

Samson, Ivan, and Xavier Greffe. *Common Economic Space: Prospects of Russia–EU Relations.* White paper. Moscow: Russian–European Centre for Economic Policy, October 2002.

Samuelson, Lennart. *Rod Koloss pa Larvfotter: Rysslands Ekonomi i Skuggan av 1900 Talskrigen.* Stockholm: SNS Forlag, 1999.

———. *Plans for Stalin's War Machine: Tukhachevskii and Military-Economic Planning 1925–1941.* London: Macmillan, 2001.

Samuelson, Paul. "International Trade and the Equalization of Factor Prices." *Economic Journal,* June 1948, 181–97.

Sapir, Jacques. "Heated Economic Debate." *Moscow Times,* November 2, 2002.

Satter, David. *Darkness at Dawn: The Rise of the Russian Criminal State.* New Haven, CT: Yale University Press, 2003.

Schroeder, Gertrude. "Soviet Economy on a Treadmill of Reforms." In *Soviet Economy in a Time of Change.* Washington, DC: Joint Economic Committee of Congress, 1979, 312–40.

———. "Soviet Economic Reform Decrees: More Steps on the Treadmill. In *Soviet Economy in the 1980s: Problems and Prospects.* Washington, DC: Joint Economic Committee of Congress, 1982, 68–88.

———. "Organizations and Hierarchies: The Perennial Search for Solutions." *Comparative Economic Studies,* Winter 1987, 7–28.

———. "Post-Soviet Economic Reforms in Perspective." In *The Former Soviet Union in Transition,* vol. 1. Washington, DC: Joint Economic Committee of Congress, February 1993, 57–80.

———. "Reflections on Economic Sovietology." *Post-Soviet Affairs* 11, no. 3 (1995): 197–234.

Schroeder, Gertrude, and Imogene Edwards. *Consumption in the USSR: An International Comparison.* Washington, DC: Joint Economic Committee of Congress, 1981, table 14, p. 25.

Segbers, Klaus. "Institutional Change in Russia: A Research Design." In Klaus Segbers, *Explaining Post-Soviet Patchworks,* vol. 2. Aldershot, England: Ashgate, 2001, 1–39.

Seton, Francis. "Pre-War Soviet Prices in the Light of the 1941 Plan." *Soviet Studies* 3, no. 4 (1952): 345–64.

Shabanova, M. A., "Institutsional'nye izmeneniia i nepravovye praktiki," Moskovskaia vysshaia shkola sotsial'nykh i ekonomischeskikh, Intertsentr, 2001, 319–27.

Shastitko, Andrei, and Vitalii Tambovtsev. "Institutionalization and Property Rights: The Reincarnation of Managerial 'Economic Authority' over State Property." In Klaus Segbers, ed., *Explaining Post-Soviet Patchworks,* vol. 2. Aldershot, England: Ashgate, 2001, 281–302.

Shatalin, Stanislav, et al. *Transition to the Market: 500 Days,* pt. 1. Moscow: Arkhangelskoe, August 1990.

Shlapentokh, Vladimir. "Is the 'Greatness Syndrome' Eroding?" *Washington Quarterly* 25, no. 2 (2002): 133–6.

Shleifer, Andrei and Daniel Treisman. "A Normal Country," *Foreign Affairs* 84, no. 2 (2004): 20–38.

Shlykov, Vitaly. *Chto Pogubilo Sovetskii Soiuz? Amerikanskaia Razvedka o Sovetskikh Voennykh Raskhodakh* (Who Destroyed the Soviet Union? American Intelligence Estimates of Soviet Military Expenditures). Voennyi Vestnik, no. 8. Moscow, April 2001.

———. "Russian Defense Industrial Complex After 9-11." Paper presented at Russian Security Policy and the War on Terrorism, U.S. Naval Postgraduate School, Monterey, CA, June 4–5, 2002.

———. *Chto Pogubilo Sovetskii Soiuz? Genshtab i Ekonomika.* Voennyi Vestnik, no. 9. Moscow, September 2002.

———. "Russian Security Policy and the War on Terrorism," paper presented at the U.S. Naval Postgraduate School, Monterey, CA, June 2003.

———. "The Anti-Oligarchic Campaign and Its Implications for Russia's Security," presented at the conference on "Russian Security and the Continuing War on Terrorism," United States Naval Postgraduate School, Monterey, California, September 16–18, 2003.

Skidelsky, Robert. *John Maynard Keynes.* vol. 3, *Fighting for Freedom, 1937–1946.* New York: Penguin, 2002.

Solnick, Steven. *Stealing the State: Control and Collapse in Soviet Institutions.* Cambridge, MA: Harvard University Press, 1999.

Solow, Robert. "Technical Change and the Aggregate Production Function." *Review of Economics and Statistics* 39, no. 3 (1957): 312–20.

Stavrakis, Peter. "Russia's Evolution as a Predatory State." In *Russia's Uncertain Economic Future.* Washington, DC: Joint Economic Committee of Congress, December 2001, 347–68.

Steinberg, Dmitri. *Reconstructing the Soviet National Economic Balance, 1965–1984: An Alternative Approach to Estimating Soviet Military Expenditures.* Vol. 1, *Technical Discussion.* DSA report no. 692. Decision-Sciences Applications, March 11, 1986. Vol. 2, *Compilation of Working Tables.* Washington, DC, March 12, 1986.

———. "Estimating Total Soviet Military Expenditures: An Alternative Approach Based on Reconstructed Soviet National Accounts." In Carl Jacobsen, ed., *The Soviet Defense Enigma.* New York: SIPRI, 1987, 27–58.

———. "Trends in Soviet Military Expenditures." *Soviet Studies* 42, no. 4 (1990): 675–99.

Steiner, James. *Inflation in Soviet Industry and Machinebuilding (MBMW) 1960–1975.* SRM 78-10142. CIA, Washington, DC, July 1978.

Stiglitz, Joseph. *Globalization and Its Discontents,* New York, W. W. Norton & Company, Allen Lane, New York, 2002.

Sutela, Pekka. "Insider Privatization in Russia: Speculations on Systemic Change." *Europe-Asia Studies* 46, no. 3 (1996): 417–35.

———. *The Russian Market Economy,* Kikimora Publications, Helsinki, Finland, 2003.

Swain, Derk. "The Soviet Military Sector: How It Is Defined and Measured." In Henry Rowen and Charles Wolf, Jr., *The Impoverished Superpower: Perestroika and the Soviet Military Burden.* San Francisco: Institute for Contemporary Studies, 1990, 93–109.

Talbott, Strobe. *The Russia Hand: A Memoir of Presidential Diplomacy.* New York: Random House, 2002.

Tikhomirov, Vladimir. "Capital Flight from Post-Soviet Russia." *Europe Asia Studies* 49, no. 4 (1997): 591–615.

———. "State Finances and the Effectiveness of the Russian Reform." In Vladimir Tikhomirov, ed., *Anatomy of the 1998 Russian Crisis.* Melbourne: Contemporary Europe Research Centre, 1999, 164–203.

———. *The Political Economy of Post-Soviet Russia.* London: Macmillan, 2000.

———. "Capital Flight: Causes, Consequences and Counter-Measures." In Klaus Segbers, *Explaining Post-Soviet Patchworks*, vol. 2. Aldershot, England: Ashgate, 2001, 251–80.

Treisman, Daniel. "How Different Is Putin's Russia?" *Foreign Affairs* 81, no. 6 (2002): 58–72.

Trenin, Dmitri. "From Pragmatism to Strategic Choice: Is Russia's Security Policy Finally Becoming Realistic?" In Andrew Kuchins, ed., *Russia after the Fall.* Washington, DC: Carnegie Endowment for International Peace, 2002.

Tugan-Baranovsky, Mikhail. *The Russian Factory in the 19th Century.* Homewood, IL: Irwin, 1970.

Unge, Wilhelm. *The Russian Military-Industrial Complex in the 1990s: Conversion and Privatisation in a Structurally Militarised Economy.* FOA-R5-00-01702-170-SE. Swedish Defense Establishment, Stockholm, December 2000.

———. *Den Ruska Militartekniska Resursbasen* (Russian Military-Technological Capacity). FOR-4-0618-SE. Swedish Defense Agency, Stockholm, October 2002.

United Nations. *Human Development Report 1998.* New York: Oxford University Press, 1998.

U.S. House Permanent Select Committee on Intelligence Review, Daniel Berkowitz et al. "Survey Articles: An Evaluation of the CIA's Analysis of Soviet Economic Performance, 1970–90." *Comparative Economic Studies,* Summer 1993, 33–56.

Weitzman, Martin. "Industrial Production." In Abram Bergson and Herbert Levine, eds., *The Soviet Economy: Toward the Year 2000.* London: George Allen & Unwin, 1983, 178–90.

Wiles, Peter. *The Political Economy of Communism.* Oxford: Blackwell, 1962.

———. "Soviet Military Finance." Paper presented at the Third World Congress on Soviet and East European Studies, Washington, DC, October 1985.

———. "How Soviet Defense Expenditures Fit into the National Accounts." In Carl G. Jacobson, ed., *The Soviet Defense Enigma.* Oxford: Oxford University Press, 1987, 59–94.

Wiles, Peter, and Moshe Efrat. *The Economics of Soviet Arms.* London: Suntory-Toyota International Center for Economics and Related Disciplines, 1985.

Wilhelm, John. "The Failure of the American Sovietological Economics Profession." *Europe-Asia Studies* 55, no. 1 (2003): 59–74.

Williamson, John. "Democracy and the 'Washington Consensus.'" *World Development* 21, no. 8 (1993): 1329–36.

Wohlforth, William. "Russia." In Richard Ellings and Aaron Friedberg, eds., *Asian Aftershocks: Strategic Asia 2002–03.* Seattle: National Bureau of Asian Research, 2002, 17–18, 183–222.

"The World Bank Confesses Its Sins: The World Bank Acknowledged That Its Activity in Russia Was Useless for the Last Decade. *Pravda,* November 29, 2002.

Yakovlev, Alexander. *A Century of Violence in Soviet Russia.* New Haven, CT: Yale University Press, 2002.

Zaslavskaya, Tatyana. "Kto i kuda stremitsia vesti Rossiiu?" Moskovskaia vysshaia shkola sotsial'nykh i ekonomicheskikh nauk, Intertsentr, 2001, 9–10.

INDEX

WMD. *See* weapons of mass destruction
Wolf, Charles Jr., 8
workers, number of, 167, 168
working poor, 172
World Bank, 97, 113, 188, 192
World Trade Organization (WTO), 101,
    108, 109, 112–113

Yaremenko, Yuri, 6
Yeltsin, Boris, 12, 61, 62, 63–64, 71, 78, 79,
    86, 128, 150
Yukos oil company, 78, 204, 205–206
Yushenkov, Sergei, 209–211

zastoi (stagnation), 26, 29, 30

Made in the USA
Coppell, TX
27 August 2020